HUNTING TALES

Ben Clingain

Maverick
An imprint of Midlands Mac Publishing

65 St. Giles Street, Northampton NN1 1JF
Tel: 0604 232262   Fax 0604 232126

First published in Great Britain 1994

© Ben Clingain

Printed in England
by Redwood Books
Trowbridge, Wiltshire

Typeset by Midlands Mac
Northampton

Limited Edition
ISBN 1 899078 00 2

Standard Edition
ISBN 1 899078 01 0
BRITISH LIBRARY CATALOGUING-IN-PUBLICATION DATA.
A catalogue record for this book is available from the British Library.

This book is sold subject to the condition that it shall not,
by way of trade or otherwise, be lent, resold, hired out,
or otherwise circulated without the publishers prior written
consent in any form of binding or cover other than that in
which it is published and without similar condition.
including this condition being imposed on the
subsequent publisher.
All rights reserved.

PROLOGUE

"Riding is the art of keeping a horse between oneself and the ground"
(Rintoul Booth)

Members of the Pytchley are largely responsible for the conception of this book. It arose out of a series of after-hunting soirees with my wife Sallyann's friends who are all pretty much horse mad. And whenever farmers and horse people are involved, there is inevitably a rich fund of earthy good humour, an extraordinary amount of ribbing, and some far-fetched stories.

It was at the end of one such long enjoyable evening last December with the Pytchley "Monday Club" that compelled me to put some of the stories down on paper. All are based in fact. All are claimed to have actually happened, some recently, some told by their grandfathers. Others have been doubtless exaggerated and, like the anglers' tales of The One That Got Away, the fences get taller, the ditches deeper, the horses wilder. As time went on members of the Pytchley, the Oakley and other hunts rang to give me stories, ripping yarns and funny tales. Several sent poems, some moving, some funny, which became so numerous that a special section was created.

Soon I discovered that Surtees was not a racing driver, but a writer on a par with Dickens; that Sassoon wasn't just a war poet but a hunting fanatic; that "Skittles" wasn't a pub game but a lover of hunting who also happened to be a leading courtesan of the late 1800's; that a hock wasn't just a German wine My education was complete when I learned that horses are not just big dogs with skinny legs and a steroid habit but dangerous animals who have caused many a broken neck over the centuries, and that a love of hunting has lost more fortunes than a dozen crashed banks.

It is undeniably true that the hunting field used to be peopled by dandies like Beau Brummel, fops, royals, courtesans and the idle rich. It has become classless nowadays with all walks of life represented and united by a common love of animals, the sport and the countryside. One magazine editor was kind enough to laud the manuscript in a review, and made the flattering point that "Hunting Tales" would in years to come be regarded as a valuable record of how life once was, as the net draws in around hunting as a legal sport. I'm sure that reports of the demise of hunting will be as inaccurate in 1994 as they were in 1909. Few foxes actually get killed through hunting. It's the dressing up, the meeting, the rich traditions, the challenge of jumping gates, fences, ditches and the warm afterglow fuelled by the many strange concoctions found in hipflasks that are the heartbeat of hunting. The legends of gates broken, riders thrown over walls and hedges are also close to the core of the sport, as much as the thunder of hooves and the gentle swearing of the riders as they fall over hedges and into ditches. These have all made up the great pleasures of foxhunting throughout the centuries, both for those on horseback as well as on foot.

Scores of people have been supportive, including international artist Joy Hawken, HRH The Prince of Wales, Joan Tice, MFH, Peter Jones, Jim Meads, Bob Andrews, (who could write a book full of his own stories), Ulrica Murray Smith, Harold Bowley, Christina McKenzie and the Pytchley Echo, and the Masters and members of the Pytchley who suffered my questions, knowing their answers would be taken down and used in evidence.

This is their book. I hope they like it.

Ben Clingain
Northampton, April 1994

FOREWORD
by
Peter Jones, Huntsman to the Pytchley

Hunting in various forms has been going on in the British Isles since the Norman Conquest, perhaps even before. It was as common in Greek and Roman times as chariot racing, and Marcus Aurelius was said to have been uncommonly fond of hunting. Reports in Chaucer's Canterbury Tales describe hunting where the quarry was the hare. The Napoleonic Wars gave rise to the Enclosure Acts, resulting in a threefold increase in the number of fences, ditches, walls and hedges. This meant the riders had to be bolder and better mounted to be able to ride the country.

All landowners and farmers are nature and country lovers at heart. Along with hunting people over the last two centuries they have developed and maintained the countryside as we now know it. Today hunting is part and parcel of the English countryside and we must do all we can to preserve it. Hunting is no longer the exclusive domain of the privileged, although that image continues to be uppermost in the minds of those who oppose it. Any local hunt now is comprised of businessmen, farmers and people from all walks of life. It costs less to hunt than it does to join the golf club, and a good horse, even these days, can cost slightly more than a set of expensive graphite shafted golf clubs. It must be said that Pings, Cobra or Yonex do not have to be mucked out or taken to the vet, but it is equally true that as golfers dream of summer, every foxhunter spends July and August dreaming of what winter will bring.

I have spent many summers in such a way, as my life has revolved around hunting for the last thirty-four seasons. I started work in Hunt service as second horseman to the Fernie after leaving school in 1958. Later I served with the South Notts, the Woodland Pytchley, the Pytchley, and the Grafton, all as whipper-in, then back to the Pytchley as Huntsman in 1971. I have had many wonderful Masters, who have given me the utmost support, and my wife Monica whom I met at the South Notts in 1960 has also been a tremendous support as my job is a way of life. Although it is not always easy, it is beyond description.

The early morning autumn mist while cubbing, the thrill of the crystal music when hounds first find sends shivers down your spine. The camaraderie and companionship of a host of wonderful friends and colleagues, and the earthy good humour of all concerned with the sport, these are the things that make the life of a Huntsman so worthwhile.

This book ranges far and wide across all the topics dear to the heart of hunting folk, from the United States to Ireland, and from Cheltenham to Calcutta. It's full of the wit, wisdom and good humour that is so much a part of every Hunt, and I hope your enjoyment of this great sport is enhanced when you read it.

Peter Jones, Huntsman
The Pytchley, Northampton,
May, 1994

ILLUSTRATIONS

List of Illustrations, in order of appearance:

Cover by Joy Hawken, "The Oakley away from Clifton Reynes". The original was presented to H.F.Bowley Esq. MFH to mark his retirement from Mastership of the Oakley Hunt. Harold Bowley had been Master for eighteen seasons and hunted hounds for eleven.
The painting depicts, from left, Bill Juffs, hon.secretary; Harold Bowley, MFH; Paul Bellamy, Kennel Huntsman; Caroline Evans, the Master's daughter and Stuart Edmunds, Field Master. The hounds are, from left, Favor, Practice, Fancy, Lavender, Capstan, Willis, Starsky, Ladle, Perfect, Comus, Wisdom and Foreman.
Copies of the limited edition print, signed by the artist, are available from:
C.J. Harris, Rookery New Farm, Preston Deanery, Northampton NN7 2DY.
At the time of going to press, each print is available at £50 plus p/p.

Captain R.E Wallace by Joy Hawken, to commemorate his 50 years of hunting foxhounds. Rights belong to the Exmoor Foxhounds Supporters Club. Copies of this limited edition may be obtained for £75 plus £5 p/p from Mrs M.B.Tate, Higher Fyldon Farm, Heasley Mill, South Molton, Devon EX36 3LF, Tel: 05984 239.

The Pytchley Hunt at Holdenby by Joy Hawken.
Reproduced by kind permission of Mr. & Mrs G. Middleton.

A Hunting Scene by Henry Alken (1785 - 1851)
(Bridgeman Art Library).

The Meet at Crick by Lionel Edwards (1952) plus key
Reproduced by kind permission of Mrs Joan Tice MFH.

The Gentlemen of the White Collar by Alfred R. Thomson, 22nd April 1960, presented to Colonel J.G. Lowther on his retirement from the joint mastership of the Pytchley hounds, which he held from 1923-1940 and 1949-1960.
Reproduced by kind permission of Mrs Joan Tice MFH.

The Red Earl with the Pytchley Hounds by John Charlton (1878)
Reproduced by kind permission of the Althorp Estate.

A Hunting Scene (2) by Henry Alken
(Bridgeman Art Library).

The Prince of Wales with Michael Farrin in 1989 at the Quorn (top) and with the Meynell in 1993.
Reproduced by kind permission of Jim Meads, the Sportsman's Photographer.

The black and white illustrations and sketches, unless otherwise named, are by kind permission of Joy Hawken, Colin Stephenson, John Summerford and Russell Martin. Some of Helen Macgregor's fine sketches from David Brock's Foxhunter's Weekend Book have been used. We are indebted to the R.S Surtees Society for their information on Surtees and John Leech, some of whose sketches we have used. Queen Victoria, who could draw, called Leech " an extraordinary artist". He drew for " Punch" almost from its inception in 1841, and no collaboration between artist and author has been more successful than that of Leech and Surtees. A list of publications is available from the R.S.Surtees Society, Nunney, near Frome, Somerset, telephone 0373-836442.

CONTENTS

Book One 9
    Quotations from the famous and the infamous

Book Two 27
    Fascinating Facts: The Unusual to the Unbelievable

Book Three 65
    Stories and tall tales of the hunting field and the characters therein

Book Four 121
    A selection of poetry from the hunting field

Book Five 175
    The Emerald Isle

Book Six 187
    Hunting around the world

Book Seven 203
    Tail Enders

A Run near Melton Mowbray, 1821, from the painting by Ferneley.

Book One

Quotations from the
famous and the infamous

Over the jump. – Illustration by Edward Ardizzone in R. S. Surtees 'Handley Cross'

WOMEN

'It was a horse woman that drove me to drink. And you know, I didn't even thank her'.
W. C. Fields

'Certain horsewomen should be struck regularly, like gongs'
Noel Coward: Private Lives 1932

'The English horsewomen is so refined,
She has no bosom and no behind'
Mark Twain: Letters 1870

'I have often observed, in women of her type, a tendency to regard all athletics as an inferior form of fox-hunting'
Evelyn Waugh: Decline and Fall Part 1 1928

'Women never look so well as when one comes in wet and dirty from hunting'
R. S. Surtees: Mr. Sponge's Sporting Tour 1849

'I ha' been at the green wood; mother make my bed soon,
For I'm wearied w'hunting and fain would lie down'
The Ballad of Lord Randall

'England is a paradise for women and hell for horses;
Italy a paradise for horses, hell for women'
Robert Burton: Anatomy of Melancholy 1620

'A Horsewoman is only a woman, but a good cigar is a smoke'
Rudyard Kipling: The Betrothed.

'Riding as an exercise for women below 45 years of age is to be condemned. Of the young married women who ride to hounds, about 60% are childless. No girl over 13 should be allowed to ride much, if at all, and then only at an amble. The reasons are obvious, but cannot be given here'
James Cantlie, Physical Efficiency, 1891

'When women do ride, they generally ride like the very devil.'
R. S. Surtees: Analysis of the Hunting Field.

'Women who ride, as a rule, ride better than men'
Trollope: Hunting Sketches (1865).

'Women have no business out hunting'.

R. S. Surtees: Ask Mamma.

This was a comment on the mores of the age when the only women who hunted were wives and daughters of the Masters. The Shires, in particular, would be invaded by wild young men and rakes and it was certainly a bachelor life. Many women did attend the meets but did not follow the hounds, and their presence caused much unfavourable comment, as it still does today at some golf clubs.

'I will refuse to give the Pytchley white collar to any woman who rides astride'.

Lord Annaly, MFH Pytchley 1902-1914 (Ladies of the Chase by Meriel Buxton, Sportsmans Press 1987)

A comment on the argument that raged about the merits of side-saddle and astride at the turn of the century.

'They say the Pytchley ladies are the greatest thrusters in the Shires'

(Dick Heathen)

Hmm . . . . I wonder what he can mean? (Ed.)

'All flesh is grass, but old women are hay.'

John Warde the 19th century MFH with the Pytchley, Craven, Bicester and New Forest.

'Sir Harold has a lot of ladies to stay at Lubbenham for hunting and generally mounts them'.

(Dick Heathen)

P.S. – I don't think Mr. Heathen meant it in the way it sounds in modern times.

'Hunting and love should not be allowed to interfere with each other.'

Quote attributed to Catherine Walters (Skittles) who was known to be very strict with her lovers during the hunting season in the 1860's when her fame was at its height.

'To make hunting more enjoyable, settle your horse behind a female with a nice rounded bottom. If there's no fox, you've still had a good view all day.'

Pytchley proverb, attributed to Bob Andrews.

'There's nothing so queer as scent, except a woman.'

An unknown MFH, quoted by The Duke of Beaufort.

'Four things greater than all things are,
Women and Horses and Power and War'

Rudyard Kipling: The Ballad of the King's Jest.

MEN

'He seems very eager both to hunt down the foxes and the Duke of York.'

A letter written by Lord Althorp's sister to her brother Robert, a sailor.

The Duke of York was being investigated by Althorp because of his involvement in a grave army scandal. Mrs. Clarke, the Duke's mistress, had been illegally selling commissions in the army.

HUNTING TALES

'A fox may steal your hens, sir...
If lawyer's hand is fee'd sir
He steals your whole estate.'

John Gray: The Beggars Opera 1720

(So not much has changed in over 250 years?)

'For what were all those country patriots born?
To hunt and vote and raise the price of corn?'

Lord Byron: The Age of Bronze 1815

'Strike me ugly if I won't go to Market Harborough'

Mr. Sawyer in Whyte-Melville's novel 'Market Harborough', having discarded Lutterworth, Rugby, Melton, Uppingham and Northampton, amongst others, as his choice for a hunting season.

'The best dressed man in the hunting field is the man whose dress attracts least notice'

Beau Brummel.

'Gentlemen who hunt for the sake of the ride, who are indifferent about the hounds, and know little about the business, if they do no harm, fulfil as much as we have reason to expect of them'.

Peter Beckford

'Like foxhunters, you should buy Old Masters. They fetch a better price than old mistresses'

Lord Beaverbrook 1940

'A privilege vested in all Masters who hunt their own hounds is to swear at their field as loud and as long as they wish.'

R. S. Summerhays

'Mr. Freeman called, and set Blaxley's sister's leg; he did the same for a hound.'

The Diary of Thomas Isham of Lamport, Nov. 17th 1672.

Mr. Freeman was a bonesetter who lived in Flore and exercised his skill on humans and animals. Bonesetters are said to have been keen followers of the hunt in the last two centuries. Presumably it was good for business!

'He doth nothing but talk of his horse'

William Shakespeare, The Merchant of Venice, 1597

'The men we have had here are principally Pytchley; which, in dandyism, are very second-rate to the Quorn or Melton men. Osbaldeston himself, though only five feet high, and in features like a cub fox, is a funny little chap.'

Creevey's description of a house party at Sulby in 1829.

HUNTING TALES

'Unfortunate turf speculation proved their ruin.'
The fate of the Andrew family who lived in Harlston (sic) House, now part of the Althorp estate.

'That feller George Washington, who discovered America, is buried there.'
Member of the Pytchley to an American visitor when passing through Brington.
Erroneous, of course, but there is a tomb of Washington's ancestors in Brington church, near Althorp, Northampton.

'Please forgive my politics. I indulge in them to neutralise my hunting which engrosses me sadly. (Hunting) absorbs my time and mind too much, and I can't do anything else with satisfaction, and politics least of all.'
The 'Red Earl', John Poyntz, fifth Earl Spencer to Lord Braye, 1878.

'I cannot see why you try to hunt this country. It is nothing but flints and forests, full of game and gamekeepers, sheep and sheepdogs, in fact everything inimical to sport.'
A disgruntled sportsman in 1930 about Hampshire.

'James Holman, a Brixworth cobbler, fell with his horse and broke his wooden leg,'
The Diary of Thomas Isham of Lamport, Dec. 10th 1672.
Even in 1672, Hunting seemed classless, and still a risky business.

'. . . the 'oss and the 'ound were made for each other and natur' threw in the fox as a connecting link. His perfect symmetry and my affection for him is a perfect paradox. In the summer I loves him with all the hardour of affection ; not an 'air of his beautiful 'ead would I 'urt; the sight of him is more glorious than the Lord Mayor's show, but when autumn comes then dash my vig how I loves to pursue him to destruction'.
Jorrocks (R. S. Surtees)

'(The Red Earl) might have been the greatest huntsman of his time only he would go to Lunnon and get himself mixed up with that there Gladstone, what couldn't do nuffin but cut down trees.'
An interesting political commentary by Dick Heathen

'From my passion for hunting and riding across country, I got into a sporting set, including some dissipated low-minded young men. We sometimes drank to much, with jolly good singing and playing at cards afterwards.'
Charles Darwin: The Autobiography of Charles Darwin (1887)

'No-one is too good to be a Master of Foxhounds. If he be gifted with the average endowment of tact, administrative talent, power of penetrating character, and all the other attributes that form the essential equipment of a successful public man, so much the better; but he should at least be reared in an atmosphere and tradition of country life, fond of sport for its own sake, a good judge of horses and hounds, and the possessor of a remarkably thick skin'.
Lord Willoughby de Broke (1920).

'A huntsman that I once knew (who, by the by, I believe, is at this time a drummer in a marching regiment) went out one morning so very drunk, that he got off his horse in the middle of a covert, laid himself down and went to sleep: he was lost; nobody knew what had become of him; and he was at last found in the situation I have described. He had, however, great good luck on his side; for, at the very instant he was found, a fox halloo'd; upon which he mounted his horse, rode desperately, killed his fox handsomely, and was forgiven'.
Peter Beckford

'There are, they say, fools, bloody fools, and those who remount after falling over a five bar gate at the opening meet.'
Anonymous

'Never believe a word any man says about a horse he wishes to sell, even a Bishop.'
John Warde, Master of the Pytchley (1798-1808)'

In spite of his taste for throwing Christians to Lions, Caligula loved horses and was, therefore, all right'.
Rintoul Booth, The Horseman's Handbook to end all Horseman's Handbooks, 1975

ANIMALS

'A horse is a vain thing for safety'.
The Bible, Psalm 33, Verse 17

'The seat on a horse makes gentlemen of some, grooms of others'
Cervantes, Don Quixote

'There used to be a rare breed of tree climbing foxes here (Kelmarsh). Climb like cats, they would, lay along the branches and watch the fun.'
(Dick Heathen)

'On what horse can we venture our lives more safely than on the Hunter?'
Nicholas Cox, quoted by Rintoul Booth

'Hounds and horses devour their masters'
John Clarke, 1639

'Horses are like sponges. They absorb all your strength and leave you limp. But give them a squeeze and you get it all back.'
Jackie Kennedy Onassis.

HUNTING TALES

'All difficulties begin with the command "Trot on......." '
W. Museler, Riding Logic, translated by F.W. Schiller (1937)

'Only cads shoot foxes'
Old saying

'Talk of horses and hounds and of system and kennel
Give me the Leicestershire nags and the hounds of Old Meynell'
Old Quorn song about Sir Hugo Meynell who founded the Quorn in 1753

'Well could he ride, and often men would say
That horse his mettle from his rider takes...'
William Shakespeare

'The brave beast is no flatterer; he will throw a prince
As well as his groom'
Ben Jonson, Discoveries, 1635

'One white foot, keep him not a day
Two white feet, send him soon away
Three white feet, sell him to a friend
Four white feet, keep him to the end'
Old English rhyme

'Oats: A grain which in England is given to horses, but in Scotland supports the people'
Samuel Johnson: Dictionary of the English Language 1754

'My horses understand me tolerably well; I converse with them at least 4 hours every day. They are strangers to bridle or saddle'
Jonathan Swift 1720

'A German singer! I should as soon expect to get pleasure from the neighing of my horse'
Frederick the Great of Prussia c. 1766
Quoted in the Treasury of Humourous Quotations

'A sleeping fox counts chickens in his dreams'
Russian proverb

'Horses should be treated like women – not to be bullied or deceived or neglected with impunity'.
Will Goodall.

'Mr. Cozier's hounds are as fierce as tigers, long as a hayband and with an amiable cast of features like the Chancellor of the Exchequer.'
Sporting Magazine, 1828.

(Were they trying to tell the Chancellor something?)

'Uncouple at the timorous flying hare,
Or at the fox, which lives by subtilty,
Or at the roe, which no encounter dare:
Pursue these fearful creatures o'er the downs,
And those thy well-breath'd horse keep with thy hounds.'
Shakespeare: Venus and Adonis

HUNTING/RIDING

'Do not ride in another man's pocket'
Old saying

'The horn of the hunter is heard on the hill'
Julia Crawford: Kathleen Mavourneen, 1840

'All are not hunters that blow the horn'
Medieval proverb

'There is no exercise that enableth the body
More for the wars than hunting, by teaching you to endure
Heat, cold, hunger, thirst, to rise early, to watch late,
Lie and fare badly'
Henry Peacham: The Compleat gentleman, 1622

'Foxhunting is a kind of warfare; its fatigues, its difficulties
And its dangers render it interesting
Above all other diversions'
Peter Beckford, Thoughts on Hunting, 1899

'The emperor who is a huntsman soon loses his throne'
Chinese proverb

'The healthy huntsman with the cheerful horn
Summons the dogs and greets the dappled morn'
John Gay, Rural Sports II, 1713

HUNTING TALES

'The world may be divided into people that read,
People that write, people that think
And...foxhunters'

William Shenstone, 1764

'When a fox gets to ground he has won and should be left alone'

G. F. Lucas 1955

'You tell me I should always kill a fox. I might answer,
I must catch him first '

Peter Beckford, Thoughts on Hunting, 1899

'When I bestride him, I soar, I am a hawk;
He trots the air; the earth sings when he touches it'

William Shakespeare, Henry V, III, 1599

'Good and much company and a good dinner;
Most of their discourse was about hunting
In a dialect I understood very little '

Samuel Pepys Diary, November 22, 1663

'Foxhunters who have all day long tried in vain to break their necks
Join at night in a second attempt on their lives
By drinking'

Bernard de Mandeville, 1714

'Tom Firr has been to hunting what W. G. Grace has been to cricket – the Champion!

Brooksby in a letter to The Field on Firr's retirement.

'The fox has much to answer for. Broken necks, maimed bodies, ruined lives and frittered fortunes by the score can be laid to his account.'

Eric Morrison, 1954.

'He was lucky enough to be born with a temperament that takes all in its stride, a physique that gives no trouble and a love of hounds and hunting that overcomes all difficulties.'

Eric Morrison on Stanley Barker.

''tis your small eater alone who chatters o'er his meals; your true-born sportsman is ever a silent and assiduous grubber. True it is that occasionally space is found between mouthfuls to shout 'WAITER' in a tone that requires not repetition.'

(Foxhunters at the trough.) R. S. Surtees: Jorrocks Jaunts and Jollities, 1843.

HUNTING TALES

'A 'regular swell' from Melton Mowbray, unknown to everyone except his tailor, to whom he owes a long tick, makes his appearance and affords abundance of merriment. He is just turned out of the hands of his valet and presents the very 'beau ideal' of his caste – quite the lady, in fact. His hat is stuck on one side, displaying a profusion of well-waxed ringlets. (Then) an enormous pair of moustaches give him the appearance of having caught the fox himself and stuck its brush beneath his nose.'

(The Melton Dandy.) R. S. Surtees: Jorrocks Jaunts and Jollities, 1843.

'Fred Earp fell in the park and had to be taken home in a dog cart,'
Tom Firr's notes, 8th November 1886.
Obviously there were no ambulances then.

'It's not that I'm afraid of horses. I'm not even afraid of falling off. I just don't want to be there when it happens.'
Woody Allen.

'Hunting makes more people happy than anything else I know.'
John Masefield.

'Hunting improves the sight and keeps men from growing old'
Xenophan.

'Foxhunting is the grandest sport of all, and reading about it is the next best thing.'
Major Maurice Barclay MFH, 1954.

'I think the horse would get along better without the man than the man without the horse.'
Leroy Judson Daniels.

'Old age is like getting on a horse on a day's hunting. Once you're aboard, there's not a lot you can do.'
Golda Meir (1898-1978)

'This being Easter Sunday, we will ask the Master's wife to come forward and lay an egg on the altar.'
Church bulletin, Sywell, 1991.

'There's no more certain test of a huntsman than the manner in which his hounds fly to him and work for him with a will'
Lord Henry Bentinck

HUNTING TALES

'Its harder to find a good Huntsman than a Prime Minister'

Henry Chaplin

'A Mr. Benton, hailing from Northampton, we believe, had frequent falls and, from his ill luck in this respect, seems to have excited considerable amusement for the field'

The Pytchley Hunt & Althorp Chase Book,15/4/1876

From the Northampton Herald, where regular full hunt reports were published. (The paper merged with the Mercury to become the Mercury & Herald, and reports were carried until the late 1970's)

'It was an exceedingly clever run of 50 minutes and the hounds did their business remarkably well. Dick Knight had a fall in each chase. In the last he was knocked off his horse by a tree! '

Northampton Herald 25/3/1876

(I presume he meant a branch?)

'A bookie is just a pickpocket who lets you use your own hands'

Harry Morgan on Point to Point racing

'Hunting is one of the most sensual of pleasures by which the powers of the body are strongly exerted but those of the mind unemployed'

Thomas Adams 1620

'Hunting is not proper employment for a thinking man'

Joseph Addison 1715

'If some animals are good at hunting and others are suitable to be hunted, then the Gods must clearly smile on hunting'

Aristotle 320 B.C.

'There is a passion for hunting, something deeply implanted in the human breast'

Charles Dickens: Oliver Twist 1860

'Hunting I reckon very good
To brace the nerves and steel the blood.'

Matthew Green 1730

'Racing and hunting excite man's heart to madness'

Lao Tzu, Chinese philosopher 600B.C.

'Hunting is fit recreation for a Pope'

Pope Pius V 1668

HUNTING TALES

'Hunting he loved, but love he laughed to scorn'
William Shakespeare, Venus and Adonis

'He that will get the better of a fox must rise early'
French Proverb

'The master of Foxhounds, to be perfect, must embody all the virtues of a saint with the commanding genius of a Kitchener and the tact of a diplomat'
Captain T. Ortho Paget 1930

'Back limped, with slow and crippled pace
The sulky leaders of the chase'
Sir Walter Scott 1820.

Obviously a bad day was had.

'It takes a good deal of physical courage to ride a horse. This, however, I have. I get it at about forty cents a flask and take it as required'
Stephen Leacock 1935 'Reflections on Riding'

'To confess that you are totally ignorant about the horse is social suicide. You will be despised by everyone, especially the horse'
W. C. Sellar: Horse Nonsense 1931

'O! For a horse with whips!'
William Shakespeare: Cymbeline

'Half the failures in life arise from pulling in one's horse as he is leaping'
Julius and Augustus Hare: Guesses at Truth, 1

'Much mixed bathing takes place when hounds cross this valley.'
A dry, witty comment by Guy Paget on the dreaded Braunston Brook, near Daventry.

'Come on, my Lord. The longer you look the less you'll like it.'
Richard Knight, Huntsman to the First Earl Spencer in 1765 at a fence near East Haddon. The 1st Earl was Master of the Pytchley from 1756 to 1783

'What with hunting three or four times a week, talking of it the remaining days, and thinking of it all the seven, with constant visits to the stable and a perpetual feud with (the) blacksmith, (the) mind is completely filled – .'
Whyte-Melville's description of Mr. Sawyer in Market Harborough (1861).

Sound familiar even today?

HUNTING TALES

'Racing men are bad enough. Politicians are sufficiently long-winded. A couple of agriculturalists will keep the ball rolling . . . on cake, mangold wurzel, shorthorns, reaping machines and guano; but I have heard ladies . . . affirm that, for energy, duration and the faculty of saying the same thing over and over again, a dialogue between a couple of foxhunters beats every other kind of discussion . . .'

Whyte-Melville (1861)

'A toss is a hawful thing'.

R. S. Surtees : Handley Cross 1843

'When we read . . . . that the Pytchley hounds will meet at Crick, we confess to the same sensation which the old coachman is said to experience at the crack of the whip. We call up a picture tinged with the colours of morning, the blood dances through (the) veins and (Earth's) children would fain leap and shout aloud for joy. What beauty is in the softened tints and shadows of the landscape . . .'

Market Harborough: G. J. Whyte Melville

Next to entertaining angels unawares, a M.F.H. may find himself giving shelter to a high prelate of the church, thrown from his horse, and yet none better for it. Of one such we asked at the time of the accident a few years ago:
"Has the Bishop regained consciousness yet?"
"I dunno," replied the good fellow, sadly, "But my butler tells me that he's found out which is my best bin of Claret!"

Extract from the Northampton Independent, April 18th 1908

'Not one man in twenty keeps his nerve for three years in the Pytchley Country, (so fearsome were the fences)'

Dick Heathen

'Hundreds of foxes owe their lives to people lighting a cigarette when they are upwind to hounds. No one ought to light a cigarette during a hunt. It's not fair on the hounds.'

Dick Heathen

'Certainly the fox likes hunting. He lives by hunting, and what is sauce for the goose is sauce for the gander. (Besides) if we hadn't the fox – or a good substitute – we should (all) be eaten up by mice.'

Sir Herewald Wake, Bart., 1908. Reported in the Northampton Independent.

'I love hunting, but I fear leaping. A king and the father of a family should not ride bold'.

George III

HUNTING TALES

'If I had my time to come over again' said the octogenarian 'I should flirt a little less and hunt a great deal more.'
G. J. Whyte Melville

'The attraction of hunting is that it acts on the mind like a poultice on a sore'.
Leon Trotsky.

'I say that hunters go into Paradise when they die, and live in this world more joyfully than any other men.'
Edward, Duke of York : The Master of the Game c.1400.

'Oh, a day's hunting will put that alright.'
Sebastian Flyte's mother on a suspicion that he was becoming a hard drinking man in 'Brideshead Revisited
Evelyn Waugh, 1945

'The peer must take a back seat if the butcher with a bold heart can pound him over a big fence.'
Ortho Paget : Hunting, (1900) on the classlessness of hunting.

'There is no sport in the world that makes men stronger, harder and tougher than hunting 3, 4 or 5 days a week for 5 or 6 months in every year.'
Hon. F. Lawley in the Daily Telegraph, August 11th 1896.

'Try to take the fences at the same time as your horse – together, not separately.'
Assheton Smith

'If you're in the mounted section of the Army, be careful when jumping fences. Do not part company with your horse, for in the Army it is a punishable offence to dismount before you are given the command!'
The Duke of Beaufort : Foxhunting.

'It's a foretaste of Heaven.'
Sir Herewald Wake, Bart., Feb. 29th 1908 on what foxhunting meant to him.

'The ideal pack of sandwiches should be capable of being opened by one numbed, gloved hand without being removed from the pocket.'
The Duke of Beaufort : Foxhunting.

'Hunting sandwiches should be so cut and packed that they can be eaten upon the back of a runaway mustang, in a hurricane of wind and cold rain, by a man who has recently broken his right wrist'.
David Brock: To Hunt the Fox.

'There is little real enjoyment on a cold December night — especially if you are already wet to the skin, tired, hungry, riding a leg-weary horse of extremely plebeian ancestry, and twelve miles from kennels — to be had out of being sent three miles in the wrong direction to search a hilly forest of some thousand acres for a lost hound. If, on your eventual arrival at the kennels four hours later, you can laugh on being told that the hound you'd been looking for had been in since half-past three, you are well on the way to being a Whipper-in.'

David Brock : To Hunt the Fox.

'It's been well observed that every man sees the hunted fox; but as we only undertake to pursue one at a time with our hounds, which are bred with the greatest care and attention, containing strains of almost every fashionable breed – the Belvoir, the Burton, the Beaufort, the Quorn, to say nothing of a dash of the old Pytchley Furrier – I say, as we only undertake to pursue one fox at a time, you'll p'r'aps have the goodness to let the hounds select their own!'

R. S. Surtees: Young Tom Hall, commenting on the discipline of the Field.

'Hunting days excepted, (the fox) parcels out the twenty-four hours after the manner of the most predatory of animals, even after the fashion of the man about-town; the nights he devotes to refreshment, plunder and love, the days to the luxury of rest and sleep.'

The Duke of Beaufort: Foxhunting (David & Charles 1980)

'I have seen a fox run along the top of a stone wall, and have heard of one running across the backs of a flock of sheep.'

The Duke of Beaufort: Foxhunting (David & Charles 1980)

'Foxhunting at its best is a wild sport; the wilder the better.'

Whyte Melville.

'"Tis a nasty varmit, I tell 'ee, and ought to be killed on a Sinday, zo well as wick days!'

Attributed to Tom French, the notorious vulpicide of the mid 1800's.

'. . . if an ill day comes, saunters about his house, lolls on couches, sighs and groans as if he were a prisoner in the Fleet; and the best thing he can find to do is to smoke and drink and play at backgammon with the Parson.'

Shadwell: Bury Fair (1689)

(Does this sound like a Foxhunter on a day when deep snow causes the Hunt to be called off? Or a golfer whose medal has just been postponed because of snow?)

'I am going to kill all your Hampshire foxes!'

Squire Osbaldeston rashly proclaimed this to the Secretary of the Hambledon Hunt. Hampshire, however, was known as the country to make or break a huntsman. The squire retired after only one season, having scarcely killed a single Charlie.

HUNTING TALES

'I should call the Pytchley the Pelican because of the large bills I have to pay!'
John Warde, MFH of the Pytchley from 1797 to 1808.

'I shall never forget one evening hunt across the (Burton) Flats with the Cottesmore, when the moon was up and there was a ground mist, covering everything like a cloud. Hounds making a tremendous cry, were quite invisible and the few remaining riders appeared like legless Centaurs – it was like a weird dream and terribly exciting.'
Ulrica Murray Smith, Magic of the Quorn .

Owing to the War, there were no second horses, therefore days were very short
The Hunting Diaries of Stanley Barker,
Second horses did not make a complete return until 1955.

'People said hunting was finished in 1918. They said it again in 1945, and some people are saying it now. But if we make it fun for people to hunt, then it will continue.'
Lt. Col. Sir Henry Tate, January 1994

Time spent on horses is never wasted. The Horse is the one certain escape from the world opf nonsense created by technologists, the envious (and the politically correct.) If you are going to be mad, you might as well be Mad on Horses.
Rintoul Booth

The Melton Train – Illustration by Edward Ardizzone in R. S. Surtees 'Handley Cross'

Book Two

Fascinating Facts
The Unusual to the Unbelievable

HUNTING TALES

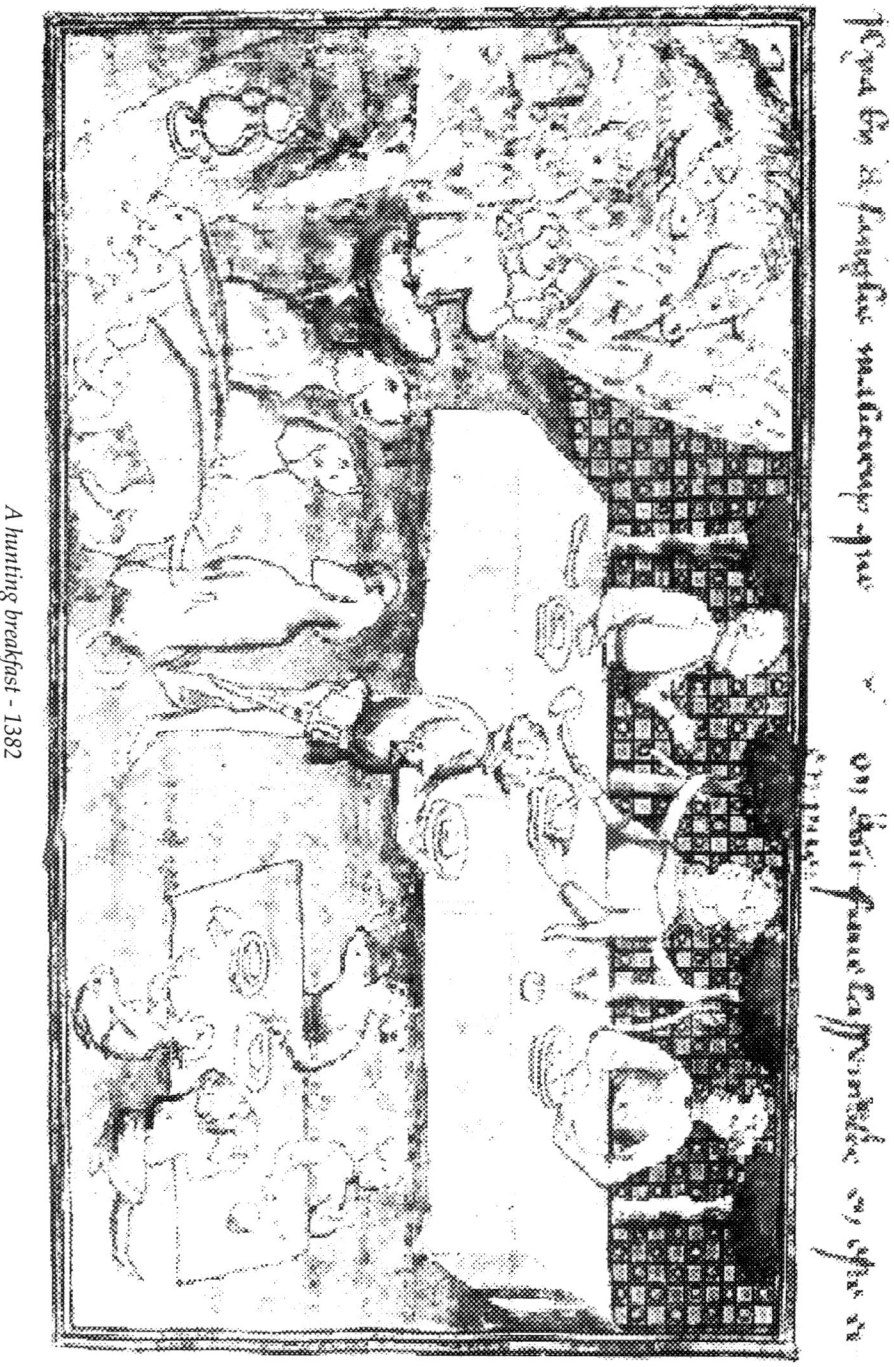

A hunting breakfast - 1382

ALFRED WRIGHT

Alfred Wright, Kennel Huntsman with the Kilkenny and first whipper-in to Major McCalmont, died in November 1993, aged 71 years. He started his career with the Golden Valley, moved to the Pytchley where he was whipper-in to the famous Stanley Barker, then the South Dorset until he moved to the Kilkenny where he stayed for 27 years.

DOONE VALLEY

Nicholas Snow (1827-1914) hunted the 'Stars of the West' country (later Exmoor) and was the owner of 'The Deer Park' on the opposite side of the Doone Valley near Badgeworthy Water. It was here that R. D. Blackmore, author of 'Lorna Doone', rode all over Exmoor with his grandfather, but there is no evidence he ever rode to hounds.

ROYAL CALPE

In Gibraltar (the Royal Calpe Hunt) in 1899, grooms and second horsemen became such a nuisance that they were charged field money. (They became scarcer after that). Hunting began there with the Duke of Beaufort's pack in 1861 when he brought his hounds to visit. The hunt became known as the Royal Calpe in 1906 with two patrons – King Edward VII and Alfonso XIII.
It is the tradition in Gibraltar to hold a point-to-point and give the farmers a free lunch. This is in contrast to the early (1891) days when there was considerable friction and not a few fist-fights with the Spanish farmers.

WHITE FOXHOUNDS

Most foxhunting hounds are a predominance of black and tan over white. But in some pure Welsh packs there are a great number of white hounds, and the Fell hounds are all white. Perhaps the most famous white pack was that of Sir Edward Curre (1855-1930), the Squire of Itton who hunted his white foxhounds from 1896 till his death.

WOMEN WELCOME

Fox-hunting was the first sport where women were allowed to 'play'. There were somewhat less objections to women foxhunting than there were to women voting!

SKITTLES

One of the most famous women foxhunters was known as 'Skittles', a glamourous courtesan of the 1860's who provoked feelings of jealousy amongst wives wherever she went. Many reports of the time refer to her only as 'Skittles', though her name was Catherine Walters.

IRON DUKE

The Duke of Wellington was a keen foxhunter (in Hampshire) and kept a pack of hounds in the Peninsula.

FORGET THE CAR

Enoch Powell, the M.P. and Classics scholar, used to travel by train from London to hunt in Melton Mowbray.

POPULAR

It is estimated that in England alone there are over fifty thousand subscribers to the Hunt, and well over a million car and foot followers.

JACK RUSSELL

Parson Jack Russell, the west-country hunting clergyman of the last century, was an ardent hunter of Stag, Fox, Otter and Hare and the breeder of the celebrated terrier.

IKEY BELL

The most famous name in modern foxhunting was Isaac 'Ikey' Bell, an American who became master of the Galway Blazers and the Kilkenny. His breeding techniques led to a lighter and more agile hound.

BEAUTY

Lady Randolph Churchill (Winston's mother) was a hunting field beauty of the 1870/1880 era and a regular follower of the Meath and other Irish packs.

ON FOOT

The Blencathra Hunt, in the Lake District, is one of six Fell packs that hunt on foot, owing to the steepness of the country. The hounds are brought to the meets by the farmers who board them.

GOODNIGHT!

When you come to the Meet, it is polite to say 'Good Morning, Master.' When you go home, you say 'Goodnight', and never 'Goodbye', even if it's only two o'clock in the afternoon.

BEAU–TIFUL

The modern hunting boot was designed by Beau Brummel (1778-1840). Baggy, long-topped boots with broad garters coming above the knee were the order of the day before he re-designed them and added white tops. It was said that the wonderful shine on his boots came from blacking mixed with peaches and champagne!

CHARLIE

'Charlie', the name given, almost with affection, to foxes, is said to derive from Charles James Fox, the 18th century politician.

NO PINK

Charles Trelawny of Coldrenick (1799-1883) was MFH of the Dartmoor. He scorned pink and rode in pepper-and-salt with brown breeches and top. His Huntsman John Roberts wore a blue coat and knee caps and carried a French horn.

GIPSY

Thomas Limpity Lavers (1800-1876) was nicknamed 'The Gipsy Huntsman' and was given to energetic, some say reckless, riding on his famous horse 'Jack Sheppard'. His recklessness, bad temper and evil tongue were legendary. He is buried at Ermington, South Devon.

STARS

The Exmoor Foxhounds were, in the late 1800's, known as the 'Stars of the West.'

JACKASSES

"Warde's Jackasses" was the name given to the pack of hounds owned by John Warde (1751-1838) because of their great size.

LONG RIDE

For sheer enthusiasm, the Rev. Griff Lloyd is hard to beat. In the early 1800's he would coach from his parish in Chester to Bicester, arrive at midnight a good 14 hours later and go cub hunting at 4 a.m., then return to Chester, always travelling as an outside passenger on the coach.

ESSAYIST

Sir Roger de Coverley, the noted Georgian essayist, was a country squire and MFH.

ECCENTRIC

George Templer of Stover (Devon) was an eccentric foxhunter. He used to hunt hares with a combined pack of terriers and foxes; he trained a monkey to ride an old hunter; and he frequently took the monkey and his stable cat (also mounted) when he went hunting. But the monkey was killed in the field by the swinging-to of a five-barred gate and Templer himself died at the age of 62 after being thrown from his horse.

BECKFORD

Peter Beckford, MFH (1740-1811) was known as the 'father of foxhunting literature' and was also the M.P. for Morpeth. He lived most of his life at Steepleton – Iwerne in Dorset. His tomb is at Steepleton, near Blandford. His 'Thoughts on Hunting', finally published in 1811, remains a classic work.

COKE

Thomas Coke of Holkham (Earl of Leicester) was one of Norfolks greatest agricultural pioneers, changing that county from one of the poorest to one of the richest. He started a pack of hounds in Oxfordshire before becoming MFH of the West Norfolk (1772) and then going into politics.

NELSON

Admiral Lord Nelson, although he first went to sea at the age of 12, was a keen foxhunter in Norfolk with the Earl of Leicester, Thomas Coke. Coke, in fact, was offered a peerage seven times, and did not accept the title of Earl of Leicester until 1837. He then appended his title and insisted on being called the 'Earl of Leicester of Holkham.

SORE BOTTOM

The Earl of Darlington (1766-1842) held the 'endurance record' for horsemanship. He is said in Nimrod's 'Hunting Reminiscences' to have hunted 5 days a week for more than 40 consecutive years. In days, that's 130 days a season, a total of 5200 days. If an average hunting day covered a modest 30 miles, including hacking there and back, he would have covered at least 156,000 miles! Simply put, he would have ridden to New York and back over 20 times!

FIRST MOBILE CAFE

A sporting parson won fame with the Cottesmore in 1826 by showing up at a meet complete with portable wine-cellar and half a hundredweight of sandwiches strapped to his waist. He was nicknamed the 'Licensed Victualler'. We believe this was the first mobile off-licence and cafe in the U.K.

JACK OF ALL TRADES

In early foxhunting days, the Huntsman was not the splendid figure he has been for the last century or so. One Huntsman in Kent was also Sir John Vout's coachman. Simon Jones, Huntsman in Herefordshire was also the gamekeeper, while an unfortunate Huntsman to a Master known only as 'Miser' Elmes was cook, valet, cowman, groom and gardener as well!

BIG HORN

Thomas Boothby (1677-1752), one of the first country squires to be a MFH, had a hunting horn which was partly silver, partly horn and was twice the length of the modern hunting horn.

DWARVES

George Templer of Stover's 'dwarf foxhounds' were known as the 'let them alones'. Templer (1781-1843) kept 20 foxes in his yard which were exercised daily. When a fox was selected he was bagged, then released, to be hunted by the dwarf hounds. The hounds were never allowed to kill and many a fox (like his legendary 'Bold Dragoon' who was hunted 36 times), returned to Templer's yard to be fed, exercised and hunted again. When Templer gave up his pack in 1826, many were sold and their blood still survives in today's Tiverton pack.

GOUT

The 9th Duke of Beaufort (1849-1924) suffered from gout from an early age. Despite the frequent bouts of pain, he would hunt with one leg encased in bandages, and use a wooden – not steel – stirrup to lessen the pain.

BIG FOX

The biggest fox killed in Britain weighed 23lbs and measured 52 inches from nose to brush-end. It was at Cross Fell, in the Northwest of England, killed by legendary Fell Huntsman Joe Bowman. Many foxes in that area are bigger and heavier and known locally as 'greyhound foxes', being the true hill sort, long in the legs and grey coated. Despite inter breeding with smaller, redder foxes, the Fell packs occasionally kill foxes up to 18lbs even today.

BAREBACK BISHOP

Dr. Gott, Bishop of Truro, was a noted horseman. Whilst at Cambridge he rode bareback over eight flights of jumps with a penny under each knee. At the end of the ride, the pennies were still in place.

RABIES

The Gibraltar (Royal Calpe) pack have twice been destroyed; once in 1898 and again in 1922, due to an epidemic of rabies. On both occasions the Master, Don Pablo Larios, later the Marquis of Marzales, managed to get fresh packs together with help from many Masters in England.

HUNTING POET

Charles Kingsley (1819-1875) was a poet, author (The Water Babies) and an early example of a Hunting Parson. Although mad keen on hunting, he never owned a horse worth even fifty pounds, so little self-indulgent was he.

RICH FARMERS

Mr. Gladstone's only appearance on the hunting field was at Althorp when the 'Red Earl' was Master and his only comment was: 'These farmers cannot be so badly off, or they would not ride such beautiful horses as those I saw this morning.'

CHESTY COUGH

Lord Spencer, the 'Red Earl' so called because of his long bushy red beard, suffered from a weak chest. It was because of this he grew the beard which he used as a chest protector!

PULP

John Chaworth Musters (Handsome Jack) and Thomas Assheton Smith, both later to become Masters, were involved in a brutal fist fight at Eton which left both their faces looking like pulp. Yet historians record that this was the beginning of a lifelong friendship!

PRODUCTIVE MASTER

Thomas Ridge of the Kilmiston Hunt (later the Hampshire) was Master from 1749 to 1784. He resigned in that year due to the prodigious expense of his family, who numbered twenty-one children!

ISLE OF WIGHT AUTHOR

Hubert Garle hunted with the Queen's Staghounds, the Garth and the Isle of Wight Foxhounds at the turn of the century. He has published various works on sport, including 'Hunting in the Golden Days' and 'A Driving Tour in the Isle of Wight', a hunting history of the island.

A JOB LOT OF STONE WALLS

County Galway is known as good hunting country with all pasture, good, light going and lots of jumping. It is reckoned that there are 30 stone walls to the mile – one every 50 yards! In the western part of the county the visitor is cautioned about the high single banks, stone walls and the continuous jumping. He must be prepared to 'throw his heart ahead of his horse!'

Jacksons Hunting Handbook 1993.

PRODUCTIVE HOUND

Jem Hills, the Heythrops legendary Huntsman, had a blind bitch hound, Affable. Because of her blindness, caused by distemper, she was never hunted to hounds, but became amazingly productive, having 90 pups in her lifetime!

ANNE BOLEYN'S BROTHER

Henry VIII made George Boleyn (Viscount Rochford) Master of the Royal Buckhounds and also the Household Pack. It was well known that he could ride, shoot, dance and fight better than most. With Anne, he was accused of treason and sentenced to be hanged, cut down alive, drawn and quartered. But the king commuted the sentence and he was simply beheaded.

THE AMAZONS

Myth and legend contend that the most complete hunters and horsewomen were the Amazons, originally from the Caucasus who settled near the Black Sea. They hunted deer, jackals, wolves and foxes with bow and arrow, riding bareback astride. The literal meaning — 'A–mazos' — means 'no breast' and it is said that they removed the right breast in order to draw their bows more easily. In modern hunting, however, it is reported accurately that this practice has now ceased.

LUCY GLITTERS

The R. S. Surtees hero, Mr. Sponge, lost his heart to the gay and fearless huntress, Lucy Glitters. She is said to have been inspired by Laetitia, Lady Lode, a famed huntress of the 1775 era who, before her marriage to Sir John Lode, was reputed to have been the mistress of a notorious highwayman.

JACK THE LAD

Capt. Jack White of the Cheshire was, according to Nimrod in 1816, 'one of the hardest and best riders in England'. On one occasion in 1842 at Melton with Lord Lonsdale, he rode back 24 miles to Melton, changed, had a chop and cup of tea, then rode 75 miles home to Derbyshire, crossing the Peak District in a snowstorm.

(Reported in Baily's Magazine)

NO GELDINGS

The Shah of Persia (before his exile and the Ayatollah took control of Iran) had large stables on the outskirts of Tehran, near the Great Salt Desert. His horses were a mixture of Persian Plateau and thoroughbreds, and all the riding horses were stallions. This is normal for the middle-east as it is considered unmanly to ride geldings.

(Riding through My Life: Princess Anne, Pelham Books 1991).

SIDE-SADDLE

The idea of riding side saddle was introduced to Britain by Anne of Bohemia, wife of Richard II around 1380. Until then, women had usually ridden astride in a split skirt, or pillion behind a man. It became the fashion for women to sit on a stuffed seat with their feet resting on a 'planchette', or wooden platform. This was quite elegant, but was only suitable for formal occasions or slow journeys. Women who wanted to enjoy the high speed of the hunting field continued to ride astride. Catherine de Medici, wife of Henry II changed the vogue when she rode with her right leg hooked around the pommel of the saddle, then added an extra horn so she could wedge her leg between the two pommels. This fashion remained for over 250 years. But Catherine inevitably caused envy at court with many wives claiming that she did it, not for security, but to show off her excellent legs!

FORGET THE CROYDON FERRY

The 2nd Duke of Grafton had to use the Croydon ferry to cross his hounds, then wait for it to return for the followers. It was infuriatingly slow, so he had London Bridge built!

CARTED STAGHOUNDS

This was an ancient practice, now long given up in England. On a hunting morning, two deer would be loaded into a cart. While the hounds were meeting, the deer would go to a meeting place and be set loose. After 20 minutes, the hounds were laid on the line and the hunt would proceed. Deer, however, were great characters. If they decided not to run, they would turn into the hounds and scatter them in all directions. Often, the deer would take refuge in a lake and defy all attempts by hunt staff to coax them out. When all else failed, a boat would be launched, a perilous expedition for all! Then the deer would be reloaded into the cart and returned to their paddock.
This practice continued until 1964 in Norwich, although the Irish packs, the Down County and the Ward Union, still continue.

Contributed by Tim Langley (Good Morning and Good Night, 1987, The Blackthorn Press, Grantham)

HUNTING TALES

DANGEROUS SPORT

Experts reckon that fox-hunting is more dangerous than motorcycle racing, skiing, boxing, or any other sport. When one considers the risks — rabbit holes, concealed tree stumps, rocks, fence wire, bogs and the unpredictable behaviour of horses and riders, it is not difficult to agree. And it is a fact that more foxhunters have been paralysed, blinded, brain-damaged, disfigured and killed than participants in any other sport!

LORD LONGFORD

The moralist, writer and prison reformer Lord Longford was the son of a Master of Foxhounds, who had always expressed a wish to die on the hunting field. He didn't get his wish but almost . . . he was killed in a fusiliers charge!

NO VULPICIDES

In the last century, if a farmer or gamekeeper was discovered killing foxes, he would be evicted or imprisoned, such was the feeling that foxes should not be poisoned, snared or shot. Even today, many tenant farmers have a clause in their leases which contracts them to do everything possible to assist the hunt, and legally restrains them from killing foxes.

FIRST CASUALTY

As noblemen copied the 5th Duke of Beaufort and hunted foxes rather than hares, the first noble casualty of the new sport of foxhunting was the 2nd Duke of Buckingham. On a wet, freezing evening he waited for hours outside a covert for the fox to emerge, and died of a fever while he waited.

ROYAL DISLIKE

The Empress of Austria, who hunted with the Pytchley, was very much disliked by Queen Victoria because she would regularly turn down royal invitations if they interfered with her pursuit of the fox. The Queen was not accustomed to such slights and was 'not amused'.

EMERGENCY STOCK

All hunting clothes are worn for a reason. The white cravats around the necks of the women riders — the stock – can be used as a bandage in the event of an accident. They can also be used as tourniquets and the tie-pin can be used to keep it tight.

SIEGFRIED SASSOON

Sassoon's joy for the hunting field is well documented in his writings and poems. When he went off to France to fight in the first World War, he even staged a mock hunt over the trenches, in earshot of the guns and shells. But he returned from the war badly wounded, completely broken in spirit and mentally deranged.

MASTER BOB PODMORE

The youngest-ever MFH was Bob Podmore. He took over from his father in 1901 as Master of the Vine at the age of 8! His father subsequently acted as his Huntsman and second whip. When the boy had finished his day's hunting, he would take his bath, have a beef tea, and then play with his baby sister and toys in the nursery!
He died suddenly in August 1907 at the age of only 14 and is buried at Charlton Kings Parish Church, near Cheltenham.

BROTH BATH

It was common throughout the last two centuries for hounds, returning from the day's hunting, to walk through a broth bath at the entrance to the kennels. This made them lick their legs and feet, so healing their sores and cuts. (And saving vets bills!)

GLUTTON FOR PUNISHMENT

Ralph Lampton represented Durham in the House of Commons and was Master of the Durham County. In 1825 he had a very bad fall, injuring his spine. Whilst still convalescing he had a fall next season, injuring his head and neck. Ten years later, while slowly regaining his health after virtual paralysis, he was thrown again and crippled permanently. He died in 1844.

STRICKLAND

A famous Yorkshire hunting name is Strickland. One of the Stricklands was lieutenant to Sebastian Cabot when he discovered Labrador. The family introduced the turkey into England, and King Henry VII gave the family a turkey for their crest. The name is mentioned in 'Tom Brown's Schooldays' as 'Martin' who acted as second for Tom in his fight with 'Slogger' Williams. And Thomas Strickland refused to entertain Queen Henrietta Maria when she landed at Bridlington. Sir Charles Strickland of Hildenley hunted with Lord Middleton in the early 1900's.

BAD BREATH

The Marquess of Winchester, later the Duke of Bolton was a strange, eccentric sportsman. He would refuse to speak for weeks on end in the winter, for fear of swallowing 'bad air'. At other times he would not open his mouth before 10 in the morning for the same reason. And he always hunted at night, by torchlight!

THE SCARTEEN HOUNDS

The unique Scarteen black and tan Kerry Beagles are now believed to have been delivered by Spanish traders before the Armada. There is a statue in Santa Cruz, Spain of three Spanish hounds so strikingly similar to the Scarteen that credence is now given to this version of their origin.

PRESERVED AS ARMCHAIRS

The legendary Master, Parson Jack Russell, couldn't bear it when his three favourite hunters Billy, Monkey, and Cottager died. Their skins were cured and used to cover the Parson's best armchair. Long before the days of horseboxes, Russell would, when well over 80, hack to meets, hunt and hack back home, doing almost 100 miles in a day.

TREAT THEM LIKE WOMEN

'Horses should be treated like women - not to be bullied, or deceived or neglected with impunity.' was the dictum of the celebrated Belvoir huntsman, Will Goodall, as he wrote in his thesis 'Goodall's Practice'.

CAMELS LIKE THE SOUND OF HORN

On their way to the Dardanelles on the S.S. Olympic, the 37 Masters on board were presented with a hunting horn. Only 3 could blow it! At Gallipoli they used the horn to summon camels when they strayed off. They came running to the sound!

A DREAM SCHOOL

Isaac 'Ikey' Bell MFH at the Galway and others, attended school at Well Vale before going to Cambridge. It was an ideal school for a boy who loved sport. The children were encouraged to bring their dogs, horses, rods, guns, even falcons!

GOOD MANNERS

Mrs. W. Hall - the Missus - MFH at Carlow for 45 years - was intolerant of any bad manners. When a youth at Punchestown spoke to her with his pipe still in his mouth, she knocked it clean out from between his teeth. She always rode side-saddle and was still cub-hunting in her 86th year. She died in 1965 and was mourned by the whole of Ireland.

BITTEN BY AN ADDER

One of Percival Williams' hounds 'Dockter' was bitten by an adder while cub-hunting, his tongue swelled up, nearly suffocating him, then completely dropped off at the base. To teach the hound to drink, Williams had to hold his head under water to the eyes and eventually he learned, and he lived for many years after and became a valuable stallion hound.

ROYAL PITSFORD

The Duke of Windsor learned his hunting at Pitsford Hall, now the home of Northamptonshire Grammar School, when a guest of Capt. George Drummond.

20 MILES HOME

The great Foxhound sire, Four Burrow Whipcord was left out one day, 20 miles from the kennels. Nothing was heard of him for 4 days when he was found 2 miles from the kennels. He had a gin-trap on his forefoot and had dragged it 18 miles to get home. He lost his two centre toes but survived many years as a stallion hound.

37 MASTERS ON BOARD

4000 troops were on their way to the Dardanelles on the S.S. Olympic and experienced a perilous voyage up the Mediterranean. On the boat, all volunteers (Kitcheners Army) - were no fewer than 37 Masters of Hounds.

EXPORT OF HORSES

'Dalesman's' Horse Fund existed in the 1920's and sought to stop the export of horses abroad. 'Dalesman' himself visited abattoirs throughout Europe and instigated a bill to alleviate most of the suffering. Shades of the 1990's indeed.

BADMINTON

The Tenth Duke of Beaufort was the inspiration behind the Horse Trials at Badminton, which had always previously been known for foxhunting. The Horse Trials, which have been held there since 1950, were the first of their kind in Britain, and the Royal Family tend to stay at Badminton House for the occasion.

THE LEGEND OF ST. ROCHE

In the 14th century St. Roche was struck down by a plague while healing the sick at Piacenza in Italy. He was found in the forest nearby by Roquet, a nobleman's hunting hound who brought him bread every day and licked his sores until he recovered. His feast day is August 16 and in some parishes in France and Italy, hounds are blessed on that day in remembrance.

FOXHUNTER

The winner of the 1952 Olympic gold medal, Foxhunter, died in 1959. His hide is buried with Sir Harry Llewellyn's book 'Foxhunter in Pictures' in a steel casket on the Blorenge Mountain in Wales. His skeleton is preserved in the Royal Veterinary College.

FURY OF A KING

James I loved hunting and kept a hound pack. His favourite hound, Jewel, was killed with a crossbow by his wife Anne of Denmark. The King was furious at her and forbade her ever to use a crossbow again.

ENDURANCE FEATS

Lord Henry Bentinck's powers of endurance were miraculous. In the 1880's he would ride 6 days a week from Welbeck to the Burton meets, some 30 miles from home. It was estimated that his Lordship covered 500 miles a week on horseback in the days before horseboxes or trailers.

BOTANY BAY COVERT

Many coverts have strange names, and knowing why can add to the interest of a day's hunting. Botany Bay Covert in Quorn country was the furthest away from the Hunt Kennels, as Botany Bay itself was the furthest exile for deported convicts.

PYTCHLEY TRADITION

Dick Saunders was Joint Master of the Pytchley until 1987 and upheld the Pytchley tradition of big fences and top-class riding. He won the 1982 Grand National on Grittar and, at 48, was the oldest rider to win the event.

HUNTING FOR ALL

Before the Industrial Revolution, the local squire owned the hounds. Invitations to hunt were given to his friends and neighbours. The squire paid all the staff himself. In the late 19th century, hunting by subscription allowed the newly wealthy to hunt and helped to pay for the sport.

PREMIER SHOW

Peterborough Royal Foxhound Show is the premier show in the U.K. Awards at Peterborough are more highly prized than at any other hound show.

HOUNDS ON THE MAYFLOWER?

Many of the early settlers of the United States took their hounds with them. The first pack was established in Virginia by Lord Fairfax and George Washington worked for him, though not in the Kennels. Washington was a keen foxhunter and set up his own pack at Mount Vernon. Unlike the U.K., American hunts do not play a central part in farming or rural life. The sport tends to be more elitist, like the golf clubs, and the social side is of great importance.

ROYAL HUNTERS

Many members of the Royal Family have had a love of foxhunting. Edward VII, Edward VIII and George VI were all keen hunting men, with George especially fond of the Pytchley. Prince Charles took up the sport in 1975 at Badminton and has since hunted all over the U.K.

ARISTOCRATS

In the U.S. State of Virginia before the first World War, the Orange County Hunt was accused of being so snobbish that its members acted like pre-revolutionary French aristocrats. Their excuse was said to be that they "thought that snobbery was socially correct."

STEEPLECHASES

The Irish gentry held races in the 18th century across country, and it became common practice to decide the horse races over an agreed line of country with a church steeple as a landmark to the winning post. Hence the beginnings of 'steeplechasing' as we know it.

FLAT TO JUMPS

Many jockeys and trainers from the world of racing enjoy hunting and jumping the sometimes daunting fences. The great flat-racing jockey Willie Carson has hunted in Cheshire and with the Quorn. Barry Hills and Peter Walwyn are trainers who love foxhunting.

AMERICAN CONNECTIONS

Americans are especially fond of hunting in Ireland. The Scarteen has had three Americans as Joint Masters – Ian Hurst, Sermon Wolf and Bill Hobby.

AFTER MASS

One can hunt seven days a week in Ireland. Some harrier packs meet on a Sunday, after Mass, of course. Sunday hunting is especially popular in Co. Clare.

BY YOUR LEAVE

During the Second World War, the hunting field was filled with many service men on leave. Men like Sir Gerald Glover's wartime memories of the U.K. consisted entirely of hunting and he, like so many officers, would spend their 14 days of precious leave chasing 'Charlie'.

ROYAL DRESS

King George III and Prince Charles wore the 'Windsor' coat when hunting, a royal blue with red collar and cuffs.

ALTHORP MUSEUM

An attempt is being made to create a museum at Althorp House with memorabilia of the family over the centuries. Old uniforms, hunting attire, weapons, books and pictures form the basis of the museum. But several artifacts and family papers are missing — sold to the British museum by Raine Spencer. Amongst the missing items is the Diary of the famous Huntsman, Will Goodall.

Hunting was a vital part of the Spencer family life, and one of the most famous was the 'Red Earl' – the 5th Earl of Althorp who held three masterships of the Pytchley Hunt. Although the 7th Earl was a keen foxhunter, he was never a Master, and the late 8th Earl Spencer and the present Earl both rode horses, but did not ride to hounds.

WEAK SHOULDER

Lord Althorp (the third Lord Spencer) had a weakness in one shoulder. He fell so often, and put it out of joint so much that a whipper-in was sent on a special course to Northampton General Hospital to be taught how to put it back.

Thereafter his lordship's shoulder was put back in the field by the young whipper-in.

LORD CHESHAM'S MONUMENT

Halfway between the villages of Pitsford and Brixworth, in Northamptonshire, stands a tall limestone monument. It was erected in 1908 to mark the death, while out hunting, of Charles W. Cavendish, Lord Chesham, who lived at Spratton Hall, later at Boughton Hall.

His horse – a hunter he was trying for the first time – caught its forefeet on a fence near Welton Reservoir, near Daventry, somersaulted over and landed on Lord Chesham, breaking his neck on November 9th 1907. It was the second hunting tragedy for the Cheshams, as their youngest daughter Marjorie Beatrice Cavendish was killed at the age of 12 after falling from her pony.

The Lord Chesham Memorial cost £230 and was erected with local subscriptions organised by the Pytchley Master Lord Annaly who then lived at Holdenby House.

MAD KEEN

Lord Gough had only one arm. A lady born without any hands rode with the Pytchley. Col. Foljambe and Capt. du Boisson had only one pair of legs between them, and a Mr. Cavanagh hunted without arms or legs. Such was the lengths foxhunters would go to, so keen were they, despite their handicaps.

Reported by Dick Heathen 'Rum 'uns to Follow'

AFTER MY DEATH . . .

When Lord Ebury fell and broke his leg while hunting with the Pytchley, he left instructions that, in the event of his death, his ashes were to be scattered near Tamborough Hill where he'd spent the happiest days of his life. Another gentleman wanted his skin to be made into a saddle and given to one of his lady friends.

BOXING DAY HORDES

At the turn of the century the Fernie used to meet on the square in Market Harborough. Sometimes there were as many as twenty thousand spectators!

SAVAGE HOUND

Lord Lonsdale's hound Sergeant had a reputation as a savage. Other packs were known to be equally savage. There is evidence (according to Eric Morrison) that the Kennel Huntsman of the Worcestershire Hounds was alarmed by the deafening din from his kennels one night. He went in to quiet them, dressed in his nightgown, and was promptly eaten! The story is believed to be authentic and very bad luck on the poor huntsman!

LOUD VOICE

Dick Knight became the first in a succession of famous Pytchley huntsmen in 1777. Amongst his accomplishments which include some amazing feats of horsemanship was his loud, clear voice. It was said that Dick Knight's voice could, on a frosty morning, be heard three miles away.

PYTCHLEY HALL

Sir Euseby Isham built the imposing Elizabethan mansion, Pytchley Hall. Members of the exclusive Pytchley Hunt would stay there during the season and stable their horses there. When George Payne first took over as Master of the Pytchley from 1835-1838 he dissipated his large fortune on the turf and actually gambled away the lead on the roof of Pytchley Hall. He eventually demolished the Hall, although the original gates still stand at Overstone. Payne came back to the Mastership in 1845, having gone to South Africa broke, made another fortune, and came back rich once more. His son blew his second fortune betting on horses!

SPENCER PERCEVAL

The only British Prime Minister to die in office was Spencer Perceval who was assassinated on May 11th 1812, shot by Henry Billingham in the lobby of the House of Commons.
His wife Jane was a horsewoman of some note, and the daughter of Sir Thomas Spencer Wilson. She married Perceval in her riding attire, and Perceval, a clever politician, was known to have bought a hunting saddle, a bridle and a pair of thistle breeches. He had been M.P. for Northampton, steward at Northamptonshire races and the nephew of Earl Compton of Castle Ashby. His wife Jane is known to have hunted in Sussex, near East Grinstead.
His popularity was questionable and church bells are said to have been rung all over England when news of his assassination was released. It is unlikely that Perceval ever went hunting, as his relationship with the Prince of Wales – himself a keen foxhunter – was, at best - a tenuous one.

FIRST PAINTER

John Wootton (1685-1765) is recognised as the earliest English artist of any repute to paint pictures relating to animals and to sport. He is said to have been the pupil of the Dutch Master, John Wyck, who was well known for his battle and equestrian pictures. Many of Wootton's pictures hang in the hall at Badminton.

WILLIAM FILGATE

Mr. William Filgate hunted with The Louth in 1875 at the age of 94, when blind. At his last meet he came out in pink, attended by a servant to hear the hounds in full cry. The Louth was started with a private pack of harriers owned partly by Col. Filgate of Lisrenny.

CAPPING

The Irish system of 'capping' for non-subscribers was started by the Quorn in 1897, as a means of raising funds and avoiding the resignation of Lord Lonsdale who was feeling the financial pressure. Each stranger was obliged to pay a pound. The system lasted a year, was dropped, then re-started in 1903, following a meeting with the nearby Hunts. Ortho Paget was given the job of prising the sovereigns loose from the strangers. It was not a pleasant job for him. Some of his old friends, out for a day with the Quorn, did not greet him with the warmth he expected. Many succeeded in avoiding him and devised many ruses to evade the 'cap'.

NO DISCIPLINE

In the late 1700's the Shires became the favourite area for hard-riding foxhunters. Their idea was to ride at each other and over each other, with the hounds only incidental. Hugo Meynell's greatest worry was keeping the hounds from being injured by these hard riders. Squire Osbaldeston once took the hounds home because he couldn't stop the foxhunters galloping directly behind the fox!

CHASING A SQUIRREL

Tom Firr's whipper-in Fred Earp admitted he'd once holloa'd the hounds onto a red squirrel. Earp saw a flash of red on a wall near a covert. It looked like a fox's brush, so away went the hounds – and the squirrel.

ERIC MORRISON

The MFH with Westerby Basset Hounds and Joint-Master with the Atherstone Foxhounds had a distinguished war career, serving with the Desert Rats (7th Armoured) and was awarded a Military Cross He is the author of 'Fox and Hare in Leicestershire', published in 1954 by Eyre and Spottiswoode.

YOUNGEST WHIP

Stanley Barker, the legendary Pytchley huntsman from 1931-1960 was England's youngest ever whipper-in at the age of 16 with the Sinnington hunt in North Yorkshire.

LARGEST CROWD EVER

At the end of 1860 there was great distress amongst the weavers of Coventry. George Baker, Master of the North Warwickshire decided that the spectacle of a meet would provide them with a little amusement (it was not designed to alleviate their distress!). He paraded the hounds for the benefit of the ladies present and accounts of the time estimate a crowd of almost forty thousand at the meet!
(British Hunts and Huntsmen, Volume II, 1909)

THE MASTER'S IMAGE

Non-hunting folk imagine a Master of Hounds to be an ogre, a hard swearing, hard-drinking man completely devoid of any moral code. 'Nothing could be further from the actual fact' said Eric Morrison in 1954 in 'Fox and Hare in Leicestershire'.

THE HATFIELDS and McCOYS

In Brocklesby Hunt country near Caistor, Humberside, lived two feuding families, Ross and Tyrwhitt. In 1603 a Tyrwhitt hunting party met up with a Ross contingent. A deadly fight was the result and many from each family were killed. When King James I, on his way back from Scotland, heard of the battle, he ordered a gallows to be built near the spot. The King promised to hang the first man who would resort to arms without royal sanction. The Tyrwhitts moved to Oxfordshire, of the Ross clan there is no further mention. This may well be the first recorded instance of two rival hunts actual killing each other.

BUCKING GIRAFFE

Field Marshall Sir Evelyn-Wood, V.C. hunted with the Essex at the turn of the century. He was a fine rider and boasted that there was no animal he couldn't ride. While in India, the Nawab of Jowra offered him a ride on a giraffe. He managed to mount it but its bucking, and extraordinary sideways gait as it bolted, unseated Sir Evelyn. He was thrown heavily and knocked senseless.

HUNTING PRINCESS

The Danish-born Queen Alexandra became very popular with the British public when she married the Prince of Wales in 1863.
She visited the Pytchley point-to-point races as Princess of Wales in 1878, with the ill-fated Empress of Austria who was later assasinated.

THE BLACK FOX

Tom Firr's notes of 1888 reveal that the Quorn found a black fox near Whatton. It was believed to be the last descendant of those imported into England by the Russian ambassador in 1815.

HUNTING IN BOSNIA

Despite the ravages of war, there are some places in Bosnia where limited hunting still takes place. Major Patrick Darling of the Light Dragoons encountered a Croat who insisted on showing him his hounds at work. He was invited to a meet the following week and the hounds were used to drag up a quarry which was then shot. Bear, wolf, hare and fox are all hunted, mostly over bare rock.

Horse and Hound, 13th January 1994

OLDEST

Lt. Col. Sir Henry Tate, 91, hunted with the Flint and Denbigh in 1915 and claims to be the oldest surviving member. He hunted till 1980 when he gave up due to hip trouble and the age of his horse. He has almost 80 years of hunting memories, over 60 of them as an active participant.

CANADA'S MASTER

Charles Kindersley was Canada's most distinguished MFH, having been Master of the Eglinton and Caledon Hunt in Ontario for 42 years until 1991, hunting hounds himself for 32 years. As a young man he hunted in the Cattistock country in Dorset in the days of Parson Milne. He died recently aged 93.

FASTER ON FOOT

Foot following can lead to some unique situations. Donough McGillycuddy of the Pytchley was out recently and, near 4 o'clock, found himself alone with hounds while the mounted followers were still three fields away!

TRUE - BLUE

The Cattistock were started up by a parson, the Rev. J. Phelips and were once known as the True Blue Hunt. Amongst the Masters was Lord Poltimore and the legendary Rev. 'Jack' Milne who, in 31 years as MFH, accounted for a total of 7882 foxes!

FIRST BOWLER HAT

Thomas William Coke, 1st Earl of Leicester, was the first man to wear the hat invented by William Bowler, the hat still known as the billycock or bowler hat.

HUNTING TALES

GENEROUS WIFE

When John Warde (1751-1838), who had been a Master for 57 seasons including the Bicester, Pytchley and Craven packs, was hard up and about to give up his hounds, he found £1000 to his credit in the bank from 'a friend of foxhunting'. That friend was Mrs. Warde, a generous lady with a private fortune. All wives take note!

From 'Famous Foxhunters' by Lionel Edwards.

NO PINK

Squire Pode, of Slade Hall, hunted the Dartmoor Country in the early 1800's. He had a dislike for Pink and rode in pepper-and-salt with brown breeches and tops and a flat low crowned hat. He hunted all seasons, the hare in winter, fox in spring, otter in summer and deer at all times.

FIRST MASTER

The title 'Master of Hounds' or 'Magister Canum Regis' was first used in the reign of Henry IV. The first Master was Sir Henry Villenove.

(History of Hunting, Patrick Chalmers)

HAPPY RETURNS

When Thomas Assheton Smith returned to the Quorn country for one day on March 20, 1840, he was met at Rolleston by a field of 2,000!

CRAFTY FOX

Hill Vixens are reputed to put each cub of a litter in a different earth, going round to each in turn to feed it.

MEET AND DRINK

In the early 19th century, 'the Meet' was a new expression, frowned upon by the country gentlemen of the day. One Master in 1827 was asked 'Where is the Meet tomorrow?' He replied sarcastically, 'There will be a leg of mutton on my table at six tomorrow, if that's what you mean'.

FROSTY RECEPTION

In 1844-45 the Belvoir lost a total of 71 days hunting due to frost.

WOMEN RIDERS

Long-time friends of my family (the Heatons and the Deakins) were the Hesketh family, who were keen members of the Holcombe hunt. Mrs. Betty Williams (nee Hesketh) played a significant part in the 1930's in the campaign to allow women to ride in point-to-points. Betty and two companions had to prove their ability to ride the course early one morning in front of six elderly ex-Army gentlemen. All three managed to complete the course and won the right to ride. The first Ladies race was run in 1934 and Betty Hesketh won her first race in the same year.

Contributed by Angela Heaton.

50 YEARS ON THE SIDE

Currently in her 55th season with the Beaufort, Mrs. Cynthia Pitman celebrated her 80th year with a meet at her home and was out with the hounds, mounted side saddle on her grey horse, Ben. She is living proof that you can continue riding actively for longer if you ride side-saddle.

Pytchley Echo, Autumn 1993

THE KING and the HOLCOMBE HUNT

My family had long associations with this pack of harriers, both my mother's side, the Deakins, and the Heatons. The following information is from my mother's 'suitcase of treasured relics and newspaper cuttings':

The event dates back to August 1617 when King James I, who was believed to be a 'great man of the hunt' visited Hoghton Tower near Preston, and was attended by several of the local gentry along with their hounds. As is quoted from the record:
"August 16th 1617. Hoghton. The King hunting, a great company, killed afore dinner a brace of stagges. Very hotte, so he went into dinner (27 courses!). We attended the Lords Table. In the afternoon a hunting ye hare". It was during this dinner that the King rose to his feet and with his sword and knife he knighted the loin of beef, since when it has been called "Sir-loin". The carvers used that day were claimed to be the property of the Deakin family though this is not fact. They now repose in Turton Tower museum near Bolton, Lancashire, and are described as used by King James I to "Dub the loin of Beef".

Contributed by Angela Heaton

70 MILE POINT

On the 8th June near Dunkeld, Perthshire, a fox and a hound were spotted, the fox fifty yards ahead. Each was so fatigued they could hardly run and were easily caught and taken to a house where the fox, exhausted, died soon after.
It was learned afterward that the hound belonged to the Duke of Gordon and that the fox had been raised four days earlier near Fort Augustus. The single hound had followed the fox all four days and the distance calculated as, without allowances for crosses, or doubling back, exceeding an astonishing 70 miles!

(Extracted from 'Rural Sports' by W. B. Daniel 1830)

TEENAGERS WANTED

Seen in a stableyard in Essex this notice:
   GIVE TEENAGERS A JOB WHILE THEY STILL KNOW EVERYTHING!'
Contributed by Paul Wolstencroft

FAMILY TRAGEDY

Scottish aristocrat and war hero, Lord Lovat, suffered two tragedies in March 1994. His son Simon fell off his horse after suffering a heart attack during the annual Drag Hunt – where hounds chase the artificial scent of a fox – at Beaufort Castle. Lord Lovat was renowned for going to war in a kilt with his own piper. He led the commando brigade that spearheaded the Normandy invasion, and his role was played by Peter Langford in the 1962 movie, 'The Longest Day'. He had lost his other son Andrew who was gored to death by a buffalo whilst on safari only a few weeks before.

THE HUNTING / ENGLISH DICTIONARY

For a stranger to the world of field sports, it's a different language, sometimes. I used to think a barbour was a hairdresser! To help your enjoyment, we proudly present the Foxhunters / English Dictionary below:

ANTI	Not the fat lady married to your uncle Fred. They're members of the Anti-Blood Sports League, (or as Jilly Cooper says Anti-Blue-Bloods)
BALL	No, you don't kick it, you give it to a horse. It's an equine pill.
BARBOUR	Nothing to do with short back and sides. Its a waxed waterproof coat, much favoured by field sports enthusiasts and its very practical (and fashionable)
BARS	No, it's not where you have a drink. They're the fleshy ridges on the upper part of a horses mouth.
BIKE	Nowt to do with spokes, wheels or girls. When used by foxhunters, it means 'BACK'.
BILLETT	No, it's not an Army barracks. It's a fox's droppings.
BLANK	Not a cheque that most wives like. A blank day is one where no fox is found.
BLOWING AWAY	You're right, it's not a Mafia hit man. It's what a Huntsman does to signal a fox in the open.
BLOWING OUT	It's not what happens at a disco when a girl refuses to dance. It's the Huntsman blowing long mournful wails on his horn to signal there's no fox.
BOTTOM	No, it's not one of those plump ones in joddies. It's a big, deep ditch, also called a dingle, a gill or a coombe. (I told you it was a different language!)
BRONX	Nothing to do with New York's most glamourous borough. Its a kind of food for hounds.

BRUSH	Easy peasy. It's not what you've just got from the girl at the disco. It's a fox's tail.
BUTTON	Each hunt has its own engraved button, worn by members at the invitation of the Master.
BYE-DAY	An extra day's hunting, above the usual quota, and not in the diary.
CAP	Nothing to do with playing rugby for England. This is money paid by non-subscribers for a day's hunting, on average £60-£80.
BULLFINCH	Not a small bird. But a hedge so high you can't jump it, but thin enough for you to jump through it.
CANTLE	Not something you light up when the electricity fails. It's the back of a saddle.
CAST	Nothing to do with broken arms, or the theatre. A huntsman 'casts' like a fisherman when he helps the hounds recover a lost scent.
CHANGE	Nowt to do with the menopause. It's starting off on the scent of one fox, then finding another one.
CHARLIE	The fox.
CHOP	No, it's not a lamb or pork meal. When the hounds 'chop' a fox, they've discovered it sleeping. Some alarm clock!
CLAP	No dear, not something you catch and don't dare tell your mother. It's a scent gone away hence 'Clapped scent'.
COOKED	A horse when it's dead beat after a hard gallop.
COOMBE	You don't use this on your hair. See 'Bottom' above.
COUPLE	No, it's not a boy and a girl on a date, or married. It's two hounds.
COVERTS	No, it's not the CIA or Watergate, as in 'covert operation'. But a wood or coppice where the fox is likely to hide.
CRIB	Not where your baby sleeps. It's a stable vice when the horse chews at the door or wall.

CUBBING	Nothing to do with the Brownies or Arkala. These are early morning hunts designed to teach young hounds to hunt.
CUT DOWN	Nothing to do with a tree. It's being harried or impeded by another rider.
DOCK	No, it's not when a ship moors. Nor a leaf you rub into a nettle sting. It's the bony part of a horse's tail.
DOUBLE	A fence with a ditch before and after. Nowt to do with Scotch.
DRAG	Not Danny LaRue, not even a man riding side saddle. It's the scent of a fox while it's on its nocturnal wanderings.
DRAIN	A ditch, large or small.
DRAW	Not the verdict of the pools panel. It's when you look for a fox with hounds.
DROP-FENCE	A fence where the landing side falls away and is lower than the take-off side.
ENTER	Nothing to do with competitions, beauty contests or a 'Sleepless in Seattle' term for the act of love. It's when you start a hound on its hunting career.
FIELD	The mounted followers of the Hunt. In cricket it's what the Aussies do better than England or any other country really.
FLESHY	The farrier's word for 'sensitive'.
FROG	A thick piece of horn on the horse's hoof which bears the horse's weight, prevents slipping and, because of its india-rubber resilience, takes the shock of impact as the horse lands.
GALL	A sore caused by a saddle, girth-strap etc. on a horse.
GAY	No, not a club you go to, or Julian Clary. It's a term applied to the back end of a hound, as in 'gay stern'. Do not say this to the captain of a cross-Channel ferry.
GELD	To de-sex a male horse or hound.
GOING	Nothing to do with auctioneering. It's the state of the ground as it affects the horses galloping e.g. soft, heavy, deep, good. Every excuse you've ever heard from your racehorse trainer includes the word going!

GRAFT	Nowt to do with hard work. It's a crescent-bladed spade.
GREEN	Nothing to do with envy, hangovers, golf or seasickness. It's an inexperienced horse (or rider).
GRUEL	A warm drink for horses or hounds.
HACK	No, it's not a journalist or writer or a taxi-driver. It's to ride to a meet by horseback, not in a horsebox.
HAND	They measure horses in 4 inch sets, it being the measurement of the palm of the hand. No-one knows why, but I suppose it would be stupid to measure a horse in feet, when he already has four.
HEAD	Americans have difficulty with this one. To head a fox is to divert him from his original course.
HEADLAND	The uncultivated part of a field near the hedge. Left by farmers so that horses won't ride on his crops.
HE-LOPE	When you talk to the hounds, it means 'come here'. When you talk to a girl, it means 'Gretna Green'!
HOLLOA	A scream to denote that a fox has been sighted. (or Spanish for 'Hi!').
HORNY	The farrier's word for 'insensitive'. Applied to horses feet. Nothing to do with farriers' wives or females in the field.
JACK	Forget the game of bowls. It's a hare.
JEALOUS	Nothing to do with love, marriage or emotion. A 'jealous' rider is one who rides recklessly.
JODDIES	Increasingly used to describe jodhpurs, mainly because its easier to spell!
KENNEL	Yes, I know it's where the hounds live. But it's also the above-ground lair of a fox.
KNEE-CAPS	Not the Mafia trick. They're wool or leather protectors for the horse's knees.
LARK	What farmers and foxhunters get up with. Also a hunting field crime if you lark, ie. jump fences when the hounds are not running.
LIFT	Not an elevator or what a bra gives you. A huntsman 'lifts' his hounds when he keeps them in an area where a fox has been sighted.

LINE	Not for hanging clothes on. It's when a fox leaves a trail of scent.
LIP-STRAP	Not what you give your Mother-in-Law for a Christmas present. It's used as part of the 'bit' to prevent the chain from riding up.
LIVERY	No it's not what you eat with bacon and onions. It's a hunt servant's uniform.
LIVERY	This is really confusing. It also means when you pay for a horse's feed and stabling at somebody else's stable.
MADE	When a horse has been broken in and also ridden to hounds. Thus a 16 year old mare would be called an 'Old Made'.
MARK	Not something you'll get in exams. It's when hounds bay outside a fox's underground lair.
MASK	The fox's head. So next time you go to a Masked Ball, you'll know what to wear!
MFH	Master of Fox Hounds. This title carries more clout than Sir, J.P., Doctor, M.P. and entitles the owner to instant obedience on hunting days. On all other days he has the same rights.
NAPPY	Not for babies. It's a horse that's known for sudden kicks, bucks or refuses to move. Like a wife, really.
OVER-RIDE	Not something on your C.D. player, or on your Mercedes trip computer. It's riding too close to the hounds.
'OLD 'ARD	STOP! Usually addressed by the Master to pushing members of the field, or thrusters. (see Thrusters) This is sometimes shouted in more colourful language.
OUTLIER	Another name for Charlie. Usually one which appears from a different direction to the one you're chasing.
PAD	No, it's not a fashionable flat. It's a fox's foot.
PECKER	Nothing to do with kissing or 'keeping your pecker up'. It's a horse that drops its head as it jumps, throwing the rider off. So requests like "Can you do something with my pecker?" are quite common on the hunting field.

PIPE	A branch-hole of a fox earth.
PIPE-OPENER	A gallop to clear the horse's wind, like a golfer's practice swing, or an athlete limbering up.
PLATE	Not what you bring your granny back from abroad. It's a light racing shoe. So racing plates are very light horseshoes.
POACHED	Nowt to do with eggs, or stealing game. It's a field that's been churned up by hooves (usually cows)
POINT	The distance between the finding of a fox and the finish of the hunt, measured as the crow flies, not as the hounds run.
POULTRY FUND	Maintained by each hunt to pay compensation to farmers for the loss of poultry killed by foxes. Often the source of argument (see Stories section).
PROVINCES	All the hunting countries of England, Scotland and Wales, except the Shire Countries (Belvoir, Cottesmore, Fernie, Quorn and Pytchley).
PUER	Nothing pure about this. It's hound dung.
PUSS	It's a term of endearment for a hare or rabbit.
PYE	Nothing to do with old TV sets, cottages or apples. It's a fox colour that's lighter than tan.
RASPER	A huge fence. Sometimes called other names.
'RAT-CATCHER'	The name given to dress worn before November 1st when cub-hunting, and after March 1st. No one knows why it's been named so.
RIBBON	What you should tie around your horse's tail (Red) if he's likely to kick. If he kicks you while you're putting it on, give up.
RINGING	Nothing to do with church bells, suspect cars or funny noises in your ear. It's a fox that runs in circles.
ROOTS	Nothing to do with Alex Haley's book. They're turnips, swedes, beets, potatoes etc.
ROUGHED OFF	It's a horse that's being gently 'let-down' at the end of the hunting season, prior to being 'turned out' (or on holiday from hunting).

ROUNDED	The practice of shaping hounds ears, now discontinued. Nothing to do with the bottoms of horsewomen.
RUBBER	Americans have trouble with this one, too. A stable rubber is a horse duster.
SCREW	Well now, you can think what you like. It's a low grade horse not suitable for hunting.
SETT	Not new mathematics. A stronghold of a badger, frequently the target of illegal badger-baiting.
SKIPPING	Picking up odd droppings in the stable. Not to be confused with 'skipping school' or 'skipping rope'. With the latter two, at least your hands stay clean.
SKIRT	No, what you call girls in discos is up to you. This is when a hound cuts corners, not working out the true line of a fox.
SOIL	If a stag stands at bay in a pond or a river, he is said to have soiled. If you were confronted by 60 hounds and 75 foxhunters, you'd soil too.
SOILED	If a covert has seen too many foxes killed there, many foxes will avoid it, and it is said to be soiled.
SPEAKER	Nothing to do with Betty Boothroyd. It's a hound with a louder voice than the others.
STALE	No, it's not bread your mother forgot to throw out. It's horse or hound urination.
STARING COAT	A dull coat that denotes general malaise in a horse or hound. Generally applied to Bob Geldorf's clothes.
STERN	No, it's nothing to do with ships or the look the Master gives you when you cut him up. It's a hound's tail.
STICKY	A horse that half-refuses at a jump, then takes it from a standstill. The rider usually comes to a sticky end.
STOUT	No, it's not a black drink from Ireland or a description of Bernard Manning. It's a horse that has strength in looks and general well-being.
STUB-BRED	Foxes born above ground, supposedly hardier.

TACK	Not something you nail your carpets down with. It means all the bits that go on a horse plus grooming kit. (Not the rider's)
TALLY-HO	'I have seen a Fox! Let's go! (Rough translation)
THRUSH	Not a bird, nor the other ailment I won't mention. It's a smell which indicates the horse's feet haven't been picked out properly. Thus the frog rots. Dust with boric powder and sack your groom. (See 'FROG')
THRUSTER	One who pushes his way regardless of other people whilst hunting. Also known as 'prats'.
TIMBER	Hunt jumps made of wood, gates or post-end-rails. Anything wooden and jumpable.
TOPS	The band of light coloured leather at the top of hunting boots. The Motown group, the 'Four Tops' were avid foxhunters, hence the name. (And if you believe that, you'll believe anything)
TRAM	No, it's not how you travelled before they invented buses. In Ireland, hay is bought by the 'tram'. Don't ask me what it weighs, but if they can drink Guinness by the bucket, they can buy hay by the tram!
TUBED HORSE	One that has a tube inserted in his wind pipe to assist breathing. Do not go into the river on one of these!
TWITCH	No, it's not a nervous disease. You put this on a horse's nose to distract him from what the vet is doing elsewhere. Owners usually twitch a bit when they're putting it on, too.
VOLUNTARY	A fall. When Napoleon fell off his horse, the trumpets blared. Hence the 'Trumpet Voluntary'
WALK	To bring up a hound puppy in your own home after he has been weaned. You also have to walk him, of course! It also means what you do for two miles when your horse bolts while you're in the middle of nowhere out hunting!
WIND	Don't be rude. It's the act of smelling a fox by the hound, and it is said to be 'winding' the fox.

And finally, the most wonderful one of all:

EU IN THEN, LITTLE BITCHES!	Means GET INTO THAT COVERT and LOOK for that FOX!

"The Oakley away from Clifton Reynes" by Joy Hawken

From: Baily's Magazine

THE BICESTER AND PYTCHLEY NEW RULES

The hunting season is over. Not for a long time has the ground "ridden" so well in March as it has done this year; nor has there been, on the whole, better sport during a month which is generally productive of more indifferent runs than any other.

The season, however, has closed with a lengthy correspondence on the subject of the virtual exclusion of strangers from participation in the sport of certain packs of hounds. The Bicester and Pytchley Hunts — with both of which large fields are the rule — have resolved that, for the future, no one living beyond the limits of their hunts shall come out unless he pays a minimum subscription of £25; and it is upon the justice and expediency of this rule that the discussion has been founded. A letter written to a weekly paper, in the commencement of last month, advocates the adoption of the rules tending to get rid of the man who is identified with no particular country; who has no land over which others can ride; who spends no money in the country of his adoption; and who grumbles if asked to contribute towards the support of the establishments which find him sport. This sort of creature unquestionably deserves exterminating. Then, says the writer of the letter, "there is another class of man who subscribes to one pack only, but lives, during the hunting season, on the edge of several, and must have five or six days a week, either to give £75 . . . or to make choice of one pack, give what he can afford to it, and stick to it, taking the rough with the smooth?" Here, again, common sense is on the side of the writer; for, there is no reason why a man who keeps a large stud of horses, and makes use of two or three packs, should not contribute equally to each; and £25 apiece would not be too much to expect from anyone, resident or not, who keeps an expensive establishment and hunts on every day hounds can go out. A not very unreasonable objection has been made to the rule on two grounds. In the first place it has been asked, why the resident can come in at a cheaper rate than he who lives beyond the limits of the hunt? Those residents who have land to be ridden over, and preserve foxes, make a contribution to the hunt upon which a money value can scarcely be placed. Without their aid — and of course that of the farmers — hunting would come to a full stop in a week; but how about the resident who lives in a house to which no land is attached, and who has not even a wood stack in his back yard as a fox-covert? Suppose he, as many do, forages his horse from a distance, and sends, a by no means uncommon practice, to the Stores for his household stuff; how does he greatly benefit the country; especially if he avails himself of his status as a resident and gives less than £25? Secondly the rule hits those who, while not living in the country in which they hunt, come out with hounds at rare intervals only— say a dozen times in the season at the outside, and in the ranks of these there may be some very good sportsmen. Mr. Haig, who wrote to the papers some time ago, is a case in point. He, it appears, has for many years been accustomed to betake himself for a fortnight or three weeks to Rugby; and in return for the hunting he had with the Pytchley during his stay, contributed £10 or £15, which, as things go, is a fair donation. But under the new rule he must pay £25 for the privilege, or an infinitely greater sum than any resident would think it worth while to contribute for the same amount of enjoyment. Moreover, the rule compels the one horse man to pay a sum which is out of all proportion to his stable expenses; while it is by no means clear that anything will have been gained by keeping away men who pay only flying visits, but who were the less ready to contribute liberally during the period of their visit. If a man is out a score of times he cannot be said to increase the field to any material extent in the course of a season of one hundred days or so.

The matter will also bear looking at from another point of view. Land is gradually passing into the hands of new men, and the shopkeeper of today is found with a place in the country tomorrow; and if, while he can only disport himself with the hounds occasionally, he finds the subscription exclude him, he may not think kindly of fox-hunting and fox-hunters when he hereafter finds himself in possession of more leisure and more money. These people may be in a considerable minority; but one fox-killer does more harm than a dozen preservers can do good. In every hunt there are estates on which game ousts foxes, and is it good policy to run the risk of adding to the number. To suggest weak points in the new regulations is one thing; to propose a scheme which would satisfy everybody is another and more difficult task — inasmuch as two different items have to be dealt with. It is impossible to judge by the same standard the man who, possessed of ample means, rides two horses a day and lives on the best of everything, and yet sets out with the deliberate intention of getting his hunting as cheaply as possible; and the man, too, who can just manage, by dint of most rigid economy, to keep one horse, but who is, at the same time, willing to regard a moderate subscription as part of the expense incidental to horse-keeping. No one would wish to deal hardly with one of this kind. But, taking a wider range, if the adoption of the rules recently passed by the Bicester and Pytchley members has the effect of making men select a Hunt and stick to it, or, in the alternative, pay the £25 for the privilege.

The Northampton Chronicle, May 4th 1889

[The questions raised above were the subject of wide and heated debate and feelings obviously ran very high!]

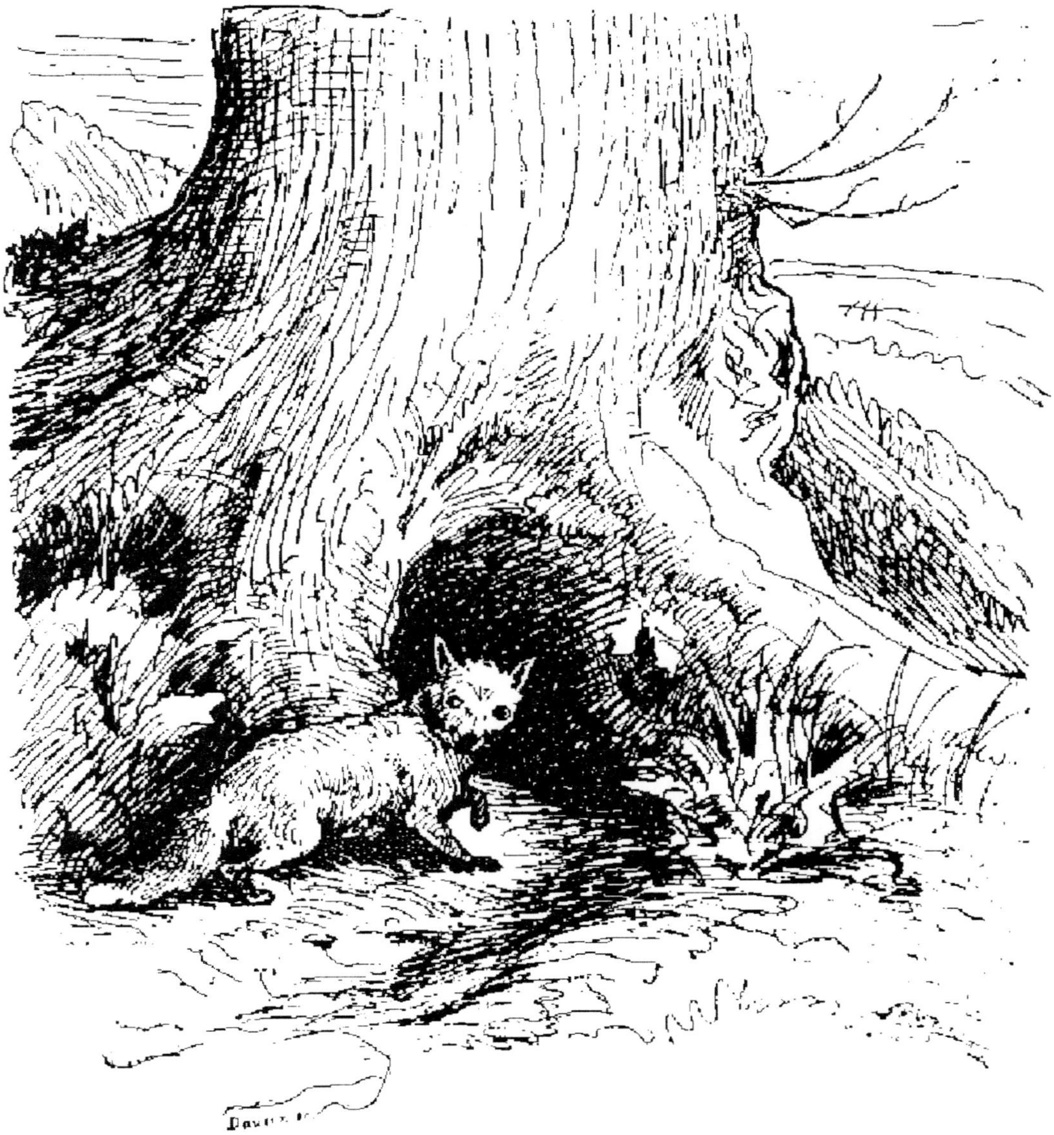

Crossing Driffield
(*British Hunts and Huntsmen Vol. 3*)

Eton College Beagles 1936-1938
Hawkstone Otterhounds 1939-1967
Captain R. E. Wallace MFH Ludlow Foxhounds 1946-1948
Cotswold Foxhounds 1948-1952 Heythrop Foxhounds 1952-1977
and Exmoor Foxhounds 1977

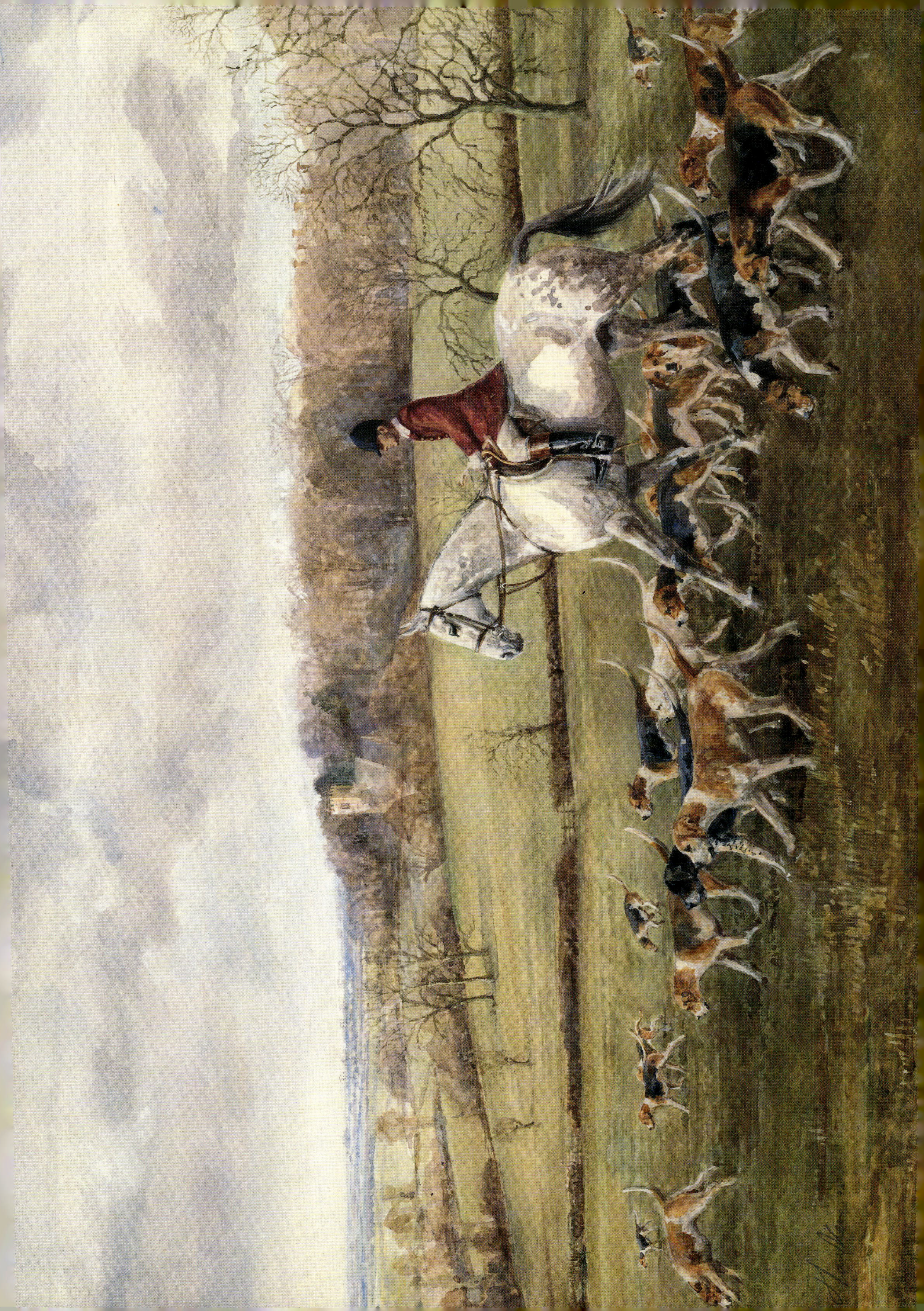

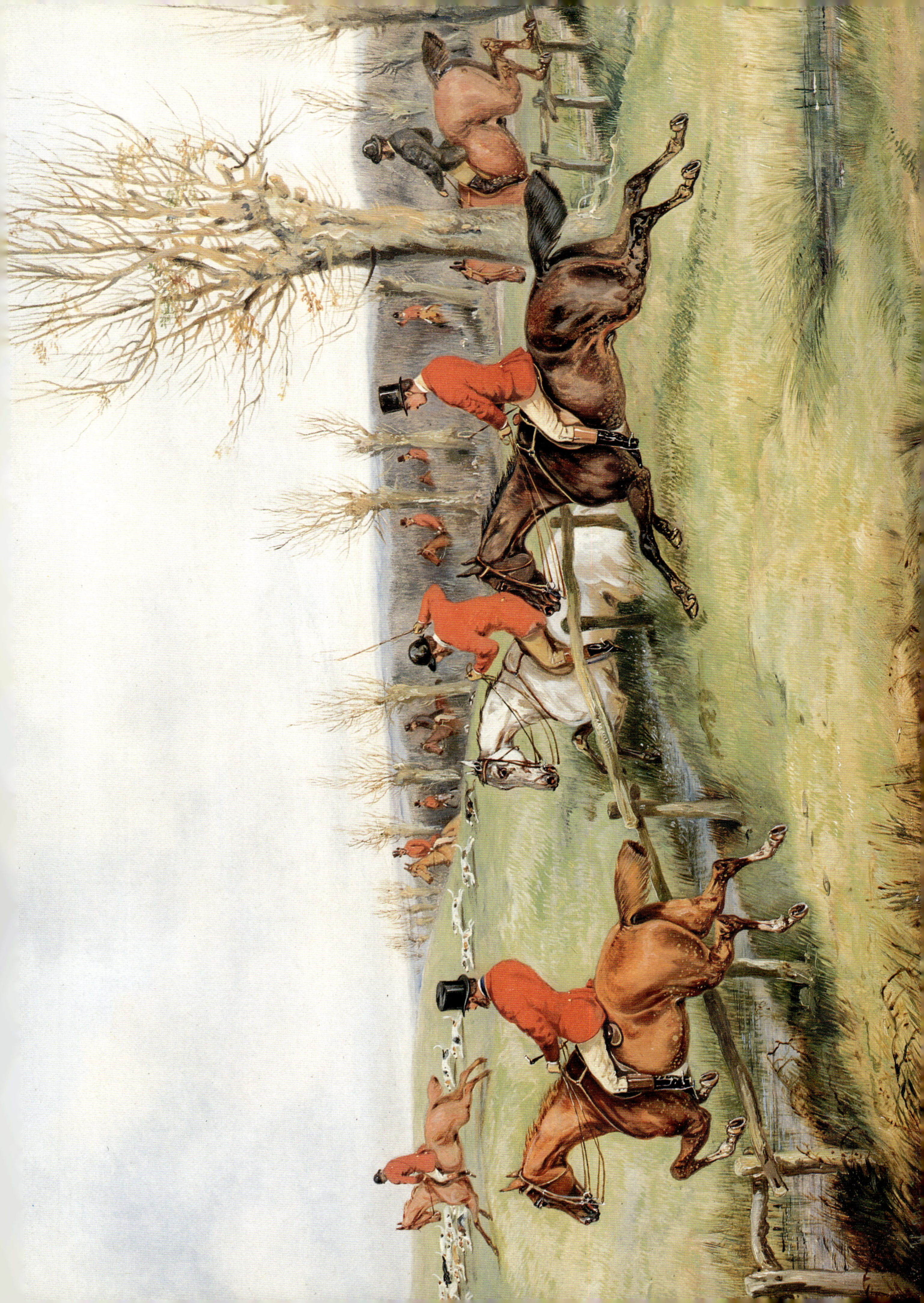

KEY TO CRICK MEET
1952

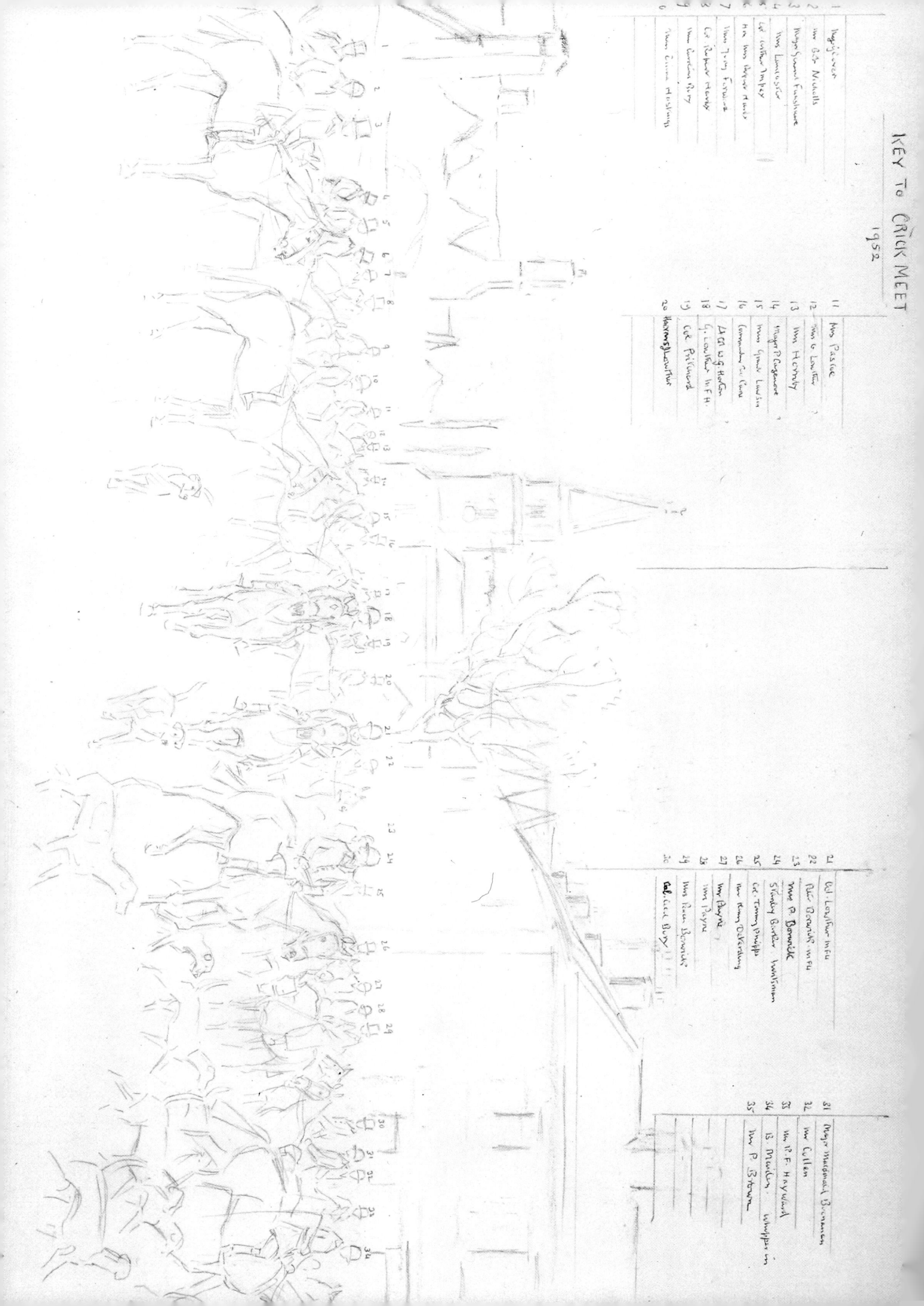

1. Major Lower
2. Mrs Bob Mitchell
3. Major Sumner Fanshawe
4. Mrs Hornby
5. Lt Colonel Lancaster
6. Lt Colonel Impey
7. Mrs Mrs Byron Hunt
8. Mrs Jenny Forward
9. Col Richard Henry
10. Mrs Simon Ray
11. Mrs Emma Hastings

12. Mrs Pastoe
13. Mrs G Lowther
14. Mrs Hornby
15. Major P Cazenove
16. Mrs Gina Lewis
17. Commander Sir Ray
18. Lt Col L.G. Horton
19. Lt Colonel Mr F.H.
20. Col Pritchard
21. Harrow/Lowther

22. Col Lowther M Fu
23. Mr Bowwick M Fu
24. Mrs R Bowwick
25. Stanley Barker Huntsman
26. Col Tommy Philips
27. Mrs Henry Okerdong
28. Mrs Payne
29. Mrs Peter Bowwick
30. Whitied Boy

31. Major Maynard Buchanan
32. Mrs Cullen
33. Mrs R F Hayward
34. B Mordin Whipper in
35. Mrs P Brown

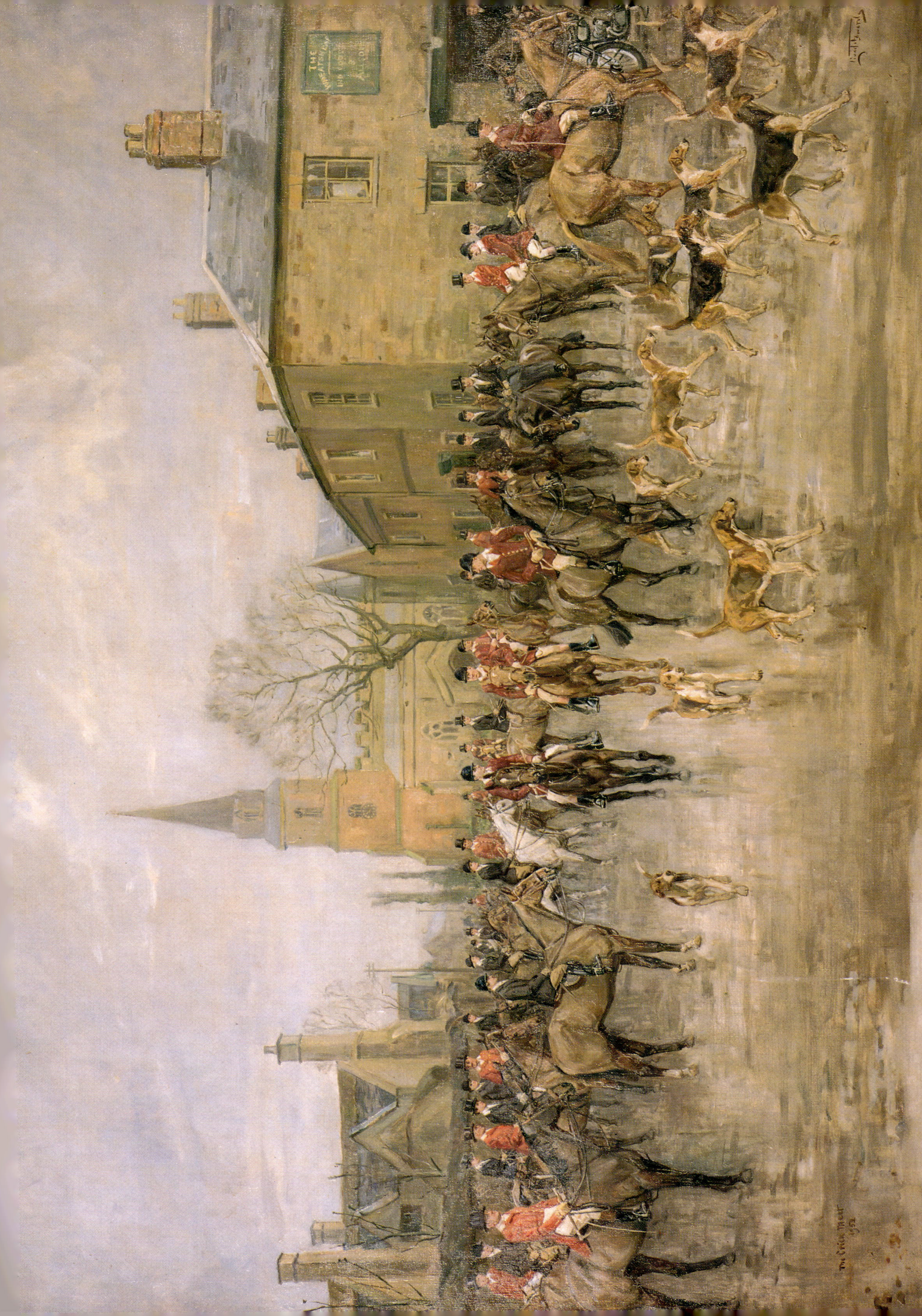

Book Three

Stories and tall tales of the hunting field
and the characters therein

The Ditch. – Illustration by Edward Ardizzone in R. S. Surtees 'Handley Cross'

A PECULIAR CUSTOM
(RAPPING - Nothing to do with the Music of the 90's)

By custom at the club, any member after dinner, on depositing half-a crown in a wine glass, might name and put up to auction the horse of any other member, the owner being entitled to one bid on his own behest. This custom was called "rapping", from the raps on the table which accompanied each bid. It was on one of these occasions that Mr. Nethercot sold "Lancet" to Mr. John Cook, of Hothorp, for the then unprecedented sum of £620.00.

THE SPORTING MAGAZINE - 1846

NO LIMIT ON DRINKING

When wine is in, the wit is elsewhere. During this period (John, Viscount Althorp) it was incumbent on every prudent man not to take part in this Post Prandial rap, for the man who could not quietly dispose of three bottles of old port was not held in much esteem as a boon companion, nor was it seen a necessity to draw the line at three bottles.
An anecdote of the times:
A lady on hearing a gentleman say that "he had finished his third bottle" of port after dinner, asked in some surprise: "What, sir, unassisted?" "Oh, no, ma'am" was the answer, "I was assisted by a bottle of Madeira!"

THE SPORTING MAGAZINE - 1846

A GRAVE MATTER

Merry Tom was the favourite horse of the first Lord Spencer. When it broke its back, the sorrowing Master ordered it to be buried with saddle and bridle where it had died, and placed a stone to mark the place. When the railway was made the bones were found, but there was no sign of the saddle or bridle. Merry Tom Lane still exists between the Welford Road and Brixworth, in Northampton.

BOXING DAY FALLERS

The custom of meeting near Northampton on Boxing Day to give the townspeople a show has been a tradition since 1775. In that year the company included "a number of holiday people from Northampton who made an immense crowd and began to fall at the leaps as soon as the chase began".

14 FOOT LEAP

Dick Knight's leap, a painting by Rowlandson, was first printed in the Sporting Magazine. It depicted a desperate and breakneck leap by the huntsman from a descent of 14 feet near Gisborough, Yorkshire. It was, in fact, at Guilsborough near Northampton while Dick was huntsman to the Pytchley.

RECORD TIME FOR SQUIRE

One of the great feats of the 19th century was by George 'Squire' Osbaldeston from Pitsford, a Master of the Pytchley Hunt. He rode 200 miles in 8 hours 40 minutes for a large wager, and became a cult figure. He was rumoured to have spent £200,000 on hunting alone before he was fifty and he was legendary for his duelling, shooting, racing and betting. He died eventually aged 79 in London forgotten, friendless and almost broke.

DEAD BEAT

Much of the comfort and pleasure depends on the master, and if huntsmen vary, how various are the types of masters. There are the jolly familiar ones, and the "speak-to-me-if-you-dare-sir" sort; there are the military-precision, and the no-discipline-at-all kind. There is the M.F.H. who notices none but his intimates, who does not take the trouble to recognise his field, nor say good morning to the farmer, or thank you to the man who opens the gate. There is the damning, cursing, swearing species—with varieties; the one that swears from bad temper; the one that swears thinking it professional: and the one that swears from pure excitement. The first sort is always offensive, the second makes a mistake, and the last is sometimes amusing. I have heard remarkable language proceed from the mouths of M.F.Hs., and heard them scream, bellow and yell, sometimes with some cause, sometimes without. We can forgive it when it is the froth of enthusiasm.

One of my father's tenants, who recently died, told me he remembered, when a boy, Ralph Lambton coming into Bishops Auckland on foot, with one and a half couple of hounds and a fox dead beat a few yards in front, calling through the streets, "Hoick to Jingler." The fox lay down in the main street, and the hounds, quite done up and unable to tackle him, lay down beside him. The master gave them a few minutes to kill him, but as they could not, he had the fox attended to, and turned down again in his native covert in the Sedgefield country.

A. E. Pease, As reprinted in the Northampton Mercury, November 1896

OUR FRIEND THE FOX

An entertaining paper on the fox was given by Sir Herewald Wake, Bart., at the annual meeting of the Northamptonshire Natural History Society on Monday. The genial baronet entered into a lively defence of foxhunting, and to prove the value of the sport incidentally said that there are 385 pack of foxhounds, costing in the aggregate £885,500 a year to maintain. Of that amount £231,000 went in wages, £196,300 on farm produce, and £23,000 as compensation for poultry. Indirectly, however, it caused £18,000,000 to be spent in rural districts; £7,200,000 was spent on wages and board for servants, and 70,000 persons were able to earn a livelihood as the result of foxhunting alone. In concluding, the baronet uttered a sentimental sigh that he supposed the days of foxhunting were numbered.

Northampton Inependant, Feb. 24th 1908

His estimate of an 'industry' generating £18 million in rural areas is a staggering amount, some 86 years ago, and at the time must have exceeded the GNP of many countries in the world!

MOUNTED BY A STEP LADDER

There was a well known lady of title who, until she was mounted, looked better fitted for a bath chair than a saddle, ... being nearly 80 years old. She arrived at the meet in a Rolls with a chauffeur and foot man, and was met by her stud groom and hunter. The footman unloaded a step ladder from the top of the Rolls and placed it in position. Her ladyship assisted by the chauffeur climbed the ladder. The stud groom held the horse. She then sat down on the horse and until the end of the day's hunting looked like she was part of it.

G. F. Lucas 1955

RUBBING A MASTER UP THE WRONG WAY

One man took to hunting in later life and was not familiar with the exalted position of the Master. One day the hounds had been running very hard and the horses were sweating freely and the field was held up by two masters in a narrow ride. The gentleman arrived with his horse rather out of control and only managed to stop with his horses head wedged in between the two masters. Now the horse thought this a good chance of a wash and brush-up so it rubbed its nose firmly against both scarlet coats. One Master turned and berated the fellow up and down in choice language, during which time the offender put his horse at attention with head up and eyes to the front. When the Master had finished his tirade, the delinquent turned to a complete stranger and said loudly 'Do tell me, who is this exceedingly eloquent gentleman?'

G. F. Lucas 1955

COMPETITION AMONGST THE PRESS

Our attention has been called by a correspondent to another foolish error in the "Northampton Herald" declaring that "in the hunting field the late Col. Renton and Major Jenkinson were sometimes called Saul (sic) and Jonothan or Damon and Pythias". Evidently our contemporary has a better memory of the Greek classics than the Old Testament, so that its plea for more Bible teaching in the schools is capable of a personal application.

Extracted from The Northampton Independent – May 9th 1908

This 'Knocking copy' was obviously long before they became members of the same press stable, first United Newspapers, then EMAP (1992).

ORDERS TO THE PRINCE

G. F. Lucas was once out with the Pytchley and, in the course of a very good hunt, encountered a very thick bullfinch. Beside him was a slim figure in scarlet on a thoroughbred horse so Lucas shouted, "Go on young fellow. Smash a good hole in it for me!" He did as commanded. Lucas was mortified when he found out later that he'd been giving orders to the Prince of Wales.

NO PARSON PLEASE

Winwick Warren on the Cold Ashby road was notorious for its sloping fences and hidden ditches. Many a rider came a cropper. Some died (Lord Inverurie and a Mr. Sawbridge of East Haddon) On the occasion that Mr. Sawbridge fell off, George Payne stopped, saw it was a very serious fall and asked 'Would you like a parson?' 'No thank you,' 'came the almost inaudible groan, 'I was at church last Sunday.'

JOHN PEEL

The famous song 'D'ye Ken John Peel' was composed by John Woodcock Graves one wintry evening at Peel's home at Caldbeck, and he set the words to the old song 'Bonnie Annie' in 1828. Peel is buried in Caldbeck churchyard beneath a tombstone bearing a hound and two hunting horns. Over 3,000 mourners attended the funeral in 1854 including ten of his brothers and sisters.

FINANCIALLY EMBARRASSED

The legendary John Peel was forced to sell small parcels of his land in order to maintain his hounds. Eventually he was so crippled financially that he had to rent out his own house at Caldbeck and live in a small property a few miles away. With a wife and 13 children to support, it was no wonder that Peel was strapped for money. At one time his friends clubbed together to give him enough to settle his debts. Peel and his bride Mary had run away to be married at Gretna Green in 1797. The couple had seven sons and six daughters.

THE ROMANTIC SQUIRE

Squire George Osbaldeston was a crack shot, a horseman without equal and an incurable romantic in the early 1880's. With a duelling pistol he once put 10 bullets in the ace of diamonds at 30 feet. When he was almost 70 he rode at Goodwood in the March stakes and was only beaten by a neck. When he was younger he rode 50 miles in the dark in 4 hours to fetch a rare orchid for the dress of a local beauty at the Northampton County Ball.
Despite all his skill and bravery, he never lost his fear of being 'jumped on.' While with the Atherstone in Quorn country he was knocked over and jumped on by Sir James Musgrave's horse, suffering a crushed leg which caused him to endure a long convalescence. His leg never fully recovered and he wore his right boot laced up at the side.
He also rode in 'steeplechase matches' which involved only 2 horses and 2 riders, with huge wagers on the side in the 1830's. The 'squire' rode in 6 matches and won them all, and the most famous was the Clasher-Clinker match. The squire, on Clasher, beat Dick Christian on Clinker, and won the £1000 bet. His powers of endurance were legendary. Once he hunted all day with the Pytchley, hacked to a ball in Cambridge - 60 miles away - danced all night, hunted all day at Sulby, then back to Pitsford. All told he had hunted, hacked, danced, hunted again and hacked home (for 36 hours and covered almost 200 miles).

HUNTING TALES

YOUR BUTTERFLY, SIR!

In an article entitled 'Please to remember the Farmer' 'Dalesman' wrote: 'How can we expect non-hunting farmers, struggling to exist, to be glad to see a crowd of horseman galloping over their land? ... Were we to find two or three people catching butterflies in (our) garden, (we) would immediately eject them forcibly or call the police. Certainly (we) would not rush to open the gate and say 'Your Red Admiral has just gone down near the onions!'

POACHED FISH

A Mr. Rowland Tree, in his last year of the Pytchley Mastership had a very wet fall near Merry Tom and when he got out of the river Nene he found a fish in his poachers pocket.

HUNTING ABROAD

Lieutenant-Colonel W. H. Buckley was sent with his regiment to India in 1924, and hunted with the packs of Madras, Peshawar, Bombay, Poona and Delhi. They hunted the jackal, an animal who is less cunning than the fox, but much faster. Buckley became Master of Bangalore. The season lasted from the end of May to March and the hounds met at 6.30a.m. twice a week.
The Christmas visits lasted for 10-14 days at the Maharajah of Mysore's palace. The Christmas Day Hunt was followed by a banquet in the palace, then Christmas Carols - with the foxhunters still in their red coats - in the small English church.
High drama was often accompanied by high comedy. One day the jackal broke cover, followed by a Sambhur (elk), followed by a panther, then a second panther. Another jackal followed, then the hounds, then the horsemen.
The hunt quickly realised the danger, turned for home, the whipper-in organised the hounds and followed the horses, followed by the jackal, the elk and the two panthers chasing everyone home. No injuries were reported but a few hearts beat faster than usual.

LONG DRIVES

Lord and Lady Willowby used to drive to Badminton from Kineton in a two wheeled trap, a distance of 66 miles. The journey took almost 12 hours in 1910. They would arrive in the evening, hunt a few days, then drive back home in their trap.

THE BIG EXPRESS

When C. N. De Courcy Parry (Dalesman) was MFH with the United in Shropshire he was reputed to have performed some remarkable feats on his one-eyed horse 'The Bean.' Amongst those was swimming a river in the dark and jumping a 6ft gate by the light of a car's headlamps. But the most fabled was jumping the level-crossing gates at Marshbrook Station and witnesses swore he did it while the Big Express was roaring through the station. 'Dalesman' denies this, but the truth may never be known.

FOLLOW THAT FOX!

The famous 'Dalesman' led a colourful life. He took passage around the world on the 'Wild Goose' and was shipwrecked. He survived but found himself on a cannibal island, went onto a penal colony, then travelled to New Zealand and Australia. One day while cattle droving in New South Wales, a fox crossed his trail and that was that. He went home at the age of 25 to Cumberland to live the life of a foxhunter - and immortality as an author.

DARTMOOR WALLS

Dartmoor is very tough county to hunt, with boulders, bogs and high walls. Major Geoffrey Mott was a widely-known sportsman in the West Country and his verdict on the height of the wall was this: 'Just ride up to them and topple off one or two storeys. Then they're quite easy to get over!'

(Famous Foxhunters: Daphne Moore)

LEAVE THE BULLET IN

Percivial Williams, Master of the Four Burrow from 1922-1964, the last nine jointly with his son John, lost his toe nails and part of his body at Sulva Bay. Near the end of the great war, he got shot up badly and had two bullets in his head. One was removed with a magnet, and the French doctor said 'Leave the other one in your brain. It won't hurt so long as you don't meddle with it!' Despite being 70% disabled, he hunted and had wonderful success in bloodstock breeding.

THE VULPICIDES

In the early 1800's there was a section of the community which was determined to kill foxes by any means. A church bell was rung in some communities when a fox was located and the 'vulpicides' appeared with guns, pickaxes, shovels and terriers to destroy the fox by any brutal method. There are numerous stories of Masters, like Jack Russell, who attempted to convince them that killing the fox with hounds was more humane. In other cases the 'vulpicides' were in no mood to be cajoled and continued their brutality.

FURY OF A PRINCE

Prince Llewellyn of Wales was fond of hunting and lived near Snowdon. On one hunting day his favourite hound Gelert was missing and they went off without him. On his return, Gelert came bounding to meet him, his paws and teeth dripping with blood.
The Prince was alarmed and raced up to the nursery where his one year old son was sleeping. The cradle was overturned and blood-spattered. In fury, the Prince ran the hound through with his sword. Then the baby cried and the Prince found him safe in the upturned cradle beside the body of a wolf, killed by the brave Gelert.
Full of remorse, the Prince buried Gelert at Beddgelert, erected a monument to him, and his grave is visited by thousands every year.

THE IRISH DRIVER

A master was taking his three horses to a hunt in Yorkshire, using his Irish groom as a driver, himself following with his wife in the car. They got stuck in mud in the field and had to give the lorry a push, having got the horses out. They pushed and shoved for an hour, and the Master was running well behind time.
They finally got the wheels free and the Master took the Irish groom aside and said sternly, 'Now don't stop for anything till you get to Yorkshire.' Well, the lad got in the truck and drove like crazy for 10 miles. The Master followed and finally overtook him and forced him to stop. 'Well, you told me not to stop till I got to Yorkshire' 'Yes, but I didn't mean you should leave the bloody horses behind' roared the Master.

SPEND YOUR PENNIES WISELY

A business friend told me the story of his first hunt some years ago. He was eager to impress and showed up in his new riding breeches, boots and jacket, all immaculate. Halfway through the morning, he was desperate to spend a penny. So he hung back near the tail of the field and waited for the chance to dismount. But the jogging up and down was causing him agony and he finally slowed down, stood up in the saddle and began to relieve himself.
But the horse took fright and bolted. My friend could not stop the flow or the horse, as he held on with both hands. Eventually the horse slowed but by then he had soaked his new joddies and filled his boots. To make things worse, some of the young ladies at the back of the field passed him, giggling, realising what had happened. To this day he winces at the memory.

THE GHOST IN GALLIPOLI

Shortly after the start of the first World War, the horses at Gallipoli were having a horrible time at night, being bitten by large mosquitoes and even bats. Someone had the bright idea of stealing a few parachutes from the nearby airfield, and making blankets out of them for the horses. They were of pink material, but the colour didn't matter. It worked well for a few nights. But one morning the six horses had vanished, so they set off to find them.
They'd driven for over an hour when they came to a small village with the tribesmen in panic and turmoil. Tents were in disarray, pots, pans and clothes strewn all over the desert. On midnight the previous evening, in the middle of a huge religious feast, six 'ghosts' had appeared in billowing pink pyjamas and galloped through the village, scaring them half to death. The horses were never found, nor the pyjamas!

ROYAL SWEARWORDS

Some years ago a friend attended a meet at Althorp House, and the Princess of Wales was visiting. He was loosening the girth of his saddle when his 17 hands horse stood on his foot. In agony, he shouted F*** at the top of his voice and turned around to find the Princess looking at him curiously. He explained, in obvious embarrassment just why he was swearing, and she held the horse while he prised his foot loose.

A STRANGE TAIL

My friend's daughter was keen to make an impression at her first hunt and for months could talk of nothing else. But six weeks before, disaster struck! Her pony had rubbed his tail on a gate, or another horse had chewed it off, leaving a stump with straggly hairs. It looked revolting, but the more his daughter cried, the funnier it seemed.

But, being a dutiful father, he took her off to a wig maker with a sample of the hairs. He did a fantastic job and they came home, and plaited it in just in time for the opening meet. On the big day they rode up proudly. 'Good Morning, Master' she said sweetly, as she'd been practising for weeks. The great man smiled at her. Just then another pony came along side and started chewing away at the tail, and pulled the wig right off in front of the astonished eyes of the assembled scarlet throng. To her credit, my friend's daughter held back the tears and completed her big day on her tail-less pony.

KICKING THE HOUNDS

Marjorie Quarton* tells the story of a man in hunting attire selling a grey at a small horse auction in Cork. Marjorie rode the grey and, after some thought, decided to buy. As she wrote the cheque, a car pulled up, a girl jumped out, ran up to the grey and patted its neck. 'Is that the horse that kicked all your hounds?' she cried to the man in hunting attire. That was the end of the sale, and no surprise.

*Breakfast the Night Before by Marjorie Quarton, published by Andre Deutsch, 1989.

MOUNT FOR SALE

In Ireland, ninety percent of the mounts at any meet are for sale. One day one of the Masters arrived at a meet on a bicycle.
'Why are you on a bike?' asked the Field Master
'Because I couldn't sell it!' was the reply.

[Marjorie Quarton, Breakfast the Night Before]

AN EMOTIONAL HORSE

In Ireland once, Marjorie Quarton* was riding a young horse on a wet day to the blacksmiths. They met an old cleric cycling down the hill in the middle of the road. He was wobbling all over the road and in one hand held a very large black umbrella, then known as a 'priests brolly'. The filly almost fainted, standing shaking, eyes rolling. Marjorie got off and held the horse till the old man passed. On her way home she met him again. 'You frightened the wits out of my horse' she told him. 'Sell it', he said, 'buy something less emotional'.

*Breakfast the Night Before by Marjorie Quarton, published by Andre Deutsch, 1989.

ONLY FLEAS AND HORSES

A well known Irish member of a Midlands Hunt was famed for his wild claims about his horses. The local Master was interested in his grey and asked him if it was a good jumper. 'Jump?' exclaimed the Irishman. 'Why, he can leap like a Dublin flea!'

HUNTING TALES

JORROCKS

John Jorrocks was the great comic character devised by Robert Smith Surtees in 'Handley Cross', first published in 1843. Surtees cast his anti-hero as a corpulent London grocer who set himself up as Master of Foxhounds. Surtees himself was a satirical genius and ranked by many as the greatest writer of sporting fiction. He co-founded the New Sporting Magazine in 1831. He was, however, insanely jealous of Charles James Apperley (Nimrod) who wrote in The Sporting Magazine (founded 1790) and some say Surtees started his magazine to try to force it out of business and then compel Nimrod to write for him.

ON A PROMISE

One Field Master was well known for his ripe language and use of Anglo-Saxon terms. He was leading the field around a covert when he spotted a female who had cut across well ahead of rest.
'F*** you, madam' he shouted in a rage.
The riders were aghast, even more so when they drew closer and realised it was the Masters wife he'd yelled at.
She smiled sweetly at him 'Right, I'll hold you to that, Field Master.'
The Field Master blushed and everyone around dissolved in gales of laughter.

SENT HOME

A Master's main sanction is to send home anyone who disobeys instructions, like jumping on to crops the Hunt has promised the farmer to protect. A Master once sent home one of a pair of twin sisters. The guilty one simply went back to her horsebox and changed into a spare coat, exactly the same colour as her sister, and then re-joined the field. The sisters made sure only one of them was near the Master at any one time.
It was only at the end of the day that the Master spotted both twins beside their horsebox and realised he'd been fooled. His response is not recorded.

IRONY

One Master was well known for sarcasm and no little wit in enforcing discipline. On a particular day, there were a few lady thrusters at the front, so he came to a halt near them and held up his hand. 'Will all the pretty ladies wait here, please. The rest can go on' he said. There were very few lady thrusters for the rest of the day.

CARPETBAGGERS AND BEASTS

Ulrica Murray Smith reports that in the 1930's life with the Quorn was very gay and social. Those up for the hunt took houses in Melton and nearby villages for the whole season. Some even arrived by private train with their servants, grooms and horses. They were known humorously as 'Carpetbaggers'. The Meltonians, in turn, referred to those who lived on the unfashionable side of the Quorn as 'beasts of the forest'.

IMMACULATE ON A COW

While serving with the Life Guards, Sam Ashton had hurried up to the Quorn to join the hounds in late afternoon. He was dressed in 'Ratcatcher' and the Master, infuriated, wrote to Ashton's C.O. complaining about his dress standards, and the officer received a rocket.
Next time Ashton went hunting, he was immaculate, but he rode a cow which he had clipped, bridled and saddled. The Master was furious, wrote again to the C.O. and Sam was confined to barracks!

Ulrica Murray Smith, Magic of the Quorn

DISABLED BY WIFE

One lady who had hunted with the Quorn for years was so upset at the thought of her third husband, who was in the Foot Guards, having to go off to the war in 1939 that, to prevent him going she shot him in the bottom with a 12 bore as he was climbing over a fence when they were shooting!

Ulrica Murray Smith, Magic of the Quorn.

SURVIVORS

Seen at the entrance to a small farm, where the 'guard' dog is less than ferocious, the notice:

'GUARD DOG LOOSE
SURVIVORS WILL BE PROSECUTED.'

THE STRANGE TALE OF THE OLD HUNTER

It was after a rare forty minutes burst with the Pytchley on the Rugby side of the country, and many of us had turned homewards that we were attracted by the somewhat extraordinary sight of a harness horse with shafts attached, jumping into the field and pulling up in our midst apparently well satisfied with his performance. The harness was poor and the shafts testified to the fact that the conveyance to which they belonged was not a Long Acre turn-out. There was a breedy, varmity look about the old beggar, which notwithstanding his trappings, could not but attract the eye. We waited sometime, thinking that the owner would put in an appearance, but as no one came we moved off in the direction from which the horse came to see if we could be of any assistance. The old horse followed and jumped the not very formidable fences not withstanding the pair of shafts. Nothing could be seen of anyone, we subsequently came upon a farm hand and asked him to take charge of the animal.
A day or so later I learned that whilst being driven home from market by an old woman, the horse, seeing the hounds cross the road became very excited, and (in the words of the old lady) "raising his head, pricking his ears and cocking his tail, he turned sharp right and attempted to jump the hedge in pursuit of the hounds. It was here that he broke the shafts and sent the old lady rolling out behind. It seems that he had been a well known hunter in his day, and the cleverest fencer in the district.

November 7th 1899 - Northampton Sporting Chronicle

HUNTING TALES

SNOW and an UGLY FALL
(Quote from one who was present)

One day at Sywell Wood we were not able to throw off till 12.30 for the snow: at that time it had sufficiently melted, and an immediate find was followed by a very sharp burst, and in the bustle the snowballs from the horses feet were anything but sport. We soon came upon an ox-fence – a very high flight of rails – a sort of hedge and a deep, wet, broad ditch on the other side. The leading man, a determined rider charged at it on a well-known hunter, whose four legs, however, the snow took from under him on taking off, and he went through into the next field, as ugly a fall as need be, where he lay, horse and all, doubled up like a hedgehog.
I made use of the fallen man's clearance, and hearing from himself that, as the Irishman says, he was not kilt entirely, rode on.

THE SPORTING MAGAZINE - 1846

WELL TRAVELLED HORSES

A dealer in Northampton sold two horses to another dealer in Kent. Off they trundled south. As they arrived in the Kent dealer's yard, a dealer in Leicester rang him, desperate for two horses to hunt at once for an American and his wife. Could they be delivered? The deal was done. A short rest later, the horses were on their way to the Pytchley meet at East Haddon, and the American and his wife, duly hunted with them.
The Northampton dealer was also out at East Haddon, recognised the horses, and asked the American where they'd got their mounts.
'Oh, the man from Melton looks after us well. He bought them last April and he has been stabling them for us since then' At the American's expense, of course!

WELHAM BOB-TAIL

In late 1928, the Welham Bob-Tail fox had become a legend. Many times hunted, never caught. She lost her tail having been cornered by a shepherd's dog in a turnip field. As she leapt for her life over a wire fence, the dog snatched her tail. The vixen went clear leaving most of her brush in the dog's jaws. She finally met her end on November 23rd 1928. Her memory is kept fresh by Stanley Barker, who mounted the brush and kept it in a trophy cabinet.

OWN FEW HORSES

There is a law well-known to all horse owners. "Have one horse and hunt three days a fortnight, not missing a single day. Own two horses and hunt twice a week. Own three or more and then there are days when there is not a sound animal in the yard.

Old Pytchley Proverb attributed to Stanley Barker.

SCRAPS WITH LORD BYRON

John Charles Viscount Althorp, was a lover of all kinds of sport and had taken boxing lessons. He had many fist-fights with his fellow Old Harrovian, Lord Byron, and so hard did he punch that it was said he was a 'prize-fighter thrown away'.

THE OLD MAN AND THE MASTER

A master well-known for his impatience and ripe language was on the way to a Yorkshire meet some years ago when he had a flat tyre on his horsebox. Luckily there was a small petrol station on the lonely road only a few hundred yards away and the owner, an equally peppery old Yorkshireman, came out to fix it. It took him a long time to get the wheel off, the Master standing behind, shifting from foot to foot, tut-tutting and generally showing signs of impatience.

The old man finally got the wheel off, and put on the spare. 'Make sure you tighten up those wheel nuts well' snapped the Master. The old man tightened them up one by one with the Master repeating his instruction as every nut was tightened. The last nut was being done and the old man gave a mighty heave and it snapped off. 'Now look what you've done, you fool, you've broken the bloody nut.' roared the Master.

The old man wiped his brow and looked levelly at the fuming foxhunter. 'Yes, and if you don't shut up I'm going to go round this ****ing horsebox and do the same ****ing thing to every single ****ing wheelnut.'

The job was finished in silence.

Contributed by P. Instrall whose grandfather was the old garage owner

WHYTE MELVILLE

The foxhunting author and poet had supreme gifts as a story-teller and his poem 'The Good Grey Mare' produced the title of the worlds most successful equestrian weekly magazine 'Horse and Hound'. He devoted the proceeds of his books to charity, being especially thoughtful of grooms in hunting quarters. His town residence, Whyte Melville Hall, is now a working mans club in Northampton. He died in 1878 when his horse fell on him out hunting.

ONE PERCENT SUCCESS

A Pytchley farmer was asked by his local Vicar, why he rode such a good horse, remarking that he should have thought he would be glad to sell it, seeing that it was worth something like 100 guineas. The farmer replied "Well Vicar, it is like this, horses are like parsons, you may breed a hundred and only get one good 'un."

Northampton Independent – May 30th 1908

HOMEWARD BOUND

A well-known Irish horse trader near Dublin had two horses which he patiently trained to find their way home.

He would take these horses to local fairs to sell. But before doing so he would disguise them by painting them with distinctive marks, the odd blaze here and there, and dye their coats black.

He'd sell them at the horse fairs then go home and wait a few days. And they'd be there, without fail, having found their way home from miles away. Then he'd hose them down, wash off the paint and dye, and start all over again.

COMING TO BLOWS

In the middle of a hunt near Haselbech in 1923, two gentlemen were seen to dismount from their horses and go at each other with hunting whips. One was George Drummond of Pitsford, the other Lord Lanburen. Drummond later confessed that he had given Lanburen a good hiding because he had criticised the Pytchley huntsman when they lost a fox. The Huntsman was Stanley Barker, whose son Ted, sister Susan and grandson Tim still live in Pitsford, Northampton.

WHEN YOUR HORSE WON'T JUMP . . . . . .

Then push it, of course. But, like all good foxhunters, don't let anyone see you . . . .
'Why you were seen, my good fellow! Seen with your back against your horse's, shoving him through a fence.' Like all stout men, Struggles was the essence of good humour. He burst into a hearty laugh, but persevered in his denial.
'Who saw me? Who saw me?'
'Parson Dove saw you. I shouldn't wonder if he put it in his sermon.'

Market Harborough: G. J. Whyte Melville

DEATH WISH

Labour Peer and ex-Member of Parliament, Lord Paget had an ambition — to die on the hunting field. Guy Paget, his father, wrote many books on the sport, including 'The History of the Althorp & Pytchley Hunt', and himself was killed out hunting.
Lord Paget's ambition, however, was not fulfilled.

BREAKING BONES

Foxhunting can be cruel, not to the fox, but to the riders, and literally thousands of riders have broken their legs, arms, necks and backs from falls over the years. "Leicestershire seemed to echo with the dull crack of breaking bones" was Alan Whicker's dry comment when he made a film about the Quorn some years ago.

THE WIFE and THE MISTRESS

Two ladies hunting in Exmoor both fell over the same fence into a bog. As they lay there, covered in mud, a horseman rode up, as if to help, then rode back. The Master saw what had happened and began to berate him for not helping the ladies.
'I can't' said the rider in some embarrassment
'Why not?'
'Well, one's my wife and the other's my mistress.'
'Oh, in that case, I'd better go and see if they're alright.' said the Master, kindly.
He rode up to the fence, peered over, and rode back, smiling.
'What's the matter?' asked the rider
'Small world, isn't it?' smiled the Master.

THE EMPRESS AT THE PYTCHLEY

Elizabeth, Empress of Austria, hunted with the Pytchley in 1877/78, and was 'piloted' by Captain Bay Middleton. She was a first-class rider and ran her own private circus in Vienna. She always carried a fan to hunting, smoked cigars and preferred the local ale to tea. One of the two most beautiful woman in Europe — the other her sister the ex Queen of Naples — she stayed at Cottesbrooke.
On her last day's hunting in Northampton on Feb. 18th 1878 there were over 500 in the field including Princess Mary of Cambridge and the Prince of Wales.

A poem at the time depicts the scene, and the varying emotions her presence caused. The poet is unknown.
"Who is this that rides down, all importance and hurry?
From his figure and face I should say 'tis George Currey.
'The Empress is coming!' – he passes the word.
With varying emotion each bosom is stirred.
But all that the Master says, speaking to Will,
Is 'Bid Orvis draw Callott, Shuckburgh Hill.'

'WHERE THE TREE FELL . . .'

Half a century before the death of Lord Chesham, another dashing foxhunter met his death in remarkably similar circumstances.
Lord Inverurie hunted from the Coach and Horses in Brixworth, Northampton and trying to jump a fence at Yelvertoft, his horse turned a somersault and fell on him, breaking his neck.
He was buried where he fell, for his father instructed 'Where the tree fell, there let it lie.' A simple tablet in Brixworth church announces that the body of Lord Inverurie lies nearby.

DIPLOMATIC MASTER

The old Master had a habit of swearing at any transgression in the field, then trying to cover it up with an innocent remark. Once he encountered a lady who was always riding over his hounds. One day she set her horse at a fence where a hound was just getting through. 'Can't anyone stop that damn bitch?' he roared. Then, as an aside to the field, 'I'm afraid she's getting in the way of that lady jumping that fence.'

'Rum 'uns to Follow' - Dick Heathen.

LOCK JAW

A politician well-known for his flowery and long-winded Lords speeches was hunting with the Quorn, fell and broke his collarbone. The local newspaper society reporter rode up and enquired as to his injuries.
'It's only my collarbone'
'Pity it isn't your jaw,' replied the irreverent newshound.

MARRIED MEN ONLY

The notorious courtesan 'Skittles' hunted with the Fernie. She was a fine rider and very pretty and unmarried. One day she had a fall and her skirt got caught in the saddle. Underneath she wore long white silk frillies to the top of her knees. There was quite a lot of discussion among the men as to who should go to her rescue. They suggested a married man. Finally Parson Thorpe of Burton Latimer was deputised to rescue her, but he said he was single, then added a prayer, before riding to her rescue.

(Dick Heathen)

HONESTY PAYS

A farmer in the 1930's sued a Master named Coupland for 'his cows slipping calf as the hounds chased 'em and bit their noses,' and demanded £500, no little sum in those days. The Master's Lawyer was able to prove the hounds had never left the Kennels on the day in question. But Coupland admitted the hounds were out the following week, and offered to pay a reasonable sum if they'd done any damage.
The jury found in favour of the farmer, but awarded him only £50.

A MISTRESS IN EVERY HOUSE

Squire George Forester of Willey had two passions — foxhunting and collecting women. As he collected mistresses, he openly moved them into his cottages in the village. When he tired of them, he replaced them with younger models and the village was soon occupied completely with old and young mistresses, all of whom bore him at least one child. The village parson was said to be fully occupied christening the squire's illegitimate children!

QUICK REPOSTE

A Master well known for swearing once met his match with a local farmer. The farmer jumped very close behind him. 'Damn and blast you!' yelled the Master, 'You'll want to ride down my back next.' 'Not if its half as foul as your mouth, Master,' replied the farmer.

THE ROMANTIC SQUIRE

Squire Payne of Sulby is riding home from a hunt when he spies a pretty girl sitting on a gate. So he stops for a chat. The girl asks him if he knows where the primroses grow, so the squire hitches the horse to the gate and goes off to see the primroses.
When he gets back, some time later, his horse had rubbed its bridle off on the gate and vanished.
So the squire had to walk seven miles home in his top boots, there being no cars or phones in those days.

(Dick Heathen)

WHERE ARE WE?

Lord Annaly had a reputation for having a poor sense of direction. Some said it plainer — he just never knew where he was. One day out cubbing from East Haddon, they had just killed outside Cank Covert.

'Where on earth are we' asked Lord Annaly.

'Look over your shoulder, me Lord', says Parson Legard, 'and you'll see the chimneys of your noble mansion'.

Lord Annaly was only a half mile from his own front door, Holdenby House.

KNOW YOUR OWN HORSES

A foxhunter from Quorn, Capt. Hartropp went to Leicester Repository, saw a horse 'the property of a gentleman', thought it was a rare sort and bought it for £25. He rode it on the Monday and it performed very well; so well, in fact, that Sir Ernest Cassel, the millionaire banker from London, quite fancied it, tried it and gave the Captain £500 for the horse.

Sir Ernest took it home after the meet and his groom was horrified. They'd only sent the very same horse up to the sale a few days before because it was vicious and had thrown the groom off in the stable yard!

(Dick Heathen: A Rum 'un to follow)

A DITCH CALLED KLONDIKE

Mr. Ortho Paget was assigned to collect the Cap Fee at the meets at the turn of the century. In those days the gentlemen carried their gold sovereigns with them, and at one meet, the day after a Hunt Ball, there were a lot of visitors, and a lot of sovereigns collected by Mr. Paget.

Unfortunately he was thrown by his horse into a ditch that was full of water. He had to hire two local labourers to hold him upside down by his feet while he fished for the sovereigns for almost two hours. The locals christened the ditch 'Klondike'.

(Dick Heathen)

KISS OF LIFE

A few years ago I was hunting at Charwelton when my horse caught a rail, threw me over and I landed heavily, a bit winded. I must have passed out for a few seconds and when I came to, Judy Wilson, Jane Bletsoe-Brown and Gloria Cockerill were looking at me a bit anxiously. These were three exceedingly handsome ladies, so I mentioned that the Kiss of Life might help me to recover in the weakest voice I could muster, and they all laughed, thinking I was joking.

'Is he hurt?' someone bellowed, and through the hedge came a huge woman, 6' tall and 6' wide, ready to practice her first aid – on me! It would have been the 'smother of life' and I leapt to my feet quicker than I'd ever done in my life, grabbed my horse, thanked the ladies and rode off. I took it very steady for the rest of the day, and, though still weak, marvelled at my narrow escape.

Bob Andrews

STOPPING FOR A WEE

In the days when Sandy Cheyne was Pytchley secretary, we were going through Badby Wood heading for Fawsley and I was dying to spend a penny. No better place than the woods, thought I, so I held the horse with one hand, unbuttoned with the other and was in full blessed relief when Sandy Cheyne came round the corner with two lady visitors in tow. They burst out laughing as I swung round and soaked my breeches, in my haste letting go of the horse which ran off. The ladies brought it back and Sandy Cheyne dined out on the story for years.

Bob Andrews

DON'T ASK STUPID QUESTIONS

A member of the Pytchley, a burly farmer, had fallen and was lying covered in mud. A novice rode up and asked if he'd fallen.
'No, of course not you fool! I do this before I come out to make the others believe I sometimes jump a fence.'

STOPPED FOR A PINT

Some years ago I came back from Draughton after a bit of a run near Maidwell. As I was near Norbert's pub, the Stag's Head, I decided to slip away for a quick pint. Norbert said I could hide Skinney, my horse – all 17.2 hands of him – in an old stable round the back. We watched as the hunt passed with Dick Saunders looking very severe, so I decided I'd better join up again. But the stable was empty – the horse had vanished.
I got a lift to Haselbech where I saw the group I'd slipped away from, with Sandy Cheyne the secretary leading my horse and laughing their heads off at me.

Bob Andrews

SMALL FOX, LARGE CLAIM

Mr. J. C. Hunter, secretary of the Grafton Hunt (poultry fund) said in 1906, that they have had claims in one year totalling over £1,000 for compensation, and 8,000 fowls have been claimed to have been killed by foxes last year. He suggests that all the fowls in the Grafton country ought by this time to belong to the Hunt, and wonders that foxes with such enormous appetites were able to run at all. Mr. Campbell, Hunt secretary, tells the story of his experience in investigating the complaint of a lady who said she had seven valuable fowls killed by a fox. On enquiring into the circumstances he was surprised to learn that twelve birds in the same fowlhouse had escaped uninjured. Knowing that it is not the habit of Reynard to leave any fowls alive which are within his reach, he inspected the fowlhouse, and judge of his surprise when on examination, he found no opening where a fox could obtain entrance, the only possible place ingress being a small ventilation pipe, not more than two inches in diameter. The circumstance he pointed out to the claimant, but she steadfastly maintained that it was a fox. "It was a very little one then," replied Mr. Campbell, "or perhaps it was a stoat." But the lady stuck to her ground, and Mr. Campbell, finding himself getting the worst of the argument, said, "Well, if you ever find that fox I think you should have it shot, for such a little one would never do the Grafton any good."

COVERTS - WHAT'S IN A NAME?

When I was away at boarding school one of my favourite little ploys was to escape to the school library for a fleeting 15 or 20 minutes and there lose myself in the pages of Horse & Hound and the Field. Hunting reports, with magic names like California Gorse and The Hermatige, transported me a million miles away from the petty and uncomfortable regime of a minor public school, with its silly rules and restrictions. The names of fox coverts form a rarely acknowledged slice of country lore. In regions where foxhunting tradition is strong — like Northamptonshire — every clump of trees has a name, easily recognised by hunt followers and supporters. The majority are named either after places — in Pytchley country like Loddington Larches or Nobottle Wood — or people, like Goodman's Plantation or Cullen's Covert. In common with other Shire Packs, the Pytchley has few woodlands called "copses". Indeed I only know of two, Loddington Copse and Pond Copse at Pytchley.

South of the border, down Grafton way, the map is littered with them. In shared country, which the Grafton hunts by long standing arrangement, there are coverts which they know by different names to those we use. For example, what we call Ganderton's Covert they call Cow Pasture Wood and what we call Meg Spinney (at Snorscombe) they call Mill Spinney. When I used to write hunting reports for both packs I found this quite confusing! Some of the covert names in our country have ancient origins. The two Merry Tom Spinneys were, like the famous lane, named after Earl Spencer's favourite hunter. Blue Covert was named after the Royal Horse Guards and Prince of Wales Gorse after an heir to the throne. Flora and fauna are well represented in covert names, there are at least three Rookeries, a Pheasantry, Pheasant Spinney, Hen Wood, Cockcrow, Cock-o-Roost, Peacock Spinney, Heronbank . . . and Bird Spinney. Beasts may be found in Hoghole, and Hogshole, Bullocks Pen, Bull Acre, Ox Pitts, Rabbithill, Rabbit Spinney and Coneygree.

There's even the prosaic Fox-in-hole Spinney and Sowditch Wood near Nobottle. Doebank is at Cold Ashby, Bullshill at Newnham. Food and drink are not forgotten, either, with Cheesecake Spinney, Brandy Spinney and Hopyard Plantation. And how about clothing? Uncle Toms Hat at Pitsford, Sir Skipwiths Grey Hat at Althorp, Miss Lloyd's Short Apron at Long Buckby, The Stocking at Fawsley. Sadly, Top Hat Spinney (at Ashby St Ledgers) has long since disappeared. Occasionally names change, sometimes with ownership. Balaclava Gorse, named after the famous Crimean battle, has long been called Sanders Gorse and Blackdown Covert has been Vanderplanks for at least 100 years.

I have long delighted in writing about Firetail and Spitfire, Sewell and Swinnell, Thornburrow and Thornborough. One day, perhaps, I shall be able to report a hunt to Solitude Spinney, the lovely name of a little clump of trees near Daventry's western bypass.

Peter Hall, writing in the Pytchley Echo.

BIG JUMP, TALL STORY

Dick Heathen (Rum 'uns to follow) recounts a story of Lord Lonsdale with the Quorn. There was a fence, a double post and rail, over 30 feet all told. Lord Lonsdale jumped it safely and was asked how he'd managed it. 'The horse was never any good afterwards. I squeezed him so hard I broke his ribs'.

HUNTING TALES

THE WATERLOO RUN
This famous hunt of the Pytchley Hounds took place on Friday, 2nd February 1866.

As with all good stories, the facts become distorted with the telling and re-telling, but Col. "Jack" Anstruther Thomson M.F.H. of Pitsford Hall, who hunted hounds that day, wrote the following account to one of the sporting papers, three weeks later.

Dear Sir,
The accounts of the Waterloo Run have been so many and so various that your readers must be puzzled to know the real state of the case, and as "Bailey" is not quite correct, I venture to send you what I believe to be the leading facts in the day's sport.
The hounds found their first fox in Loatland Wood, and ran in and out of cover for one hour and five minutes, and ran hard to ground at Arthingworth. They found again in Waterloo Gorse, at a quarter to two o'clock. The time from Waterloo to the earths at Keythorpe was one hour fifty minutes. The total time was three hours and forty-five minutes; but we had a long check, twenty or twenty-five minutes, at the Windmill at Medbourne, and hunted on slowly afterwards. I take the distance to be — from Waterloo to Kelmarsh, three miles; Kelmarsh to Keythorpe, eighteen as we ran it — twenty-one miles in one hour and fifty minutes. There were only four ploughed fields in that distance. The hounds were only off the line once, between Kelmarsh and Keythorpe, when I lifted them one field to a holloa at little Oxendon. As to changing foxes, I don't think we did, as it was quite in the same direction our fox was travelling. I think we changed at Keythorpe Wood, as another fox was viewed there besides the fox which we followed to Medbourne. We may have changed anywhere in the hedgerows, but I saw no perceptible change in scent, or anything to cause me to think so.
Some of your correspondents have asked where I managed to get five horses during the run. They will see in "Bailey" that I was indebted to the kindness and sportsmanlike feeling of my friends Mr. Hay and Mr. Walter de Winton, and I beg all of them to accept my most grateful thanks. Both Co. Fraser and Col. Whyte on getting fresh horses also most generously offered them to me. Capt. Clerk was the only man who rode the same horse to the end of the run, and then rode home with me to the kennels. I left two and a half couple of hounds out (not four and a half in the covert at Fallow Closes), but they all came home next day except one, and he came home on Monday. The only men present when I stopped the hounds were – Capt. Clerk, Col. Fraser, Col. Whyte and Mr. John Chaplin.
This I believe to be a correct statement of the leading facts. I can only add I never saw hounds carry on so far at the same pace, and so straight, and over so fine a country.

Yours truly, J. A. T.

Northampton Sporting Chronicle

POLITICAL HOUND

Some years ago at this show, brought before me was the most mis-shapen hound I have ever seen. Later the lady owner of the hound complained to me that I hadn't given her hound a fair chance. "Why?" "Because you didn't put him through all his tricks." "What tricks?" "Why, if you put a lump of sugar on his nose and say 'Gladstone' he won't stir, say 'Salisbury' he'll up and take it like a shot."
I then had to assure her that foxhounds are bred and trained to hunt foxes, not to entertain party political views.

As told by a Judge at the Peterborough Hound Show of 1908.

DEAD RIGHT

The Pytchley Hunt Kennelman, Russell Martin was out collecting flesh earlier this year when he was greeted by some rather chilling words as he drove into one farm yard. The small boy watching him ran off shrieking "Its the dead man, Grandad".

Pytchley Echo, 1993.

WILL HE SHOW? AND WILL HE BLOW?

Certain hunts used to attract Masters who cared little about hunting or hounds. The Marquis of Hastings was a legend, not for his foxhunting but for his drinking sprees and parties. Often he wouldn't turn up for a hunt at all, after a late party. When he did manage to show up, the members of the Quorn feared he couldn't blow his horn in case he was sick in front of everyone.

GET OFF MY COAT

A well known farmer was out with the Grafton with a friend. He was a well-known thruster and was merciless with anyone who fell through bad horsemanship. At a certain fence, with a friend at his side, he lined it up and made to jump. At the last second his horse skidded in the mud, and the farmer (who shall be nameless, but his first name was Mike) was thrown off sideways.
A group gathered round, concerned when he lay there, unable to get up. Several times he made an effort to rise, but fell back in the mud. By now the group was worried he'd broken something.
'Are you all right?' enquired his friend (who also shall be nameless, but his first name was Bob)
'Of course I'm all right. Any fool can see that.'
'Well, get up then.'
'I can't.'
'Why not'
'The bloody horse is standing on my coat!'

HANDSOME JACK

In the legends of foxhunting Masters, Jack Musters was notorious for his instinctive skill, his womanising and his rudeness in the field. John Chaworth Musters spent a good part of his life with the South Notts, the Pytchley (6 years), back to the South Notts on the death of his father in 1827, and later with any subscription pack that would put up with him. He was known to have an incurable desire to make love to every woman he met. Whether he did so is not recorded but he lived to the age of 72.
Whilst with the Pytchley he resided at Pitsford Hall, and had a reputation of being a stern disciplinarian, giving short shift to anyone who overrode the hounds. It was during his time with the Pytchley that a somewhat lame parson overrode his prized bitch-pack. 'You're as deformed in mind as you are in body!' he is said to have bellowed at the unfortunate.

GREASY FARMERS

Beau Brummel – the epitome of a dandy – hunted with the Belvoir and never troubled to ride too far. If the day's hunting was some distance away, he'd stay in bed. If close, he'd ride a few miles, then stop at a farmhouse and cadge a meal.
But his aversion to long hunting days were nothing to do with his appetite or laziness, simply his wish to take care of his immaculate clothes. 'I cannot bear to have my tops and leathers splashed by the greasy, galloping farmers' he would often say.

Extracted from A Foxhunters Anthology, (1934)

UPSTAIRS, DOWNSTAIRS

Melton in the 1920's was awash with glamourous foxhunters and their ladies who hunted hard, partied even harder and made outrageous bets with each other. One of these (Peter Flower) made a bet over a Saturday night late dinner that he could ride a horse up a flight of stairs to the first floor. One of his horses was saddled and Flower galloped upstairs to the landing. There the horse stopped and refused to go up or come down.
The horse stayed there all through Sunday and the only subject in Melton that day was how to get the horse down. Finally on the Monday, he was lowered out of the landing window using a hastily constructed wooden platform and ropes. The horse was later purchased by Lord Annaly and re-named 'First Flight'. Whether this is because it was the first flight of stairs or the first airborne jaunt by a horse is unknown.

Extracted from Lady Augusta Fane: Chit Chat 1926.

WORN OUT HORSES

During the famous 'Waterloo Run' of the Pytchley in 1866, Capt. Thomson, riding twenty stone in the saddle, tired out five successive horses and experienced several falls. He wore out his mare Valeria, then borrowed the first Whip's horse Usurper, then commandeered two horses that were already being ridden, and finally his own second horse Rainbow.
The run ended at 10'o'clock in the evening whereupon the worthy captain donned his evening dress and set out for the Market Harborough ball, where he got a rapturous reception.

Reported in a review in the Daily Telegraph, March 1887

TEN LORDS A-LEAPING

'Lord Althorp had a fall in leaping over a hedge and a blind ditch; Lord Cavendish's horse put its foot in a cart rut and fell on its side; the Duke of Devonshire's mount slipped backward into a ditch, throwing him off; Mr. Samwell fell into a bog; Mr. Poyntz fell backward into Brampton brook trying to jump it; Mr. Grenville's horse fell at full speed though he was not 'essentially hurt' and his face was much bruised; Lord Westmoreland's horse rolled over him; Mr. Isted's mount threw him into the swollen waters of Kingsthorpe Mill and he was forced to retire.'

[Extracts from various diaries December 1774 November 1791 in which the fences jumped (or not) and the falling bodies are faithfully recorded in great detail.]

STOUT QUEEN

During William and Mary's reign, the latter's sister Anne was a fanatical hunter. When she came to the throne in 1702, every meet of the Buckhounds was honoured by her presence until she became so stout that she could no longer ride upon horseback. Then she took to hunting on wheels and was seen in 1711 by Dean Swift driving furiously through Windsor Forest.

Reported in the Daily Telegraph February 12th 1894.

FOX JUMPS THROUGH WINDOW

'Weds. Nov. 28 1781.

A fox of unusual resource was found. In the course of the chase, lasting 2 hrs 40 mins, the fox came out of Mr. Samwell's house at Upton through a pane of one of the windows, in view of the whole company'.

Pytchley Hunt and the Althorp Chase Book, Part V

SHOPKEEPERS DELIGHT

Frank Beer's diary recalls that in 1889 the Grafton pack ran a fox into the village grocer's shop in Ravenstone. The incident was a rather lucrative one for the lady who kept the shop. Lord Penrhyn and Lord Spencer, besides giving her something (for the damage the hounds had done), purchased all the oranges and biscuits in the shop.

JACKIE ONASSIS and the MIDDLEBURG HUNT

The former First Lady, Jackie Kennedy Onassis, often rides with the Middleburg Hunt in Virginia. She is a noted horsewoman who is a regular rider with the Middleburg and has a reputation for aggressive galloping and jumping.
On November 22, 1993, the 30th anniversary of the death of her first husband President Kennedy, she was staying with relatives for Thanksgiving on an estate in Virginia Hunt country. She went out for a ride early in the morning and estate staff raised the alarm when her horse was seen running free near some jumps. They found Mrs. Onassis lying unconscious in a field after a heavy fall. She was kept in hospital overnight before being released into relatives' care. She later returned to work in New York as a book editor with the Doubleday company.

Extracted from London Daily Mail 25/11/93.

THE PIG

A master well known for his ripe language and bad temper berated a visitor for riding too close to him at a gateway.
'You haven't got the manners of a pig.' he bellowed.
'That's alright, Master, you have!' replied the young man smartly.

HUNTING TALES

THE JUDGE AND THE EIDERDOWN

Peter Bletsoe-Brown recounts the story of the High Court judge in the 1940's who hunted near Althorp. Peter met him at the station with his horse one bitterly cold morning.
'I don't think I'll have my second horse today, Peter. I'll meet you back here at 3 o'clock.'
Peter went home and at 1 o'clock the phone rang.
'I've tethered the horse to a drainpipe at the Fox and Hounds. Can you fetch him home?' asked the judge.
'Certainly, your honour. But he'll be a bit cold, won't he?'
'Don't worry about that. I've covered him with an eiderdown.'
'Where did you get the eiderdown?'
'The landlady was very helpful. Don't worry about the horse, the eiderdown's warm. The landlady and I spent some time under it! And I've got to rush now. I'm expected for tea at the Palace at three o'clock.'

SLOW HOUNDS

John Warde had a career as a Master for over fifty years and hunted the New Forest, Pytchley, Craven and Bicester countries. He bred a large heavy hound lacking any speed or dash. He was a huge man of over 20 stone who liked the hounds to go at a slow pace and he was reported to have fed his faster hounds a diet of meat and suet, known as 'stopping balls' to his quicker hounds.

STRANGERS INVADE HUNT

Hunts and farmers were beginning, even in 1896, to resent the "intrusion of countless strangers, many of whom are neither gentleman, nor sportsmen nor good equestrians. At a recent meeting (February 1896) of the South Staffordshire Hunt, the field consisted of almost 400 horsemen, only 53 of whom were members. Many of these jumped on the hounds, nearly knocked over the hunt officials, and rode with entire disregard for the farmers and their interests."

Hon. F. Lawley, Daily Telegraph August 11th 1896.

TOM FIRR'S DEATH

On the last day of 1897, Tom Firr fractured his skull in a fall near Wymeswold. Following a long convalescence, he went back to the saddle and cub-hunted. But he fell again, hitting his head on a stone, and his career was over.

By this time Captain Burns-Hartopp had taken over the Mastership from Lord Lonsdale and Firr had become bent and frail. He tried to write his memoirs but gave up because of persistent headaches. When throat cancer was diagnosed, the end was rapid and he died near Christmas 1902 aged 61. Firr is buried in the quiet cemetery at Quorn within the sound of the hounds.

He left a legacy as a brilliant huntsman, singer and writer of songs. In April 1899 several hundred people attended his retirement ceremony at Quorn Hall and he received £3200 and a silver salver.

JOCK O'MILK

In the reign of James VI one of the celebrated characters was 'Jock O'Milk'. King James described him as 'a tight huntsman who could holloa to a hound till all the woods rang again'. Despite the fact that the King had a soft spot for him, Jock O'Milk's — or John Urwin's — name was held in considerable awe as a 'Border Raider' and he usually got the blame for any misdeeds committed in the area. He met his end from Lord Torthowald's lance.

(British Hunts and Huntsmen, Volume IV, 1911)

BOGGED DOWN

Thomas Spiers was a horseman of great ability but a dangerous man to follow in 1868 with the Lanarkshire and Renfrewshire Hunt. When he was in a jovial mood, he revelled in the fun of leading the inexperienced into difficulties. He would gallop right into a bog if he saw a chance of landing anyone in a predicament and no jump was too big for him!

(British Hunts and Huntsmen, Volume IV, 1911)

[Does this sound like anyone you know?]

THE ARTIST and the FOX

The artist Glover, some of whose works now hang in the National Gallery, was visiting the Cumberland Foxhounds, staying with Major Colomb. The Hunt was at breakfast in Colomb's dining room as the Master went to see what Glover was doing in his painting-room. Glover was doing a portrait of a live fox which he had boxed up in a corner by two chairs. The window was open and Colomb said 'If that fox escapes, we're in the breakfast room. Just yell 'Tally ho!' and we'll be after him'.

The fox duly made his escape through the window and Glover wiped his brushes, cleaned his palette and then walked slowly to the breakfast room. 'Gentlemen, tally-ho, the fox is gone!'

There was a loud cheer, much scraping of chairs, and mounting in hot haste. But the fox was never found.

(British Hunts and Huntsmen, Volume IV, 1911)

I BREED THEM

In 1849 when the Prince Consort visited the Brocklesby on his way to opening the Grimsby docks, he was impressed by the fine class of the farmers there, some fifty of them hunting in 'pink'. He asked the Earl of Yarborough where he got such tenants from. 'I don't get them, I breed them. When a tenant dies, it passes to his son,' replied the Earl.

AN OLD QUARRY IN THE FOG

Major Colomb was a Master with the Cumberland, a man of iron frame and constitution. One day during thick fog Colomb and his whipper-in rode straight into a quarry, falling about 20 feet down. Both were injured and could not move. The whipper-in began to shout as loud as he could to try and save the rest of the hunt from disaster.
Colomb bellowed at him: 'Hold your tongue, you bloody fool, and we'll have the whole place full of them!' He obviously thought there was safety in numbers!

(British Hunts and Huntsmen, Volume IV, 1911)

HEARING UNDER WATER

When a Huntsman or a Master is thrown from his horse, it is the subject of much mickey-taking from the rest of the field. On one occasion Borderer (of Baily's Magazine) recalls the look of disgust as Tom Firr was catapulted into Twyford Brook. The famous huntsman surfaced smiling, saying 'I could hear your laughter even when I was under the water!'

I SAW MY FIRST CUCKOO!

When you are on the receiving end of the field's mirth, because your horse has thrown you, or you're upside down in a hedge, there's not much you can do except laugh at yourself. One rider was thrown into a brook swollen by rain. As the other riders jumped safely over, the bedraggled rider raised his head above the water and warbled 'Cuckoo! cuckoo!' at them! Another horse approached, stopped in alarm and threw its rider into the same brook. The two then put their heads under the water and sprang up in unison, warbling 'cuckoo! cuckoo!' Not another horse jumped that fence for the rest of the day and the two warblers were given a severe dressing down by the Master as they returned in their now soaking attire.

THE HARE AS A WITCH

In some parts of the British Isles, the hare is credited with the power of the Occult, and it is said that witches take on the form of the hare. On the moors of North Yorkshire in the last century, a hare was being hunted down by the hounds as darkness fell. They'd trapped the hare near a remote cottage and the huntsman arrived to find the hounds snarling near the back door, trying to get into the cottage.
The huntsman knocked and went inside to investigate and found a very old woman sitting in the kitchen nursing a badly mauled leg! The only way to kill these witches was with a silver bullet, or a sixpence rammed down over the charge.

WAGERS BY THE SCORE

In the Kilkenny Hunt Club in the 1850's, there was apparently nothing in the rules to prevent any escapade, however outrageous. For one wager Lord Waterford rode his horse up the brass-bound staircase of the Club House Hotel, jumped over the dining room table and returned the way he came. Captain Machell used to win bets that he could jump onto the mantel shelf of the Adams fireplace in the hotel and stand there for a prescribed time. The feat seemed impossible as the mantel was five feet from the floor and only four inches from the wall.

British Hunts and Huntsmen (Vol. IV 1911)

THE DEVIL RIDES OUT . . .

When Squire Connolly (1738-1803) was Master of the Kildare, a stranger joined the hunt. He went wonderfully well and cut down the Squire who complimented him on his riding and asked him back to his home, Castletown, for dinner.
When the wine was circulating the Squire perceived that his guest was possessed of the cloven hoof, whereupon he sent for the parson and the priest. The parson arrived and threw a bible at the hard-rider, the priest began to pray over him. His 'Satanic Majesty' then disappeared through a hearthstone, and the crack remains in the dining room at Castletown till this day!

British Hunts and Huntsmen (Vol. IV 1911)

STAY IN THE BOG

Giles Eyre, one of the original Galway Blazers, was challenged to a race by a 'jealous' (i.e. reckless) English captain during a hunt. Away they went, each trying to cut the other up (and down). Eyre led the way at a bank, on the other side of which was a bog, jumped it, fell off and managed to scramble out with his horse, and remounted.
As he did so the English captain jumped, fell off and landed in the bog. His horse scrambled out and cantered past Eyre and away. The captain floundered around, wiping the mud out of his eyes.
'Where are you, Eyre?' he shouted.
'In and out', was the reply, 'but you can stay there.' Whereupon he galloped off.

CHARLES SHOULD BE SO LUCKY

The Prince of Wales in the late 19th century was a frequent follower of the Pytchley. On his first visit there, he astonished followers with his horsemanship. Earl Spencer, the Master and Charles Payne his huntsman noticed this.
'What do you think of the Prince of Wales?' said the Earl.
'He'll make a capital King, my Lord.'
'I'm glad you think so. And why?'
'He's sure to. Sure to do that, my Lord. He sits on a horse so well!'

(British Hunts and Huntsmen, volume II, 1909)

If only things were so simple one hundred years later!

ALMOST A ROYAL SUICIDE

The Prince of Wales went out with Parson Jack Russell to a meet with the Exmoor Hunt in August of 1879 at Hawkcombe Head. Nearly 5,000 people were present. The stag made a run for the sea, then turned back to Badgworthy Water where the future King administered the coup de grace. A young reporter, eager to impress, rushed to the nearest telegraph office and wired The Times as follows:
'Clipping run. Deer taken Badgworthy Water. Prince cut his throat 4.30 p.m.'
The item was received at the subs desk and there was consternation. Deadline was approaching and the subs took the news to the circulation department who immediately started work on the contents bill for the next issue, announcing the awful suicide of the heir to the throne. Fortunately the editor was a hunting man and soon realised what had happened!

British Hunts and Huntsmen, Vol. II 1909.

LEAVE HIM THERE

There is a deep ditch in Cottesmore country, notorious for being difficult to get out of, once in. A parson was out riding one Wednesday in 1799 with William Lowther and his huntsman, A. Abbey, who was a bit of a wit. The parson fell into the ditch, then tried to scramble out and fell back in again. Abbey watched the struggle with some amusement, then told Sir William, 'Leave him there, he's not wanted again till Sunday,' a comment very characteristic of an age when sport was at a high and the church at a low ebb.

ANOTHER DITCH STORY

The third Duke of Suffolk in 1745 was thrown from his horse into a notoriously deep ditch near Euston Park. A hard-riding parson, close behind, called out, 'Lie still, your Grace, I'll clear you!'
He then leapt over the prostrate Duke and galloped off without a look back. The Duke was not amused, especially when he was forced to stay there for an hour before a horseman stopped to help him out!

MIS-MATCH OF THE DAY

Jimmy Hill, of 'Match of the Day' fame, was being given riding lessons by his friend Ted Edgar, a brilliant rider and well-known practical joker. On one occasion Edgar took Hill across hunting country, encouraging him to jump some low fences. Hill took to this with relish and after a few hours, was sufficiently keen to try a larger hedge.
Edgar, some yards ahead of Hill, approached the fence gingerly, 'I know this fence, so I'll just take it steady. You kick on and take it at speed' he yelled to Hill. Edgar popped over the fence, turned his horse swiftly to the left and waited.
Hill's horse gathered speed and flew the fence, landed on terra firma, then, unable to stop, ran straight into the Grand Union canal! Edgar sat on his horse laughing, Hill struggling in the canal, soaked through. 'What'd you do that for?' he roared at Edgar. 'That'll teach you not to believe everything you hear' laughed the great man.

HOME, DOBBIN

Squire Boghurst of Frinsbury, Kent, was a noted foxhunter with the West Kent. He retired after the death of his wife and sought solace in his friends, the bottle, and his old hunter. He would ride to the White Hart tavern nightly on Old Trusty and, hours later, the waiters would carry him to his horse and the old hunter would find his way home unguided.

One night an arch of the Rochester Bridge gave way, leaving a yawning chasm, passable only to passengers via a 9-inch wide plank. The Squire had already ridden home when news reached the tavern in the early hours of the morning. The landlord, fearing for the health of his best customer, immediately walked all the way to Boghurst House, where he was ushered into the Squire's presence.

'Though I was drunk, Old Trusty was sober and got me home safely', he explained. The good old horse had walked the plank across the river!

UNLUCKY PIG

During the Mastership of Squire Osbaldeston the Pytchley chased a fox in 1830 from Kelmarsh to Stoke Albany where they lost it due to darkness. The following day they raised the same fox which they chased almost twenty miles into a pigsty, where 'both he and the pig were eaten by the hounds'.

British Hunts and Huntsmen, Vol. II 1909.

LUCKY FOX

In 1907, the Fitzwilliam chased a fox from Lilford to Barnwell village, then back to Stone Pits where the fox raced into a pigsty. The hounds followed and ate the pig while the fox watched in astonishment, then made his escape.

THE CAPTAIN, THE BROOK, AND HIS FAT MARE.

The majority of the regular followers of the Grafton and Pytchley Hounds are acquainted or familiar with the figure of Brooksby (Captain Elmhirst, of Daventry), a clever contributor of hunting notes to the "Field." The appended is an extract from his account of what he experienced at a brook between Weedon and Wappenham whilst out with the Grafton last week.

WISTFULLY I GLANCED

for the Huntsman's directing form, but he too was for the moment nonplussed on the bank. So, with a fat mare and a Fainting heart, I took the plunge–for hounds were already a furlong away, fairly laughing at us with their merry cackle. I hated to get in; but I should have hated myself far worse had I turned away. Or, to put it otherwise, I hadn't the pluck to funk though I would. The steeper bank was on the side of the hounds: the mare could not climb it; and all hope of progress was dashed to the waters. The little band of horsemen–intent on their own escape–hurried up on the stream in search of a bridge (which, by the same token, they found only a field further on!)–and I was "left blooming alone." One young gentleman, to do him justice, came back, and had a flick at the mare with his lash. But, finding this of no avail, he gladly availed himself of the invitation to go on. A rustic stood on the further bank–but the mare of course had to be got back whence she came. "Capital–so glad of your help! Get over quick, and here's half-a-crown." The rustic forthwith ran up and down the bank like a terrier seeking for water rats, and the mare meanwhile subsided like a dead log, as blown horses in water always will.

"GET OVER YOU FOOL! SHE'S DROWNING!"

–and with a one-legged hop I placed myself on the shore whereon I meant to beach her. But Rusticus stayed where he was; and neither entreaty nor plain speaking would make him venture into the water. He merely scratched his head, and shook it, murmuring "I'd be watchered (Anglice, wetted), I ca'ant joomp that fur." From entreaty I went to objurgation; and, as the mare played dolphin in the deep water–hemmed in, too, by bushes growing on either bank–I grew angry, and sinned. In a state of fury almost excusable, I emptied my vocabulary (no slender one, but enriched from travel in many countries) at his cowardly head–till

HORRIFIED AND TERROR STRUCK

he slunk off and disappeared. Now came another phase of the situation. The afternoon was fast closing in; and all around was solitude and silence, save for the chirping of the busy pack as–not half a mile away–they hunted backwards and forwards on a tired and dodging fox. Slipping one stirrup leather round her neck, and lengthening my hold with the other, I hauled the mare's languid head on to terra firma, and then proceeded to review the position. The watch told me it was now close upon four p.m.–the date being near the shortest of days–and it was forty-five minutes since we had left Tite's Copse. Not a living soul within sight; the evening still and dark and warm; good day for a wetting, anyhow. Let me see, how much did she cost me? Halloa, there's a man cutting a hedge only 300 yards away. Hey, you! Now for a view halloa. He's sure to hear; or–who knows?–perhaps it may fetch hounds back for news of their fox.

TALLY HO! YOI!! YOI!!!

Help you fool. Why the fellow's deaf! Of course he was deaf–did you ever know a man mending a hedge or a road who wasn't? He never moved, or even looked up from his work! In sheer despair I soused the mare's head under water; and implored her by all her ancestry and by the soul of St. Patrick to make an effort. She made one or two–then subsided lower than ever; and I played her by the bridle as if she were a great white trout. Again I lifted up my voice, halloaed–I think I should have wept, had not I been so angered with Rusticus and his base cowardice. I halloaed to the rising moon, I halloaed to the dim grey horizon, and I bawled to the unknown distance. And the latter at length gave succour. A whole village-full of wreckers suddenly dashed into view, bringing at least willing hands and sturdy hearts. Six men on to the stirrup-leathers; a crack with the whip, a pull altogether–and the mare was on her legs on the turf, her back up and every fibre quivering; but alive. A quart of hot ale, and a handful of ginger quickly brought back the circulation, and so ends my tale of woe.

Extract from the Northampton Mercury December 21st 1889

A NOTE TO THE FAIR SEX
Thank you for missing my spine.

WANTED.–Lost, stolen, or strayed, the name of the lady–presumably young–who at Spratton Brook on Friday jumped right on to the back of Major Z., of Market Harborough, and who galloped away at top speed, perhaps for home for fear of recriminations, without any inquiry. Major Z. offers sixpence reward (in acid drops), and the mark of the shoe of the lady's horse can be accurately seen and compared, within an inch of his spine, if and when desired. He is very grateful to the lady for missing his spine, and so avoiding his death. Applications can be made to "The Sign of the Horse Shoe" at Great Bowden.

From: Coronet, Wit and Wisdom of the Shires

THE NEWBY FERRY TRAGEDY

One of the most tragic incidents in the annals of hunting took place in 1869, on February 4th. The York and Ainsty had chased a fox for an hour when they came to the wide River Ure where the fox swam across. The hounds followed and, though many were washed over a nearby weir, crossed safely. Sir Charles Slingsby saw the Newby Ferry boat coming in and led the field on. Thomas Clayton recalls the Master shouting 'Don't overload', but the ferry was crammed full with eleven horses and thirteen men. The ferry began to lean and sank only thirty yards from the shore. Sir Charles and his horse Saltfish were both drowned, as were two boatmen, Orvis his huntsman, Edward Lloyd and Edmund Robinson.

A memorial window in Knaresborough Parish Church was raised and is still there.

CONDOM JOHN

A gentleman, a motor dealer by trade, was visiting the Pytchley in 1992. He was very affable and anxious to make a good impression.

Two lady members of the hunt were sporting their new show hats, fitted and measured in London, and more pointed than the normal hunting ones. 'Those are fine hats you're wearing' the stranger said courteously. 'But why are they that pointed shape?' 'Oh, that's for keeping our condoms in' replied one of the ladies with a straight face. The stranger nodded with a new understanding and rode away, muttering to himself. Everytime the ladies see him now, they refer to him as 'Condom John'.

THE FIGHT

When Tom Assheton Smith went into a bank in Leicester, he tethered his horse outside. A passing coal-heaver gave the horse a cut with his whip and it almost jumped through the bank window. Smith raced outside and the pair, well-matched, squared up. No science, just punching, a real rough and tumble until the police interfered.
'You will hear from me again' roared Smith as he rode off. That evening he dined with some friends, a beefsteak over one eye, but told the tale with some gusto.
The following morning his groom discovered the coal-heaver's address, knocked on the door for some time before it was answered by the wife.
'Does the man live here who fought the gentleman by the bank yesterday?'
'He does if he is still alive after the terrible beating he got' answered the woman.
'Mr, Smith sent me to give him this five-pound note and to tell him he is the best man he ever fought' said the groom.
The coal-heaver jumped off his bed and came to the door, for he was more frightened than hurt.
'Thank him a thousand times. But tell him he hits like a kicking horse' said the relieved man. 'To show my gratitude, tell him I will fight him any day he likes for love!'

STRANGE ADVERTISEMENT

WANTED: A flash, high-stepping SCREW. Must be very fast, steady in single harness and the price moderate. Blemishes no object. Apply by letter to George Gallon, Rose and Crown, Four-Lane-Ends, Herts.
    R. S. Surtees reports that the above advertisement appeared around 1840, (Hillingdon Hall, Methuen & Co 1904).
The Times wouldn't allow it these days.

GENTLEMANLY FOX

The Heythrop Hounds met at Ranger's Lodge near Charlbury, found in Hazell Wood went away through Great Cranwell, turned into Kings Wood near a manor house, with the hounds close to the brush, where the fox disappeared in a mysterious manner. After a lapse of a little time, he was discovered by a maidservant in the ladies dressing room, from which he immediately bolted on the appearance of the petticoats, without doing the slightest damage to person or property.
(Bell's Life 1840)

HUNTING ON A DONKEY

Amongst the many colourful figures in Yorkshire in the mid 1800's was Jack Smith. He was an eccentric known all over the East and North Ridings and was a rat-catcher by trade. He became a regular hanger-on of Lord Middleton's Hunt, always turning up mounted bareback on a small donkey. Finally his services were recognised and he was given a pink coat and cap and allowed to attend all the meets. Lord Middleton, considering a donkey was not in keeping, provided Jack with a pony. Smith politely refused and continued to hunt on his donkey until his death.

DOWN THE WELL

In 1851 on Christmas Eve, a fox was found and raced off to Fairfold Park in the Vale of White Horse country. In the corner of a meadow was an old pump and nearby was a gap in the hedge. Mr Harry Van Notten Pole made for the gap but, as he neared it, the horse's hindquarters sank out of sight, followed by Mr. Pole, then the horses neck and head. The rest of the field rode up in some alarm to find the unfortunate rider and his horse stuck down a disused well! Getting Pole out was no problem, but the horse was stuck. After a council of war, ropes were passed under the horse, round his forefeet and neck and he was eventually pulled out after several hours unharmed by a large crowd. Mr. Pole then got back on his exhausted horse and rode him back home gently.

UNDER THE TABLE

Lord Kintore took the Mastership of the Old Berkshire in 1826, living in Wadley House. He was a hard rider and a harder drinker, keeping a virtual 'open house' for foxhunters. Once he entertained his guests on Scotch ale to such an effect that they all fell asleep on the floor. Kintore had them wrapped in rugs and laid side by side outside on the lawn, to recover by morning. But a dozen Berkshire squires were more durable and Kintore fell asleep. The squires summoned the butler, bade him take Kintore to bed and bring more wine. He woke up a few hours later, went downstairs and rejoined the party, only to fall asleep again and to be put to bed for a second time. The squires drank till morning, and then rode off.
Kintore was so impressed that he chalked the names of the squires – and the wine they drank – on the cellar walls, where it is said they still remain!

THE HOLE IN THE WALL GANG

Surtees reports (in Handley Cross) that the manoeuvres of the hunted hare are truly astonishing. On one occasion a hare had led the hounds a merry dance, but was all but exhausted as it approached a high loose stone wall. A few stones were out in the middle, and the hare jumped in. The quarry was concealed from view, the scent lost and the hounds frustrated.
The field were puzzled, then decided that someone from a nearby gypsy camp had stolen their quarry, rode down and searched the cooking pots. The gypsies were annoyed, half a dozen stout wrenches emerged from one of the carts and a royal battle ensued. The Master was drenched with hot soup and the hare forgotten!

AUTO PILOT

Squire Osbaldeston always disliked having anyone ride close behind him. A friend of his was constantly annoyed by a gentleman who continually used him as a 'pilot'. So he determined to get rid of the nuisance.
One day he found the gentleman at his horse's tail. He said nothing, but took another line. An hour later, the follower said, 'I don't see the hounds, Sir Charles'. 'Of course you don't. I'm on my way home across country'.

'Autobiography': Squire Osbaldeston.

HUNTING TALES

LUCKY WHIP

G. D. MUCKLOW was an amateur whip of the Holcombe Harriers, and always rode an excellent jumper. Sometimes however he was apt to test his mounts ability to alarming limits especially when the well being of his hounds was at stake. On one occasion hounds had checked along a railway line at Holcombe Brook.

Mucklow, finding the level crossing gate closed against him, without a second thought, leapt the gate onto the railway line, gathered up his precious hounds and trotted safely back through the gate which had been quickly opened by the level crossing attendant. How rider and horse escaped turning over on the hard, stoney surface of the railway track must be put down to sheer good fortune, but hardly a feat to attempt again and hope to be so lucky.

Contributed by Angela Heaton

BROTHERLY LOVE?

Two brothers of a well-to-do family were in conflict with each other, so much so that their only exchange of conversation was in vicious argument. An intense rivalry existed in all aspects of their daily lives; houses, horses, cars or similar possessions, the competition for the more powerful model being fierce. The story goes that on the day in question, the brothers both had a party of guests out to enjoy the Otterhunting activities, their cars laden with the usual splendid picnic fare ready to lay out at the appropriate hour.

As the day's sport progressed, the two brothers driving their respective parties, and as usual wishing to avoid all possible chance of contact with each other, trundled slowly along opposite sides of the river as far as they could, until the river's course made it necessary for one of the parties, brother 'A', to cross over a bridge to keep the river in view. Unfortunately, brother 'B' had decided to park his party on the incline of the same bridge, to have good sight of the hounds progressing up the river towards them and they were enjoying their grand stand view when party 'A' slowly made their way over the bridge. The two brothers glowered at each other, brother 'B' had no intention of giving up his prize place to allow brother 'A' to complete his crossing. Both stood firm, and a fierce exchange of words ensued which became hotter by the second until one of the other car followers, who found himself stuck behind brother 'A' and likewise wishing to cross over, became irritated and decided the only resolution was to call the police.

The arrival of the police caused much excitement throughout all the hunt followers, who certainly had not expected such variety to their day. By now it was lunch time, and the occupants in each car were ready for their food. Browned off with the trivial arguing between their drivers, the guests climbed out of their respective carriages, laid out their drink and fodder on the most suitable river bank and, joining forces, enjoyed their feasts together. As for the two brothers, both were so deeply involved in their battle as to who was going to give way to the other, that the highlight of their hunting day, the lunch time picnic, was ruined and their performance the subject of much amusement to all who witnessed the event.

The matter was eventually resolved by one brother being ordered to give way to the other, who, I never learned. The occurrence did not, however, improve the brotherly relationships.

A story related to Angela Heaton by an old gentleman Kit Wright, regretfully since died, about an incident whilst out with the Otterhounds. She cannot be positive which pack, or, unfortunately exact date but believes it could have been the Kendal & District sometime in the early days of Otterhunting.

THE RUNAWAY HOUNDS and THE LEGLESS HOSTLER

Labordor Hall was a Markyate hostler of the last century who, when changing horses for the Woburn coach, had been struck by the speeding Manchester coach and lost both legs. Thomas Pickford - whose name is synomynous with travel - had widened the road from St. Albans to Dunstable to improve coach travel but unfortunately the new road had encouraged a craze for speed and Markyate's long High Street had become the scene of many accidents.

Pickford was resolved to alleviate the plight of the now legless Markyate man and the result was the building of a dog cart to help 'Old Lal' as he was known, get around. More astonishing was the arrival of three foxhounds who were trained to harness and pulled Old Lal around the village. The legless man found he could earn money running errands and delivering small packages. He thus became an early version of TNT.

There being no television or radio to distract the locals, Old Lal became a celebrity and a business success, and the locals turned out to watch the man with no legs and his foxhounds delivering items in Markyate and the surrounding area. Soon, the locals started challenging Old Lal to 'chariot races' and Markyate High Street became even more of a hazard for pedestrians as they now had to deal with racing stage coaches, horsemen in a hurry and Old Lal's chariot races. His fame grew and races were held every Wednesday and Saturday at noon.

Thomas Pickford was finding the situation a pain in the neck, but there was nothing he could do. But providence intervened in the form of the local hunt.

One Saturday, just as Old Lal had emerged from the Sun Inn for the start of yet another chariot race, the whole village was thrown into uproar as a fox, hotly pursued by hounds and the hunt in full cry, chose Markyate High Street as its best escape route.

Old Lal's foxhounds immediately forgot their long months of training and gave chase. Despite the legless man's attempts to stop them, they overtook the hounds and got right up on the fox's brush. The fox then left the road for the safety of fields, ditches and hedges, followed by Old Lal's foxhounds and the cart and the rest of the field.

Some hours later, a group of subdued foxhunters returned to the High Street and deposited Old Lal's legless and now lifeless body at the Sun Inn. They had found him in a wood where his foxhounds had crashed the cart, wedging it between two fir trees. The coroner decided on death by misadventure, Markyate High Street returned to relative normality, chariot racing ceased and a relieved Thomas Pickford got on with his stagecoach business.

ROLL OUT THE BARREL

In the early 1950's, hounds' excrement was saved, put into barrels and transported to a tannery where it was used to tan leather. Tim Langley and Billy Cook would load the barrels on the kennel lorry and take them to Ruabon station. They treated the barrels with great respect because of their weight and, in the warm weather, they were liable to explode. The porters at the station were no help, they would recognise the Kennel lorry and scatter in all directions, leaving the two unfortunates to heave the barrels onto the goods platform.

One very hot day, they were struggling with a barrel, when it fell. There was a loud bang and the contents flew in all directions, smothering them and everyone in sight with the evil smelling manure. An old porter heard the bang, came out looking concerned, then convulsed into fits of laughter. He yelled for the other porters to come and look and view the entertainment with the only words Langley had ever heard him utter - SHA - HA - HA - HE - IT. SHIT - HA - HA.

Tim Langley (Good Morning, Good Night, 1987)

HUNTING TALES

THE OLD SKITTLES MARE
The strange story of an Encounter in Calcutta.

I was dining with my old friend Brigadier Clayton of Pytchley late one evening just after the Great War which we had both fortunately survived. The Brigadier, unhappily, had lost a leg and an eye in the campaign and couldn't hunt anymore, and the conversation turned to the golden days of the turn of the century.
He'd hunted with them all. He'd been the 'pilot' of the Empress of Austria. 'That damn'd Middleton', the Brigadier fumed. 'I had the Empress all lined up for a night frolic at Boughton Hall. Her dance card was full when up stepped Middleton, cut in and swept her off her feet. Never saw them the rest of the week. She was shot of course. Served her right!' 'What about Skittles?' I asked curiously. 'Whatever happened to her?'
His one good eye glowed and his black eye patch jumped up and down with excitement. His one good leg shot out and kicked over the spittoon. The memory of Catherine Walters obviously affected him greatly. He leaned forward confidentially and put his hand on my own.
'Calcutta,' he said hoarsely.
'Calcutta?' I repeated dumbly. 'Yes, you fool. Calcutta.'.
I sat silent, the brigadier's mouth worked furiously like a toothless granny chewing chestnut stuffing. I'd seen him in this mood before and stayed silent, knowing he was about to impart some dark secret of his past life. He'd been quite a dashing figure in his younger days with the ladies when he had two legs and two eyes.
'Ah, Calcutta', he whispered. I waited.
'I was in Calcutta in the company of the 71st Horse. My father was acting as adviser to the colonial administration, a tricky job at the time. We were located in the Government White House – our idea before those dammed Americans swiped the name for themselves – in the Northern part of the city and one day we were strolling through the local bazaar when suddenly my fathers eyes widened, his moustache twitched violently and he stared open-mouthed.
'Good God, look'
I followed his pointing finger and beheld a most unusual sight. An old skinny nag, ribs protruding through the flesh, plodded with its head down along the dusty street. Leading it was a creature in rags, bare feet blistered, unkempt hair falling down over a dirty tunic and what appeared to be torn, ragged trousers hung from the creatures legs.
My father stood erect, 'Look at that horse! Who on God's earth would allow a horse to be in that condition?'
He stood in the middle of the dusty street, planted his feet directly in the creatures path.
'Stop there, my man'.
To the horse 'Whoa, there, I say, whoa?'
Both creatures stopped, still with their heads down, and my father circled the two pitiful figures. He stared at the horse in rigid concentration, eyeing it all over.
'Good Lord. By all the saints. Heavens above. My sainted aunt', he exclaimed. 'It can't be. It is. It must be. It's Queen of the Chase!'
At my father's voice, the creature holding the horse fell to the ground in a dead faint. Father hardly glanced down, but reached for the mare's halter rope and stroked its muzzle. The mare's eyes seemed to glow with a new recognition and lifted the head and neighed. Father beamed at me.
'See, she knows me. How on earth did she come to be in such a state? And in Calcutta, too, of all places.'
I shook my head dumbly. We all knew that animals in India are used for three things, riding, hunting and eating. Anything you catch, you eat. And when a horse gets too old for riding, it ends up in the tribal soup-pot. How a hunter from England could arrive in

Calcutta and survive the pot in the present emaciated state was beyond me.

'Perhaps this filthy creature knows?' bellowed my father, poking the bundle of rags with his foot.

The bundle didn't move. My father gave the rags a cut with the hunting whip he always carried as protection against flies and the local tribesmen. It was motionless for an eternity or as long as it took to read 'Horse and Hound' from cover to cover in those sad depressed days when it took 6 months to reach us in Calcutta.

Father wrinkled his nose, then turned the bundle of rags over with his highly polished riding boots. The wretch was still in a swoon. We gasped. It was a white man. Young, apparently with small hands and feet.

'Yes, by thunder, it is the Queen of the Chase,' bellowed Father.

'And I'll prove it.'

He threw back his head and roared 'Halloa, halloa!' at the top of his voice. The effect was dramatic. The mare laid its ears back, bared its yellowing teeth, and lashed out with its back feet, then set off at right angles to us, jumping two carts full of trinkets being peddled by two local traders, wheeled around in a circle, and screeched to a thundering halt, hooves not a foot away from the prostrate bundle of rags.

'See that?' said father. 'Its got spunk, though it looks a mangy creature now. You should have seen it with Skittles on its back. That was a sight to make red-blooded men tremble.'

I know the feeling well. Had Bay Middleton not introduced me (before he dallied with the Empress) I should never have made the ladies acquaintance. I shall always remember her handshake, cool but full of warmth, and her blue eyes boring into my soul.

The creature in rags stirred. Father gave it another push with his foot. 'Just how, you little runt, did this mare get in this condition?' He kicked the bundle again. He threw a sovereign down at the pitiful figure. 'That'll pay for the horse. We'll keep her better than you will, although God knows it looks like a hopeless case.' He looked thoughtfully at the bundle of rags again. 'I suppose we'd better take care of you, too. At least till we know how the horse got from Pytchley to Calcutta.'

He arranged for both the nag and the rags to be moved to the White House and there, in the stables, they were both fed and watered and settled down for the night. It took both almost a week to recover and only then did we learn of the strange story of horse and rider. The erstwhile bundle of rags was given stable boys clothes and, washed and deloused thoroughly, sat at our dining table one night and told the story in his low, almost female voice. There was something strange in his manner and his hands, though small, had long fingers like those of a piano player.

He and some friends of Lord Hartingdon had been hunting with the Quorn. He had been riding Queen of the Chase.

'Just a minute', interrupted father. 'Queen of the Chase was always ridden by Skittles, you know, Catherine . . . .'

'Catherine Walters', said the figure in stableboy cloths, 'I know. It was Hartingdon's horse, but I always rode it.'

The voice had changed. It was no longer a feminine man's voice, but a husky low woman's voice. We stared in amazement. 'But, but, who the hell are you?' father bellowed.

'They used to call me Skittles. I'm Catherine Walters.'

'I don't believe you.'

'Ask me anything', she shrugged, 'the Quorn, the Pytchley, the Cottesmore, I know them all.'

And so did father and I. We shot questions at her for an hour, and she answered every one accurately.

'But how did you come to be in Calcutta?'

'Hartingdon brought his regiment 500 miles north of here 2 years ago, and several of his hunting horses. He asked me along, as he didn't trust me alone in England.

Unfortunately, I had an affair with the Maharajah of Bangalore, and Hartingdon began seeing the Empress of Burma. One day he just announced that he was sending me home on the next ship. I took Queen of the Chase that night and rode to the Maharajah's palace. But he'd left for the summer for his place in the mountains. I tried to find him, but got lost. So the Queen of the Chase and I rode south, I think. By that time I had decided it was safer to dress like a man and stole the rags you saw me in. We begged and stole food until you found us two weeks ago.'

We were both flabbergasted. What an extraordinary tale of treachery and deceit on both parts. She had long been Hartingdon's mistress, but a known courtesan as well. The Times had once lampooned her as 'The Prostitute on a Horse.' And yet, here she was in Calcutta, dressed as a stable lad, having almost died of starvation!

'What will you do with me now?' she asked in a low voice. 'I'm not sure', father blustered. 'We'll have to see. You can sleep in the stables tonight, then we'll find you some better accommodation'.

The brigader's voice trailed off. There was a faraway look in his eye, a smile on his lips. 'So what happened?' I gasped.

There was no reply. The old brigadier was still smiling. I got up slowly, found another decanter of port, and poured him a glass. He was still smiling. I waited, convinced that the long-ago incident that had brought a smile to his face would soon be related.

The smile stayed in place, the faraway look still in his eye. I sighed. The brigadier was notorious for falling asleep in the middle of a good story. There was a long sigh from the chair and his chin dropped onto his chest. 'Damn' I thought, 'I'll have to wait till morning,' covered him with a blanket and stoked up the fire. I rang the bell for his old valet, who was familiar with the old boy's habits, then, tiredness overwhelming me, went off slowly to bed.

When I awoke, the house was pandemonium. The doctor, the nurse and, it seemed, the whole of the hospital had been called. All to no avail. The old brigadier had died smiling, the memory of Skittles still in his eye and on his lips.

And for myself, I was sad for him, but sadder at not knowing the final outcome of the strange story of Catherine 'Skittles' Walters. Perhaps I wasn't meant to know. . . .

GREATEST DANDY

Beau Brummel's extravagant exploits in the hunting field have been mentioned elsewhere in this book.

Brummel was pre-eminent as the greatest dandy of his time, the 'arbiter elegantarium' of fashionable society. He resigned his commission when the Hussars were ordered to Manchester to suppress a riot because he could not tolerate the idea of 'being exiled to a provincial town'. Though his father was a self made land agent and his grandfather a humble valet, Brummel set out to cultivate a personality and manner superior to everyone else. By a combination of outrageous impertinence, sarcasm and extreme arrogance, he managed to succeed beyond his wildest dreams.

Tailors, hatters, glovemakers and shirtmakers were all prepared to give Brummel extensive credit in exchange for his patronage. Hoby, the most famous of all the bootmakers in Piccadilly, made a fortune thanks to Brummel and his society friends, the Duke of Argyll, Lord Worcester, 'Poodle' Byng and other members of White's Club inner circle.

Brummel's debts eventually caught up with him and he was forced to make a hasty escape across the Channel. He died in poverty and squalor in a Brittany boarding house, ignored by his hunting and society friends, and pursued by his debtors.

HUNTING TALES

BRING ON THE CLOWNS

My young son heard me talking about hunting and the people I rode with for most of his eight years. One day I decided to take him to a meet. I introduced him to my fellow riders, the Master, the Huntsman, but he seemed unimpressed. I tried to amuse him by telling him the names of the horses and hounds, but he remained bored. As we drove home I was perplexed at his lack of enthusiasm and the sullen look on his face. Finally the penny dropped when he complained, "I never got to see the clowns you said you hunted with!"

Name and address withheld.

NO TALKING

A M.F.H. arrived back from the Second World War with a French lady in tow, who was to become his wife. He spoke no French, she not a word of English. I asked him how he would communicate with her.
'Apart from hunting, there's only three worthwhile things in life', he replied. 'That's eating, drinking and making love. If you need to talk during any of these, there's something seriously amiss!'

Contributed by Bob Andrews, Pytchley Hunt.

TRADING PLACES

An old Master, well known for his dry humour, was wakened in the middle of the night by a telephone call from his young whipper-in. The young man blurted out 'I'm sorry to wake you, but your Huntsman has passed away. We're all very saddened, but I'd like to know if I can take his place?'
The Master thought it over for a moment, then replied 'Well, I guess it's all right with me, if it's all right with the undertaker!'

BACK TO FRONT?

A member of the Polo playing fraternity was trying to encourage his more than reluctant pony to jump a very small cross-pole. Unsuccessful, he dismounted and attempted to lift each leg over in turn, both he and the pony becoming steadily more confused. Eventually he called out despairingly to an instructor, 'Do horses jump with their back legs or their front legs first?'

ONCE BITTEN

'My first taste of doing post mortems in hunt kennels was in Kirbymoorside in Yorkshire. It was the habit at these kennels to let the pregnant hound bitches have the run of the flesh yard, so I had to hoot the horn to alert the huntsman who would put the bitches out of the way while the carcass was being examined. Having more than once been bitten on the backside while concentrating on a post-mortem, I made very sure the bitches were always locked up.'

P. D. Foster, Spratton, Northants

HUNTING TALES

THADDEUS RYAN AND THE WHITE FOX

When 'Thady' Ryan was born in the late thirties in Ireland, the midwife had just delivered him when she gave a great shriek and rushed to the bedroom window. She saw the great White Fox of Guryspillane sitting in the middle of the lawn watching the window, apparently approving of the birth of a man said to be one of the most brilliant foxhunters in history.

HENRY VIII's EXECUTIONER

A hunting party of the King's nobles arrived at Scarteen. Henry VIII sent his Chief Executioner to tell the Ryan Family to donate some of their best hounds to the Royal Kennel, or the eldest Ryan would have his head chopped off. He refused but persuaded the nobles to allow him a last hunt, and was then beheaded. The nobles, however, had such a great day's sport that they decided to remain in Ireland. The executioner himself became Kennel Huntsman to a new pack in Cork!

WHO DUNG THAT?

At the turn of the century, before the car replaced four-legged transport, some of the most beautiful cities in Europe had streets littered with horse manure. The French humourist Alphonse Allais once said that 'the most striking thing about Venice is the complete absence of horse dung!' But Horace de Vere Cole, a notorious London practical joker on honeymoon in Venice in 1919, determined to put this right. He spent his honeymoon night spreading vast quantities of manure all over the Piazza San Marco. The locals were astonished. No-one knew where it had come from. The local newspaper even guessed that it might have been put there by sea horses!
Cole later confessed to the prank, once he was safely back in England.

HELL IS . . .

A noted horsewomen, soon to be married, was crying to her mother. 'I can't marry Robert. He's not as religious as I used to think. In fact, he doesn't even believe in Hell!'
Her mother thought for a moment, then replied. 'Go ahead and marry him. Between the two of us we'll show him how wrong he is!'

Name and address withheld

CLEVER MASTER

'Only two things are necessary to keep your wife happy and be a successful Master. One is to let her think she is having her own way, and the other is to let her have it!'

Anonymous MFH, Pytchley Hunt.

THE HUNTING CLERIC AND HIS WIFE
A strange tale of Wartime Espionage

The history of foxhunting has been constantly distinguished by its long association with the men of the cloth. Until 1940, that is.

How many country parsons have officiated at the solemnization of marriages and the baptising of month-old screaming babies while secretly wearing under their robes their hunting coats and riding boots?

I recently attended a service at the parish church of Pitsford Prostate and the vicar there is an old friend, a hunting fanatic named Rev. John-Joe Osbaldeston Russell. He had taken up residence in the village after serving several years as Parson General to Sealink and had achieved immortality as the only man to be seasick while giving holy communion to Lord Vestry. Fortunately milord saw the christian side of it and transferred him to Pytchley country where my friend became a collector of priceless hunting memorabilia. It was also for his safety as war had just broken out.

He showed me his treasures one evening after vespers, and they filled a whole room. George Osbaldeston's hunting whip which the Prince of Wales had used to flog him after discovering the squire bedding his wife in a hay barn in Brixworth; Nimrod's pen but no ink, Mike Bletsoe-Brown's driving gloves; one of Peter O'Sullevan's support hose, discovered amongst lost property items at Ascot; and Peter Jones' personal toenail clippers. Other minor items included a copy of Lester Piggott's draft tax returns, the Imran Khan guide to Cricket Cheats and the Ian Botham Golf Swing Tutor.

These treasures he held in great esteem along with dozens of books and prints, horseshoes and hunt buttons. He was he said, saving all of these items up to sell at an auction, the proceeds to go to his retirement party. His treasured item was Barbara Cartland's hunting hat, ivory white with a trace of lipstick on the visor which he hoped would pay for his world cruise.

You'll gather from all this that Parson John-Joe was not a wealthy man. Worse than that, he seemed quite poor and his meagre Church of England salary was augmented only by the collection that he held after services. And that hardly paid for his subscription to the Hunt. As for a horse, well, he kept it in the stable behind the rectory and rode everywhere upon it, disdaining to follow the fashion and buy an expensive motor car. This enabled him to save thousands a year on insurance and petrol and provided a bonanza for the rose-growers of Pitsford Prostrate. On his daily rounds he collected cabbage, carrots and Polo mints for his horse so his food bill was kept low. I have dined with him many times. An excellent cook, his favourite meal was carrot soup followed by a rare vintage cabbage wine with a slightly minty flavour.

His wife, however, was mean lipped and treble chinned with a tendency to bellow. The last time I dined there, I excused my self to go to the toilet. As I re-entered the room, she bellowed 'I hope you've shaken that Thing properly!' I looked in some amazement, then realised she was talking to the reverend who was about to put Heinz Ketchup into his carrot soup. The reverend did confess that she would bellow at him if there was more than two inches of hot water in his bath, or if the horse did biggies on their lawn. But, he sighed mildly, this was understandable as she was rather a large lady who didn't ride (or bathe). She had been a good understanding wife until his spell as Sealink Parson General, as their rectory had been a small outside cabin with only one porthole and no garden. In her younger days she had been a fine athlete, keeping wicket for Yorkshire Colts and had been renowned for her invention of the box and ladies chest protector. When she gave up trying to break into the Yorkshire first team, she went training with Millwall Football Club. Unfortunately, the twelve months of heading a heavy wet leather football had caused an unsightly bald patch above her forehead, of which she was quite proud.

But the reverend's wife had one serious drawback. She was the sister of Mr. George Drummond, the well-known Pitsford Prostate landowner and Nazi sympathiser. She would open after-dinner conversation with 'If Hitler invaded England, do you think the Master of Foxhounds Association would allow Germans to hunt?' I usually said they would as their committee seemed to consist of members of the Gestapo and cousins of Heinrich Himmler. 'Dear George' she would say of her brother, 'he is much misunderstood.' Drummond, indeed had been almost deported in 1940 and forced to live in Ireland. My friend often hoped loudly that his sister would join him. But, strangely, Parson John-Joe, had been invited to be Home Guard Chaplain before the crucial Opening Meet in 1939 and refused the honour on the grounds of overwork. This I know to be nonsense. He was simply afraid of his wife.

Now the parson would hunt every Monday with the Pytchley, Wednesday with the Quorn and Saturday with the Cottesmore. On some occasions he would venture out with the Grafton, the Belvoir and the Oakley. I found this decidedly odd as he had little money, but I know that his love of hunting was genuine and that it was customary for the hunts to give a reduced subscription to parsons. In exchange the Church of England allowed Meets to be held on their huge tracts of church owned land. So even at the start of wartime, with most of the Masters away commanding regiments, the parson would hunt as often as he could. When the Land Army was formed, the parson's wife refused to join. One can see her point, when you consider the horrors that this institution — and giving women the vote — has inflicted upon all of us — big strapping farm girls throwing their bulk all over tractors and soldiers on leave, ugly sisters incessantly sucking spangles, mixed ballroom dancing and – worst of all – the tradition of village hall dances where the girls put their overloaded handbags in the middle and dance around them. This practice started with the Land Army and continues today, along with dandruff and fair isle pullovers. I thought it a shame she refused to join as her bellowing voice would surely have guaranteed her the rank of Colonel, at least.

Shortly thereafter I was out with the dandies at Melton and happened to notice my friend the parson hobnobbing with the Master Brigadier Plumbley 'Digger' McGann. He had left for the war only two weeks before and was obviously having a spot of leave. 'There's plenty of time', I'd heard him say at his drinks do on the eve of his departure. 'He's just invaded Poland, Denmark's next and it'll take the frogs a few months to surrender. He won't get to us till May next year, well after the end of the hunting season. And when we line up a few hundred foxhunters with their hounds on the cliffs of Dover, well, that'll make him think. And if Hitler ever sees the Land Army women he won't come anywhere near us'.

The parson had certainly improved his appearance and looked very well turned out with new boots and one of those new fangled hats with a chin strap. Disgusting things, they were, rubbing against the Remington Lectric shave all the time and causing chafing. I put his smart appearance down to his new fund raising efforts with manure. He had started bagging it up and was advertising it for sale with some success, in the local newspaper. As the field moved out I saw the parson riding side-by-side with Group Captain Ingleby-Dogsworth Andrews who was in charge of the RAF base at Hackleton, and who was also on leave. I didn't think any more of this, even when I saw him hob-nobbing with Rear Admiral Bletsoe-Butt Jones who was in charge of the North Sea Fleet, also on leave. But as we all trooped home, weary and muddy, I saw deep in conversation with Commander Fields-Fitzgibbon Gurney Wilson, the man in charge of our Red Berets, also on leave. That was the final straw. There was something afoot.

Two days later with the Cottesmore I watched him chatting to Colonel Frost-Feiffer, Vice Admiral Michael Adams-Black, Group Captain Brudenall-Donald and Brigadier Dexter Worthington-Bass – all on leave. Something was decidedly iffy. The following morning with the Pytchley at Sywell he was in deep conversation with Rear Admiral (WRNS)

Leslie Bailey-Heather (also on leave) as they approached the first fence. The parson wasn't much of a thruster but he made a valiant attempt to jump, fell off sideways and banged his head on the side of the thick blackthorn. His helmet fell off and rolled towards me as my mare skidded to stop. The parson was lying, only winded, as I picked up the hat. Then I noticed something strange. The name 'Braun' was stitched inside and a short wire protruded from the buckle. Braun was a name I knew well - Werner Von Braun - a German scientist who after the war, fled to America and invented the hair drier and curling tongs, becoming best friends with Victor Kiam (Lord Remington) about whose life Yul Brynner and Deborah Kerr starred in the movie 'Anna and the King of Kiam'.

Other riders rushed to aid the parson. I hung back and thoughtfully examined the hat. Discreetly I wheeled my mount and rode back to Group Captain Gerald Simmons-Monica, (also on leave) who was head of MI5. He had arrived late for the meet with his wife Lady Gabriella de Grose-Cundell Pyke due to petrol rationing.

'Good heavens, man, this is sensational!' he exclaimed, examining the hat.

'What is?' I asked

'It's one of these new-fangled ones with straps. And so well made, too' I gave up on MI5 and walked across the field to Brigadier Stepford-Instrall, head of the SAS, also on leave. He was a known loather of cricket, zam-buk, Vera Lynn, knitting patterns and continental holidays. The moment he saw the riding hat, his eyes narrowed and his moustache twitched violently and I knew this was my man. He fixed his monocle in and examined the wire.

'Von Braun, eh? Dashed clever chaps, these Germans, what?' He took me into the back of his horsebox, arm around my shoulder. 'Know what this is?' 'Some kind of recording device, I suppose?' 'Close, but not that close, old boy. It's a wireless. It's transmitting all sounds to a receiver somewhere. Where did you get it?' I explained about the parson and how I'd come to possess his hat. He stroked his moustache thoughtfully. He ordered me to hand it back to the vicar and he'd set a trap for him.

I did as instructed and caught up with the parson as he was walking slowly back, leading his horse, still a trifle dazed. 'Thank you', he said weakly, and started off on the long hack home to Pitsford Prostate.

The rest of the day was a daze for me. Six armoured cars and twelve brawny foxhunters still on horseback surrounded the vicarage as the Brigadier, moustache still bristling, led the raid, finding the parson's wife eventually in the attic at the top of the church transmitting the day's conversations to Germany, using the church's lightning rod with the wire from the end of the hunting hat plugged in to the receiver.

She was no easy capture, however, and it took six MFH's and two whippers-in to carry her down the church's stone steps. She then bolted and, in the ensuing melee, the poor brigadier and my friend the parson got kicked by the frightened horses. The parson, alas, failed to recover from his injuries and the brigadier was never the same afterwards.

Shortly after I took his place as head of the SAS and the parson was buried with full church honours. His wife was deported to Ireland with her brother George Drummond and the Master of Foxhounds Association passed a special wartime resolution banning all men of the cloth from the hunting field. Which is a long winded way of explaining how I passed the war as head of the SAS and why you never, to this day, see a parson on the hunting field.

From an unpublished manuscript 'My Ten Years with the S.A.S.' by Philip Kinell, Pitsford Prostate, July 1955

TRUE TO FORM

A lady called on a Scottish Master to solicit a charitable donation. She handed him a card that read 'Charity Fair – Give Till It Hurts'.
The Scotsman read it carefully and genuine tears seemed to well up in his eyes. He handed her back the card 'Lady, the verra idea hurts!'

BURY A BOOKIE

George Payne who made and lost two fortunes through bad bets at racing, was approached by a town committee to give a donation towards the burial of a man.
'What was he, a writer, an artist?' he asked.
'Not exactly,' came the reply, 'but he was well-known to many of us, he was our local bookmaker'.
'How much is the burial?' asked Payne.
"A guinea'
Payne pulled two guineas from his pocket.
'Here's two. Go bury two bookmakers'.

HORSES' UNDERWEAR

H. L. Mencken, the notorious Baltimore practical joker, invented an organisation called the 'American League for Animal Decency'. The League declared itself to be opposed to the flagrant displaying of horses' genitalia, and campaigned against this moral laxity! Newspapers all over the U.S. gave the League editorial space, and soon horses were being equipped with cod-pieces!
The practice spread to dogs (breeches) and cows (brassieres). Even after Mencken confessed that the whole thing was a joke, animals all over the U.S. appeared in fields, dressed in an assortment of gaudy underwear.

HOIST WITH HIS OWN PETARD

The famous French Essayist Guy de Maupassant was a habitual practical joker, even writing 'Memoirs of a Joker' in 1883. But once he was the butt of his own joke.
He went to stay with friends in Picardy for a hunting weekend, and he knew them all to be keen pranksters. So he was on guard right from his arrival. Their welcome seemed too effusive; everyone was in high spirits at dinner — too high, Maupassant thought. He suspected a set-up when they all accompanied him to his room, bade him goodnight amid much laughter.
Once in the bedroom, Maupassant looked in cupboards, wardrobes, under the bed, behind the drapes, everywhere. Finally he decided to go to bed. Another close inspection revealed nothing, but Maupassant remained convinced that whatever trick had been played on him was in some way connected to the bed. So he took the mattress and bedclothes and settled down on the floor, near the door.
He lay awake for an hour, then sleep finally came. He awoke very suddenly. Someone heavy had fallen on him, and he heard the sound of the crashing of crockery. Hot liquid spilled all over him. The servant bringing in his morning tea had tripped over the mattress near the door and spilled breakfast all over him. Maupassant's careful precautions made him the victim of a joke that never was!

WIFE'S LOGIC

A farmer walked into his house, completely out of breath.
'What's the matter, darling?' asked his wife, still in joddies, after a day out with the Pytchley.
'It's a great new idea I have to save money. I ran all the way home behind the bus and saved 50 pence.'
'Well, that wasn't very bright' snapped the wife. 'Why didn't you run home behind a taxi and save £5?'

CHANGING HORSES

An old Master was over 90 and in poor health. He had been a staunch supporter of the Conservative party all his life. When his doctor confirmed that the end was near, he called his son and asked him to drive him to the nearest office of the Labour Party, and that he wanted to register as a Labour supporter.
His son protested and reminded the old man that he had voted Conservative for the last 70 years, and that the whole family were Margaret Thatcher supporters. Finally the old man explained his logic.
'Look son, I'm dying. Now I reckon that if someone has to die, it might as well be one of them!'

Contributed by Dennis Thatcher

OVER THE WATER

Two foxhunters went on a hunting trip to Ireland, taking their own horses and a loaded horsebox. Trying to find the meet at Galway, they got hopelessly lost. Finally, they pulled up to a man working in his field along the road.
'Excuse me, sir,' said the driver, 'could you tell me if we're a long way from Galway Town?'
'Yes, siree,' was the answer
'How far?'
The farmer thought for a minute, then replied 'About 20,000 miles the way you're pointed, and I don't know how you're going to get over all that water!'

Contributed by Dennis Ryan, Kissimmee, Florida

TWO OF EVERYTHING

Two foxhunter were bitter business rivals. St. Peter was dispatched to rectify the situation and appeared to one of the men.
'You are very cruel and bitter to a fellow foxhunter, he should be your friend. To cure you, the Good Lord has promised to give you one of anything in the world, if you will let your rival have two of the same thing'.
The man thought carefully. 'You mean, if I ask for a gold Cadillac, he will get two?'
'Yes,' replied St. Peter.
'And if I ask for a horse-ranch in Kentucky, he'll get two?'
'That's exactly right'.
'Then I'll take one glass eye!'

Contributed by Michael Linville, Cleveland, Ohio.

STAY AWAKE

A hunting parson died and arrived in heaven. He noticed that a London hackney carriage driver had been given a higher place than him. He complained to St. Peter. 'I can't understand this, when I've devoted my life to my flock'.
'Our new policy here is to reward results,' the great man explained. 'Tell me, Vicar, what happened when you gave your sermons on Sundays?'
The Vicar admitted that a few of the congregation would regularly fall asleep.
'You see?' said St. Peter. 'That's exactly the point, when people rode in this man's hackney carriage, they not only stayed awake, they actually prayed!'

SWEAR WORDS

A little boy was caught using a forbidden 4-letter word. 'You shouldn't use that word', said the teacher. 'Where did you hear it'? 'My daddy said it'.
'Well, that doesn't matter,' the teacher explained, 'you don't even know what it means.'
'I do, too,' replied the boy, 'it means the horse wouldn't jump.'

CLEVER DOCTOR

'My doctor is a wonderful man. Once in the 1950's I fell off a horse learning to ride and cracked two ribs. I couldn't afford the operation, so he touched up the X-rays!.

Jack Benny.

MISSING HAT

A Master, not one for standing on ceremony, lost his hat and decided the simplest way to replace it, as all the shops were shut for the holidays, was to go to the cloakroom of the local church and pinch one. Once inside, he heard a sermon on the Ten Commandments. As he left the church, he said to the vicar, 'I want you to know, Vicar, that you have saved me from committing a crime, I came here to steal a hat, but after your sermon on the Ten Commandments, I changed my mind'.
The Vicar was flattered. 'What did I say that made you change your mind'.
'Well, Vicar, when you got to the part about 'Thou shalt not commit Adultery', I suddenly remembered where I left my hat!'

NO HOPE

Three hunting couples had gone on holiday together and died in a tragic accident. They arrived at the pearly gates and St. Peter said to the first man, 'It's true you lived a good life, but you also drank too much. You even married a woman called Sherry. I'll send you to Purgatory for a few centuries, then we'll consider your case.'
The second man had also lived a good life, 'Yes,' said St. Peter, 'but you were also much too fond of gold and jewellry. You even married a woman called Pearl. I'll send you to Purgatory for a century or so, then we'll review your case.'
The third man turned to his wife, grabbed her arm and started walking towards Purgatory. 'Come on, Fanny, we've got no chance of getting in!'

Contributed by Sarah Puri, Forest Hills, New York.

FIRST LADY JOCKEY

A noted hunting lady, Alicia Thornton, was the only female to appear in the Racing Calendar in the nineteenth century. She entered a 4 mile race against her brother-in-law Capt. Flint at Knavesmire, York, in 1804. The news spread like wildfire and the course was thronged with 'old rakes, magistrates and swells', according to a poem of the time. Her horse went lame after 3 miles and she lost the £1,000 wager.
She then challenged Capt. Flint to a re-match which was never held because the £1,000 bet from the first race had never been paid. At the York summer meeting, there was a terrible row in the stand when Flint proceeded to lay his whip across Col. Thornton's back, demanding his money. He was arrested on the orders of the Lord Mayor and several magistrates who were at the meeting.
Alicia did ride — and win — in 1805, but that was the last time she or any other woman rode under the auspices of the Jockey Club until 1970 — 165 years later!

WHAT A DAY!

A farmers wife tells how her husband, a noted Master, was ecstatic on the day their first daughter was born, bringing her huge bouquets of flowers. Five years later, after the birth of their fourth daughter, he got to the hospital after a day's hunting, around 5 o'clock, slumped in a chair beside the bed and groaned, 'Hell, what an exhausting day I've had!'

NICE ALMONDS

A farmer's wife worked at a geriatric hospital in Oxford. One of her favourite patients was an old Master, now well past his dotage, who always gave her small presents.
One Christmas she received a bag of almonds from the gentleman. As she particularly liked almonds, she ate them in her tea break. Just then she was joined by the Sister.
'Old Squire. Bailey gave me some almonds as a present' she said in delight.
'Where are they?' asked the Sister.
'I've just eaten them'
'Oh' said the sister, 'that's bad luck.'
'Why?'
'Well, they were given to him by his son and they were chocolate almonds. The old man's sucked all the chocolate off and given them to you!'

STOCKING SURPRISE

A Master with the Cottesmore had two sons, Peter and Thomas. Peter was a pessimist, his brother the opposite.
The Master and his wife were concerned about their sons difference in outlook and determined to try and redress the balance. On Christmas Eve they filled Peter's - the pessimist's - stocking full of chocolates, Kinder eggs and other goodies. At the foot of Thomas's empty stocking they placed some horse manure.
On Christmas morning they eagerly watched their son's faces for reaction. Peter wasn't impressed with his stocking, it was the wrong kind of chocolate, he didn't like Kinder eggs, and he wasn't all smiles as they had expected. When Thomas appeared, he was all smiles, much to their astonishment.
'I haven't seen it yet,' he yelled in delight,' but I think I've got a pony!'

SILENCE

The horsewoman was well-known for her women's liberation views. 'For centuries, women have been mistreated and misjudged,' she thundered to her fellow hunters at the Opening Meet. 'They have been oppressed and suffered in a thousand ways. Is there any way they haven't suffered?'
'Yes', said the Master, who overheard. 'They have never suffered in silence.'

A BETTING TAIL?

In the 1920's, the Grafton were justifiably proud of their fox-catching exploits. At the Hunt Ball in 1918 the local gamekeeper struck a 5 guinea wager with the Grafton Master that he could breed foxes that the Hunt would never catch.
Now the gamekeeper knew where there was a vixen who had recently had cubs, and made a point of throwing her the odd rabbit for the cubs. Shortly after, Vic Edwards, aged 8, was sent down to the lair and brought up all the cubs to the gamekeeper.
The gamekeeper then cut off all their tails, returned them to the lair and they learned to run without having to worry about the weight of their brush. When they grew up, they ran like the wind and were never caught. The gamekeeper collected his five guineas.

Contributed by Vic Edwards, aged 84, and his son Dave of Hartwell, Northants.

THE STOMACH PUMP AND THE CAT

A Master's wife in Bicester found her cat lying outside her back door early one morning when she went to get the milk. As she picked it up, it was very sick all over the floor. She called the vet, 'What did you give it to eat?' the vet asked.
'Same as my husband. A tuna fish salad.'
'It looks like food poisoning. You'd better get your husband to the hospital.'
So she rang her husband at his office, explained what had happened, and the Master rushed to the local hospital, saw the duty doctor and was rushed in to have his stomach pumped out.
He was still feeling groggy the following morning when his wife answered a knock at the door.
'Is your cat alright?' asked the milkman.
'Yes, we've had the vet out. But how did you know?'
'It's just that yesterday morning, I dropped the crate of milk bottles on the cat and knocked it out. I left it on the back door step for you.'

SKITTLES AND THE MASTER

I have been told that 'Skittles' was the last of the great 'demi-mondaines' of the 'sixties, and that she was a well-educated, clever woman, devoted to riding and hunting. She went to Melton Mowbray with Lord Hopetoun to hunt with the Quorn when Lord Stamford was MFH. Now Lady Stamford, his second wife, was reported to have come from a different social set to 'Skittles' and to have started life as one of three handsome daughters of a Norfolk keeper. This tale may be true or not, but anyhow Lady Stamford objected to a rival in the hunting field, so she sent for her lord and master and insisted that he should 'dispatch that improper woman home,' declaring that it was a scandal that so notorious a person should dare to hunt with the Quorn Hounds.
On being told of this discussion by a friend, 'Skittles' at once turned her horse for Melton, being too keen a sportswoman to wish to make trouble in the hunting field and embarrass the MFH. As good luck would have it, before she had gone far, a fox crossed the road in front of her, followed by the hounds in full cry. This was too much for 'Skittles'; she jumped the fence and joined in the chase and rode so straight and well that at the end of the run Lord Stamford congratulated her, and swore that she must always hunt with the Quorn 'and damn all jealous women.' To show her displeasure Lady Stamford never went to another meet whilst her husband was master.

Lady August Fane : Chit-Chat (1926)

POLITE LORD

Lord Spencer could deliver rebukes in the most polite language. In 1877 he had requested a Captain Riddell to give him a lead over an awkward place out of a wood. The Captain did so. But before Lord Spencer could follow, a thrusting stranger jumped right across him and 'scattered him'.
Instead of bursting out into a torrent of abuse, Lord Spencer said quietly, 'I am very much obliged to you, sir. Upon my word, I am. But may I ask you – did you come far to do this?'

From 'Kings of the Hunting Field' : Thormanby

HUNTING TALES

TROLLOPE AND THE AMERICAN
(The Senator found the whole scene incomprehensible!)

'Now they are hunting,' said Mr. Morton to the Senator.
'They all seemed to be very angry with each other at that narrow gate.'
'They were in a hurry, I suppose.'
'Two of them jumped over the hedge. Why didn't they all jump? How long will it be now before they catch him?'
'Very probably they may not catch him at all.'
'Not catch him after all that! Then the man was certainly right to poison that other fox in the wood. How long will they go on?'
'Half an hour perhaps'.
'And you call that hunting! Is it worth the while of all those men to expend all that energy for such a result? Upon the whole, Mr. Morton, I should say that it is one of the most incomprehensible things that I have ever seen in the course of a rather long and varied life. Shooting I can understand, for you have your birds. Fishing I can understand, as you have your fish. Here you get a fox to begin with, and you are all broken-hearted, (because he's been poisoned) Then you come across another, after riding about all day, and the chances are that you can't catch him!'
'I suppose,' said Mr. Morton angrily, 'the habits of one country are incomprehensible to the people of another. When I see Americans loafing about in the barroom of an hotel, I am lost in amazement.'
'There is not a man you see who couldn't give a reason for his being there. He has an object in view, – though perhaps it may be no better than to rob his neighbour. But here there seems to be no possible motive.'
But just at that moment, while the hounds and the master, and Lord Rufford and his friends, were turning back in their own direction, John Morton came up with his carriage and the Senator. 'Is it all over?' asked the Senator.
'All over for to-day,' said Lord Rufford.
'Did you catch the animal?'
'No, Mr. Gotobed; we couldn't catch him. To tell the truth we didn't try but we had a nice little skurry for four or five miles.'
'Some of you look very wet.' Captain Glomax and Ned Botsey were standing near the carriage; but the Captain as soon as he heard this, broke into a trot and followed the hounds.
'Some of us are very wet,' said Ned. 'That's part of the fun.'
'Oh; – that's part of the fun. You found one fox dead and you didn't kill another because you didn't try. Well; Mr. Morton, I don't think I shall take to foxhunting even though they should introduce it in Mickewa. What's become of the rest of the men?'
'Most of them are in the brook,' said Ned Botsey . . .

Anthony Trollope : The American Senator, 1877

'WARE DRINKS'

'Try some,' the Squire said pleasantly – though resenting the familiarity – at the same time offering his flask, at which the other took a long pull, thinking it was sure to be something good. But he made a wry face when he swallowed it, and a still sorrier one when the Squire said, laughing, 'And now I advise you to be off home as quick as you can. It's my gout mixture.'

J. Randall, A History of the Meynell Hounds and Country, 1901

SECOND CHANCE

The Master of the Puckeridge, Nicholas Parry, was on his death bed. He was asked what changes he would make to his life, if he were given the chance to live it over again. After lengthy consideration he replied, 'I should put in a few more days hunting before Christmas'.

BEFORE SUNRISE . . .

I had gone through the dreary routine of the cub-hunter. The alarm clock had shrilled its exulting and age-long summons in the pitchy dark. I had burnt my fingers with the spirit-lamp, and my mouth with hot cocoa; I had accomplished my bathless toilet, I had groped my way through the puddles in the stable yard, and got on to my horse by the light of a lantern, and at 5.30 a.m. I was over the worst, and had met Flurry and the hounds . . . at the appointed cross-roads.
It was still an hour before sunrise, but a pallor was in the sky, and the hounds, that had at first been like a gliding shoal of fish round the horses' feet, began to take on their own shapes and colours.

E. Somerville and Martin Ross, Further Experiences of an Irish R.M., 1917

AND BLANK DAYS . . .

A story is told of a veteran sportsman who was asked upon an occasion as to what he thought were the three most enjoyable things in the world. As to what was the best, he had no doubt, it was a good day with hounds. He hesitated a little before replying to the query as what was the next best thing, but it was only for a short time, and then he replied, 'A bad day with hounds.' What was the third best thing was a bit of a poser after that, but after a long and careful consideration he shouted out to his tormentor in answer to the question '——it, sir, a blank day with hounds.'

W. Scarth Dixon, The Sport of Kings, 1900

THE RUNNING PHOTOGRAPHER and ELEVENSES

Jim Meads has been photographing and writing about hunting since 1950. He became known as " The Running Photographer" because of his style of crossing country on foot to be where the action is. In 1956 he co-authored a book with his father, (himself a former staff photographer at Country Life), called "They Meet at Eleven", followed in 1979 by "They Still Meet at Eleven", then in 1991 "They Will Always Meet at Eleven" was published.
In his 44-year career, he has been out with 414 packs of hounds all over the world, and visits the USA three times each hunting season, writing and photographing fox and coyote hunting. When Lionel Edwards came to Crick to paint the now famous scene, 100 years after the original, Jim Meads was with him to photograph all those at the meet, and his association with the famous Pytchley huntsman, Stanley Barker, goes back some fifty years.

HUNTING TALES

BRIEF CAREER

Henry Green (1905-1973) was a novelist who, as a boy, hunted with the Ledbury. His heart, however, was never in it and his career was short.

'All I remember of those days is the excessive cordiality my elders used towards each other at the meet, the terror with which most of them waited while the covert was drawn, and in that first gallop there after the hounds have found after which I would be left. Chipping, the groom, and I would make our way diagonally across the circles foxes usually make their way by; if you know where the coverts are and what they call the line foxes take them by diligently trotting, with time to spare to shut open gates, you come upon the field quite often and then as likely as not be in danger of heading the hunted fox. My Mother's father I believe went out with a servant who carried two axes in his saddle and because there was so much wire in his country (they were his own hounds) every variety of wire clipper as well and yet he saw as much as anyone of what went on. Those who, galloping hard and jumping everything, were seldom out of sight of hounds, were seldom out of earshot of his voice encouraging his man as he chopped the fences down, for my grandfather had lost his nerve and would not jump. After hunting so they say he would go out in his pink coat, still in his boots and play golf in the park with his butler in a bowler hat carrying the clubs'.

Henry Green: Pack my Bag, (Hogarth Press Ltd. 1940)

WOMEN IN THE FIELD

Arguments, previously noted elsewhere in this book, raged about women riding astride. Lord Annaly's views were extreme. But despite women riders being generally welcome, not everyone approved, as Surtees reported:

Like many things in this world it makes all the difference who the party is that hunts. If a pretty woman hunts we are all glad to see her; if an ugly one comes we wonder what 'brings her out.' Certainly dishevelled hair, ruddy and perspiring face, and muddy habit, are more likely to be forgiven in the bloom of youth than in what ought to be the orderly sobriety of mature years. We had dotted down a lot of names of first-rate female performers across the country, but in looking it over we find it contains such a curious medley, that we think it better to suppress it altogether than risk the chance of offending by publishing an unpalatable assortment.

Never having been a woman, we cannot understand how it is they manage to keep their seats. We see what are called 'washball' seated men rolling about constantly, and yet women, to whom the term as well as the form is much more applicable and becoming, manage to keep on. Keeping their seats on the road, and keeping them in the field are very different things, about as different as riding horses on the road and riding them with hounds. 'Still, where there's a will there's a way,' and pretty dears who would scream at the sight of a frog or a mouse, will face a bullfinch fence from which many men would turn away – indeed that is one of the palpable inconveniences of ladies hunting, for it is almost a point of honour for men to go over what ladies have taken. If it were not their great desire for pace, we would rather be a woman's horse than a man's. Women have much finer, and more delicate hands than men, and they never fight or bully their horses as men do – neither do they ever pull them into their leaps – by which means nine-tenths of the annual falls are procured.

R. S. Surtees. Analysis of the Hunting Field, 1846

Some Masters like Lord Ladythorne did not welcome women at all:

'They say she's the finest 'oss-woman that ever was seen.'
'Indeed' mused his lordship, thinking over the pros and cons of female equestrianism – the disagreeableness of being beat by them – the disagreeableness of having to leave them in the lurch – the disagreeableness of seeing them floored – the disagreeableness of seeing them all running down with perspiration; the result being that his Lordship adhered to his established opinion that women have no business out hunting.

R. S. Surtees. Ask Mamma, 1858

AND THEIR LANGUAGE . . .

Before Mr. Mowbray had recovered his composure a shrill cry from the end of the wood let loose the avalanche of horsemen. Galloping downhill, Silas noticed everyone converging to the corner, leaving the line of the hounds; so concluding the next obstacle was unjumpable he wisely followed suit, and arrived at a hand gate on the far side of a ford. Beside him was a lady for whom he politely pulled back to let her through. 'Damn your soul, can't you get on,' from one rider behind, 'Where the hell are you pushing,' from another in front. 'Blast you, putting me on to the damn post,' from a third.

Too late, Mr. Mowbray realised his mistake as he was swept aside and found himself in an eddy in the stream of horseflesh forcing itself through the narrow outlet. At last, crushed and bruised, he managed to get through, and voiced his woes to a farmer next to whom he found himself. 'Oh, them ladies don't mean what they say. You must forget you're a gentleman if you want to keep your place at a hand gate here.' Mr. Mowbray was shocked to the marrow. He had never heard a lady swear before.

Extract from 'Mr. Silas P. Mowbray Returns to Melton' by Guy Paget
(Edgar Backus, Leicester, 1940)

MISSING FOX...

John Watson was ten years old when out cubbing with the Quorn in the 1950's with his father Dick, now over 90. He stood near Botany Bay covert with the Huntsman, waiting for the fox to appear. "I don't think Charlie's coming out," said the Huntsman, after a long wait.
"You won't find a fox in there, sir," said the youngster.
"How do you know that?" asked the Huntsman.
"I saw the farmer shoot him last night!" replied young John.

Contributed by George Watson, now 84, of Marston Trussel, who hunted with the Fernie and Pytchley, and recalls the days of Stanley Barker and Major Borwick with razor sharp memory and great affection.

The Empress of Austria

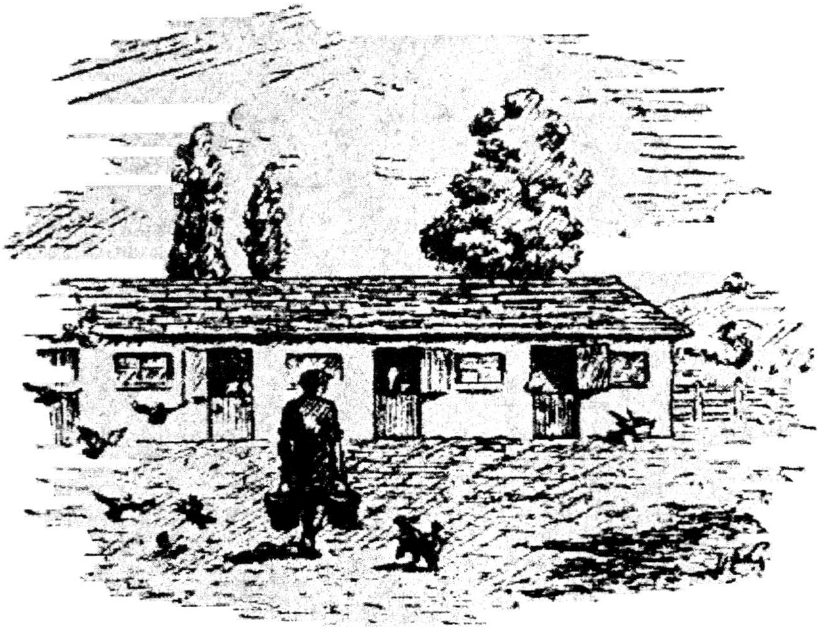

Book Four

A selection of poetry
from the hunting field

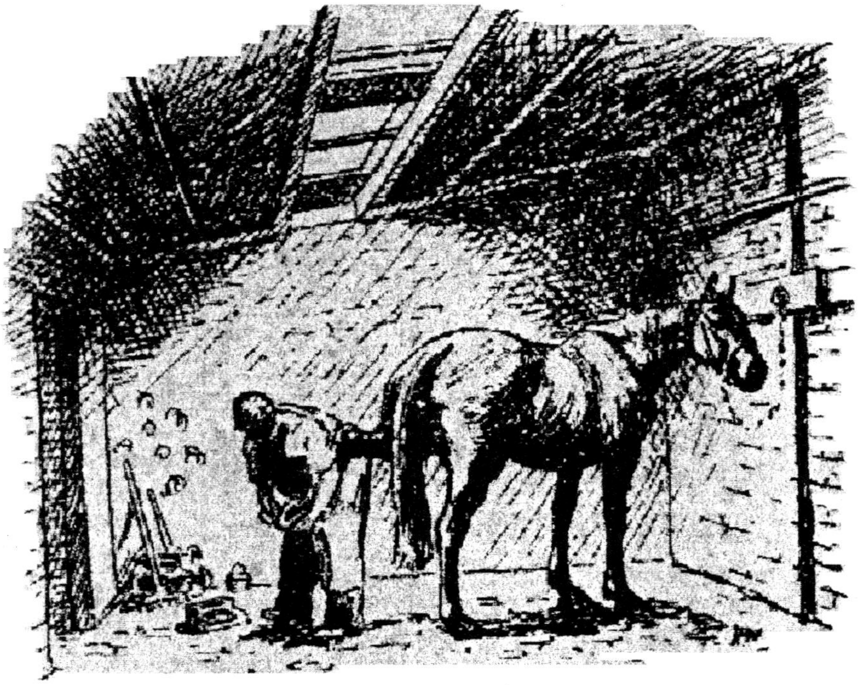

HUNTING TALES

IF

(with profound apologies to Rudyard Kipling)

If you can keep your head when hounds first open.
And a holloa tells you they have gone away,
If you can ride a four year old half broken
And lie up with the thrusters come what may.

If you can go to anyone's assistance,
Catch a loose horse when hounds are just ahead,
Or fetch a doctor, never mind the distance
When some poor devil's lying out for dead.

If you can buy your wife a stud of horses,
And hear she's meanly crabbed them one by one,
And sold or traded them at fearful losses,
Then hear her say, "you've more to learn my son".

If you can force your heart and nerve and sinew,
To follow her over a daunting five barred gate,
When you have got that sinking feeling in you;
Perhaps the time has come to meet your fate.

If you can bear to see your income dwindle,
And have to part with special things you like,
Through taxes on your land or some such swindle,
And have to sell your car and buy a bike.

If when you've parted with your faithful hunters,
You raise a bit of cash and buy a screw,
And show the field they're really mostly funkers,
(Which is not very difficult to do).

If in the evening when the wine flows faster,
And unforgiving things are being said,
About your friends, the Huntsman and the Master,
You presently say something nice instead.

If you can go from field to field as hounds ran,
And never breath a word that you alone were there,
Then my opinion of you as a sportsman,
Is greater far than most who hunt can share.

*(Given to the late Judy Forwood by the late Sir Harold Nutting
M.F.H. of Quenby Hall, Leicestershire).*

HUNTING ATLAS?

There are many roads in Britain,
    Roman roads and new:
But the best my heels have smitten,
    Lead to Pytchley and to you.

Season report 1923/24 - no author

PASS THE PORT . . .

When you've emptied a glass to "A lean on the grass"
    When you've toasted the Horse and the Hound,
And the Master and Huntsman, I'll ask you to pass
    The decanter another time round.

Season report 1923/24 - no author

RE : SQUIRE OSBALDESTON

The Fox from the covert has broke ice at speed:
Away goes Vere Isham as straight as a reed.
At score off he goes, O'er every fence bounds,
Till at last he rides over the scent of the hounds.

Northampton Sporting Chronicle - January 2nd 1899.

MACHO . . .

O give me that man to whom naught comes amiss,
One horse or another, that country or this;
Through falls and bad starts who undauntedly still
Rides up to his motto - 'Be with em, I will'

Egerton Warbarton

TOM JOHNSON

Here Johnson lies; What Hunter can deny
Old honest Tom the tribute of a sigh?
Deaf is that ear which caught the opening sound,
Dumb is that tongue which cheer'd the hills around.
Unpleasing Truth: Death hunts us from our birth
In view, and men like foxes, take to earth.

On a Head stone in Singleton Church, Chichester, to the memory of Tom Johnson by the Second Duke of Richmond.

THE PYTCHLEY HUNT
(*Extract*)

I believe I've gone through the whole of the list,
Oh no! I beg pardon, Bob Andrew I've missed,
To pass such a hero a man would be slack
So in the next verse he joins the gay pack!

The lad's a gay sportsman and rides well to hounds,
And when there's a run he goes straight o'er the grounds,
He never gets off and the reason is plain,
For his legs are so short he can't get on again.

Gyles Isham, The Pytchley Hunt 1796
[*The poem was written almost 200 years ago, but it bears a striking similarity to a member of the Pytchley of similar name in 1993*]

OSBALDESTON

Long since in days of yore, no doubt
You've heard of famed Squire Western
He for antiquity can vie
With bold Squire Osbaldeston.

He's huntsman, jockey; at all games
His powers are quite a riddle
He's musical and some folks say
He likes to play first fiddle.

The hounds now fly, he speeds his course,
Nor cares for bush or thorn;
And, if he does not blow his horse,
He's sure to blow his horn.

Extracts from 'Osbaldeston' by John Chaworth Musters,
Master of the Pytchley 1821-27.

A GOOD DAY

We've had the run, the fox has won,
The day has been quite perfect.
The judge's duty yet remains
To take the jury's verdict.
Now, foreman of this jury true,
What is your verdict then sir?
We find my Lord, of Master all
There's none as good as Spencer.

Written by Mr. Justice Grantham, a visitor to Maidwell Hall,
after a good day's hunting from Hardwick to Althorp in 1891.

THE FLATULENT HORSE

There was once a Yorkshire Master (so says my story)
Who was fond of his wife and hunting field glory.
He hunted the moors, the covets and gorse
And his only undoing was his flatulent horse.

Now he didn't realise how serious the noise,
And he'd always thought it had been the rude stable boys
Or the hounds or even his young groom called Jen
Who was known to be a bit windy now and again.

He was chatting at a meet to the Princess of Wales
When the horse's tummy rumbled, and he passed wind in gales;
Then he did it again, and they all held their noses
As the horse made a heap on the Althorp prize roses

'Excuse me, your Highness, I'm new in these parts,
And I didn't appreciate the number of farts
That can come from a horse, I'll just take him away
And I'll be back on another one later today.'

Now that was some years ago, I've not seen him since
But the memory of that day still makes me wince,
I've seen Charles and Di hunt in all kinds of poses
But never with handkerchiefs over their noses.

Philip Kinell, Pitsford, 1993

THE ONE THAT GOT AWAY

*Anglers may boast about the one that got away. Shooting men may brag,
but hunters should never lie. So advised 'Punch' in the following verse.*

And the awestruck nations listened, and swiftly the proverb grew;
Fishers are sly and shooters lie, but a hunter's tale is true.
But oh! ye latter-day hunters, ye cannot hope to vie
With the many hunting Washingtons who knew not how to lie;
So when ye fare to the hunting, my council is plain to you –
Though foxes may lack, at the least bring back a tale that is slightly true.

[Reprinted in Wit & Wisdom of the Shires]

EPITAPH FOR A LADY RIDER

A lovely young Lady I mourn in rhymes
She was pleasant, good-natured and civil (sometimes);
Her figure was good, she had very fine eyes
And her riding a mixture of foolish and wise,
She had chased many foxes, and one of them said
'She hunted rather well - it's a pity she's dead.'

*Anonymous poem written after the style of George John Cayley in 1890,
Printed in the Brighton Morning Argus in 1896.*

HUNTING TALES

THE HUNT BALL TRYST

We were dancing there on New Years Eve
All the Hunt were there
The fairy-lights at the castle
Shone on many a maiden fair.

The Elizabeth Taylor look-alike
Came on to the floor to twist
With not her husband - but the man
With whom she had a tryst

After a dance, they sauntered off
They climbed the ancient stair
She was dressed in a pink silk ballgown
With three roses in her hair

In true Elizabeth Taylor style
Her hair was piled on top
She'd back-combed it till it looked like
A stylish bee-hive mop

The music was good, we waltzed away
Her husband came to dance,
He looked agitated 'You haven't seen
My wife, by any chance?'

Just then the lovers walked downstairs,
And rejoined the merry throng
She turned around, I saw her hair—
All the flowers had gone

And what had been a beehive
Was now completely flat,
It was obvious she'd been on her back
And her lover on top of that

So wives, just heed my warning if
With another you want to roam
Keep the flowers out of your hair
And leave your beehive at home.
Contributed by Howard Futterman, South Dakota, USA, written in 1989

MELTON DREAM

And when the run's over of earthly existence
And you get safe to ground, you will feel no remorse
If you ride it – no matter what line or what distance
As straight as we rode it from Ranksboro' Gorse.
(extract) Dream of an old Meltonian : Bromley Davenport.

IN MEMORIAM, WILL GOODALL

No more November moons in hearty greeting his voice will hear,
No more across the Cottesbrooke Vale the flying pack will cheer.
And tho' his place is void, and silenced his voice for evermore,
He surely has not passed away, only gone on before.
For day must ring to Evensong, and when life's work is done,
We too must turn our bridle rein and follow where he's gone.

*Henry Bentley, 1895 after Will Goodall was stricken with a fatal illness.
Goodall was mourned by the whole country, having been the Pytchley huntsman for 22 years and universally popular. He was only 48 years old.*

THE FOX'S PROPHECY

The woodland where my race has bred
Unto the axe shall yield
Hedgerow and copse shall cease to shade
The ever widening field.

The manly sports of England
Shall vanish one by one;
The manly blood of England
In weaker veins shall run.

The furzy down, the moorland heath
The steam plough shall invade;
Nor park nor manor shall escape
Common, nor forest glade.

The sports of their forefathers
To baser tastes shall yield;
The vices of the town displace
The pleasure of the field.

For swiftly o'er the level shore
The waves of progress ride;
The ancient landmarks one by one
Shall sink beneath the tide.

A chilling prophecy by D. W. Nash (1870)

THE HUNTING DAY

There is only one cure
For all maladies sure
That reaches the heart to its core;
'Tis the sound of the horn
On a fine hunting morn
And where is the heart wishing more?

Extract from 'The Hunting Day' by William Williams

THE OBITUARY POET

Max Adeler reported these unusual verses in the Morning Argus (Brighton) in 1896 by a scurrilous obituary poet named James B. Slimmer.

This is one about a hunting woman, Lady McGregor:

Lady McGregor has gone from this life
She has left all its sorrows and cares;
She has caught the rheumatics in both of her legs
From hunting the fox in Broadstairs,
They put mustard plaster upon her in vain,
They plied her with Whisky and Rum.
But Thursday out hunting her spirit had left
Her body entirely numb.

HARK!

Far on the hill is the horn still blowing
Far on the steep are the hounds still strung
Good men follow the good men gone
And Hark! They're running!
They're running on!

W.H. Ogilvie, The Hunt

MY BEST HORSE ...

You may put on his clothes; every sportsman, they say,
    In his lifetime has one that outrivals the rest,
So pearl of my casket I've shown you to-day,
    The gentlest, the gamest—the boldest, the best;
And I never will part, by sale or swop,
    With my Clipper that stands in the stall at the top!

G. J. Whyte Melville

IN FULL CRY

Over the top come the lean white hounds
Screaming to scent and view;
The hill is walked to its furthest bounds
As they clamour and drive him through;
And the joy of the far-flung challenge sounds
Till it shivers against the blue.

Coronet : Wit & Wisdom of the Shires.

A SIMPLE WISH

All I ask is a fox on the hills that he knows
And a heart-stirring Holloa and 'Yonder he goes!'
The pack in full cry and the moor lying wide
And Woodpecker taking the walls in his stride.

W. H. Ogilvie (1869-1962)

FRANK FREEMAN

Frank Freeman sleeps, and surely finds a worthy resting place
Beneath where Brix's steeple points the spirit's path to grace,
Where waves the grass beside the walls, whose ashlar Saxons dressed
With lintel bricks of adamant that Roman crafsman pressed!

John Orr Ewing, 1949

THE FOX SPOTTED

'Hark, Rauter, Hark' the huntsman cries,
They have him off again!
A sheet would cover all the pack now
Racing o'er the plain
A view! It is the hunted fox:
I know by yonder crow
Oh, 'tis pure delight in foremost flight
In a run like this to go

The Badby Wood Run, J. Anstruther Thomson.

AND AFTER DINNER . . .

Three jolly gentleman
In coats of red
Rode their horses
Up to bed.

Walter de la Mare: The Huntsman c.1938

FARMERS, DON'T GRUMBLE

And should his steed with trampling feet
Be urged across your tender wheat,
That steed, perchance, by you was bred,
And yours the corn on which he's fed.

R. E. Egerton Warburton.

GET UP and DIG . . .

Rouse thee! Earth stopper! rouse thee from thy slumber!
Get thee thy worsted hose and winter coat on,
While the good housewife, crawling from her blanket,
Lights thee thy lantern.

Clad for thy midnight silent occupation,
Mount thy old doghorse, spade upon thy shoulder,
Wire hair'd vixen, wheresoe'er thou wendest
Ready to follow

Through the chill rain drops, driven by the north wind,
Pelt thy old jacket, soaking through and through thee,
Though thy worn hackney, blind and broken winded,
Hobble on three legs;

Finish thy night-work well, or woe betide thee,
If on the morrow irritated Huntsman,
Back'd by a hundred followers in scarlet,
Find the earths open!

R. E. Egerton Warburton.

THE DUKE OF BEAUFORT'S HOUNDS

How they drive to the front! – how they bustle and spread,
Those badger-pied beauties that open the ball!
Ere we've gone for a mile, they are furlongs ahead,
As they pour like a torrent o'er upland and wall.
There is raking of rowell and shaking of rein
(Few hunters can live at the Badminton pace)
And pride of the stable's extended in vain,
And the Blues and the Buffs are all over the place.

G. J. Whyte Melville

POSERS . . .

T'aint the red coat make the rider
Leathers, boots nor yet the cap.

They who come their oats to show, know they
Better were at home in bed;
What of hounds and hunting know they?
Nothing else but 'go ahead';

R. E. Egerton Warburton.

AT LEAST YOU'RE DRY...

Trotting homeward in Spring on the hope we rely
That we reach it ere dark with our hunting-coat dry;
The horse undistress'd by the work he has done;
The rider well pleased with his place in the run.

R. E. Egerton Warburton.

TO A HOUND, 'LADY'

Exult, foxes, for your foe
Lies beneath this Pillar low.
Yet exulting, tremble too,
Fleet your brushes to pursue,
From her blood, behold another,
'Lady' rises, like her mother.

*Inscribed on a monument in Bainton, in Bicester country by
Sir Thomas Mostyn, Bart. in 1812.*

*The inscription is no longer on the monument which was brick faced with cement
and may have been defaced more than once.*

RESTING TIME

The gold is on the gorses,
The leaf is on the plane
There's rest for all good horses
Till cubbing comes again.

The beaches throw new shadow,
Wild flowers the pasture fill,
There's clover in the meadow,
And round the sheltered hill.

And shoeless feet go lightly,
As slow our favourites pass,
And forehead stars gleam whitely
Among the cool wet grass.

The bright spurs languish idle
Through many a sunlit day,
The saddle and the bridle,
Are cleaned and laid away.

Yet who but will remember
The rides that went between
The red leaves of November
And April's early green?

W. H. Ogilvie

HUNTING TALES

JOE BOWMAN

When the fire's on the hearth, and good cheer abounds,
We'll drink to Joe Bowman and his Ullswater hounds,
For we ne'er shall forget how he woke us at morn
With the crack of his whip and the sound of his horn.

Dr. G. F. Walker: Joe Bowman
A song to the Fell huntsman who carried the horn for 32 years with the Ullswater.

WOORE COUNTRY EXTOLLED

A Fig for your Leicestershire swells!
While Wickstead such sport can ensure,
Long life to the varmint old Wells,
Success to the country of Woore.

R. E. Egerton Warburton: Woore Country (1830)
(Woore Country is a portion of Cheshire and Staffordshire)

ON SQUIRE OSBALDESTON

Who is that trumpeter coming from Quorn?
The very worst huntsman that ever was born.

Opinions on the Squire's abilities seem varied.

WHEN IT'S SUNNY . . .

Upon some little eminence erect,
And fronting to the ruddy dawn; its courts
On either hand wide opening to receive
The sun's all-cheering beams.

E. Somerville: Notes of the Horn

MY GOOD GREY MARE

With a hopeful mare and a conscience clear,
I can laugh in your face, Black Care;
Though you're hovering near, there's no room for you here
On the back of my good grey mare.

Extract from G. J. Whyte Melville

MASEFIELD COPY

I'll not go down to the seas again, to the lonely sea and sky,
For I'd rather have the hunting news, and know my feet feet are dry.
A horses kick, a huntsman's cheer, and a big field running;
The grey look on Freeman's face, and an old fox's cunning.

Coronet 1925

HUNTING TALES

EARLY MORNING NOISES

England in her autumn sleep turns about and stirs,
Hears the click of bridle rings, hears the chink of spurs;
Sees the gleam of spotted flanks moving in the gorse,
Sees the flashing scarlet of a whip upon his horse!

Coronet 1924

THE CAMARADIE

But one who has wandered over the world
By East and South and West,
He knows the worth of a hunting face,
And he finds old friends the best.

Coronet 1924.

AND THE FOX . . .

There's a shadow gaunt in that shadowy frame –
'Tis the great fox comes, 'tis the fox of fame
With his long wolf jaw and his coat of flame,
Down in his den to lay.
But when he comes to his lodging's door,
They've stopped him out, as they've done before
And a horn shakes far and away.

Coronet 1923.

THE HOUNDS

Raging they came like a torrent of flame
There were nineteen couples and over,
And the huntsman grey, who blew them away
With the note of a true hound lover.

Coronet 1927.

LIKE PEARLS . . .

Now didn't I tell you they'd draw no blank
Before a hound had spoke?
For Cross's wet gorse with fox was rank
And he ran at them like smoke;
And hounds came tumbling down the bank
Like pearls off a string that's broke.

Coronet 1926.

SWEET MUSIC...

Everything is music when you hunt
The crash of post and rail,
In a sort of running scale
The thunder as gallopers go by,
The raining 'FORRARD ON'
That is swallowed up anon
In the chorus of the pack against the sky.

Coronet 1925.

ON DEATH

And when the shadows fall
You can hear the old rooks call
And their plaintive crying mingles with the storm before the lea;
They will tell with bated breath
Of strong huntsmen gone to death
And how their souls still haunt the land where they so longed to be.

Coronet 1925.

GETTING UP EARLY...

The happiest man in England rose an hour before the dawn;
The stars were in the purple and the dew was on the lawn;
He sang from the bed to the bathroom – he could only sing 'John Peel';
He donned his boots and breeches and he buckled on his steel.

He chose his brightest waistcoat and his stock with care he tied,
Though scarce a soul would see him in the early morning ride.
He hurried to the stable through the dim light of the stars,
And there his good horse waited, clicking rings and bridle bars.

Extract from W. H. Ogilvie : The Happiest Man in England, (1925).

AND THE RESULT...

He had a quality uncommon
To early risers after a long chase,
Who woke in winter ere the cock can summon
December's drowsy day to his dull race
– A quality agreeable to woman
When her soft liquid words run on apace,
Who likes a listener, whether saint or sinner –
He did not fall asleep just after dinner:

Extract from Lord Byron: Don Juan (1822).

HUNTING TALES

THE CHASE...

As we cram down our hats for the cream of the Vale,
By the ghosts of old comrades the pace will be set;
And the brave ones who broke for us rasper and rail,
Will be riding the grass land in front of us yet.

Coronet* 1922.
*Col. Walter Faber, MFH Tedworth (1908-11) Pytchley 1918-19.

A DANGEROUS SPORT?

Three ribs hath he broken, two legs and one arm,
But there hangs, it is said, round his neck a life-charm;
Still, long odds are offer'd that Dick, when he drops,
Will die, as he lived, in his breeches and tops.

*R. E. Egerton Warburton: Hard-riding Dick
from Hunting Songs (1877).*

STAND A ROUND?

Hunting folk don't like standing around
And the Huntsman doesn't like standing a round...

Rintoul Booth

AND SOMETIMES FATAL...

I was up in half a minute, but he never seemed to stir,
Though I scored him with my rowels in the fall;
In this life he had not felt before the insult of the spur,
And I knew that it was over once for all.
    When motionless he lay
    In his cheerless bed of clay,
Huddled up without an effort on his side –
    'Twas a hard and bitter stroke,
    For his honest back was broke
At the place where the old horse died.

With a neigh so faint and feeble that it touched me like a groan
'Farewell', he seemed to murmur, 'ere I die;'
Then set his teeth and stretched his limbs, and so I stood alone,
While the merry chase went heedless sweeping by.
    Am I womanly and weak
    If the tear was on my cheek
For a brotherhood that death can thus divide?
    If sickened and amazed
    Through a woeful mist I gazed
On the place where the old horse died?

*Extract from G. J. Whyte Melville: The place where the Old Horse died.
Whyte-Melville himself was killed when he fell whilst hunting in 1878.*

THE HUNT PASSES BY ...

And scattering horses, going, going,
Going like mad, White Rabbit snowing
For on ahead, a loose horse taking,
Fence after fence with stirrup shaking,
And scarlet specks and dark specks dwindling,
Nearer were twigs knocked into kindling,
A much bashed fence still dropping stick,
Flung clods, still quivering from the kick,
Cut hoof-marks pale in cheesy clay
The horse-smell blowing clean away.
Birds flitting back into cover.
One last faint cry, then all was over.
The hunt had been, and found, and gone.

John Masefield: Reynard the Fox 1919.

IN THE SMALL HOURS ...

I like the calm of the early fields,
The ducks asleep by the lake,
The quiet hour which nature yields
Before mankind is awake.

I like these things and I like to ride
When all the world is in bed,
To the top of the hill where the sky grows wide
And where the sun grows red.

W. S. Blunt: The Old Squire, 1914

LADY LOWTHER

Horses she loved, and laughter and the sun,
A song, wide spaces, and the open air;
The trust of all dumb living things she won,
And never knew the luck too good to share.'

Coronet 1925 on the death of the popular wife of Sir Charles Lowther.

CLEANLINESS IS NEXT TO ...

We ride to our places
With clean gloves and faces
To be a thruster or a nuisance, we won't make so bold.
We daren't go any faster
Than our venerable Master
Fox hunting is greater than silver or gold.

A rhyme that used to be repeated in the 1930's Pony Clubs in Devon.

AND IF THEY FALL, LEAVE 'EM . . .

With a quick, shortened stride as the distance you measure
With a crack of the nostril and the cock of the ear,
And a rocketing bound, and were over, my treasure,
Twice nine feet of water, and landed all clear.

What! Four of us only? Are these the survivors
Of all that rode gaily from Ranksboro' ridge?
I hear the faint splash of a few hardy divers,
The rest are in hopeless research of a bridge;

Vae Victis! the way of the world and the winners!
Do we ne'er ride away from a friend in distress?
Alas! we are anti-Samaritan sinners,
And steaming past Stapleford, onward we press.

Extract from W. Bromley Davenport:
The Dream of the Old Meltonian (1864).

AND SOME LIE WHERE THEY FALL . . .

Still I recall it, that fearful disaster,
The fence where the wire was obscured from the eye;
Gamely they tried it, the mare and the Master,
Gamely they fell, with the hounds in full cry.

Such a sad spectacle, Oh! so unsightly,
Mangled and bleeding he lay on the plain.
'Steady!' they gave the word, 'lift him there lightly,
Spread the coat over him, let him remain.'

So did he die with his comrades around him;
Dairymaid licked the strong hand as he lay;
Perfect as Master and huntsman we found him,
Now the strong life has gone down to decay.

W. Phillpotts Williams: The Grave in the Vale (1894).

HUNTING TALES

SOME FALL FURTHER THAN OTHERS... 'WARE HOLES

'E was a stranger to the 'unt
There weren't a person as 'e knew there;
But 'e could ride, that London gent –
'E sat 'is mare as if 'e grew there.

They seed the 'ounds upon the scent,
But found a fence across their track,
An' 'ad to fly it, else it meant
A turnin' an' a 'arking back.

'E was the foremost at the fence
And as 'is mare just cleared the rail
'E turned to them that rode be'ind,
For three was at 'is very tail.

''Ware 'oles!' says 'e, an' with the word
Still sittin' easy on 'is mare,
Down, down 'e went, an' down an' down,
Into the quarry yawnin' there.

Some say it was two 'undred foot
The bottom lay black as ink,
I guess they 'ad some ugly dreams
Who reined their 'orses on the brink.

For mind you, 'twas a sportin' end,
Upon a right good sportin' day;
They think a deal of 'im down 'ere,
That gent that came from London way.

Extract from Sir Arther Conan Doyle, 1898.

"Ware holes" is a cry to warn following riders of deep ditches and unseen obstacles, and a cry some foxhunters dread.
Few, however, are as serious as the 'hole' described above.

THE HUNT BALL

Then round the room the circling dowagers swept,
Then in loose waltz their thin-clad daughters leap:
The first, in lengthened line, majestic swim,
The last display the free unfettered limb.

Surtees, quoted in 'Wit & Wisdom of the Shires' 1923

HUNTING TALES

THE GHOSTS OF THE HUNT
A poem by Mrs. Morland (Dulcie Wroughton)

While I dream by the fire on a winter's night,
    The branches groan and sigh,
As the wind goes whistling through the trees
    And the clouds race over the sky;
The Ghosts of the Hunt come up from the wold,
On milk-white horses with hoofs of gold,
And ride again as they rode of old
    When hounds were in full cry.

Out of the mist they keep their tryst,
    Unheedful of cold and rain,
For love of the chase is in their race,
    And they ride as they rode;—again
I hear the sound of the Huntsman's horn,
Of galloping hoofs, on wild winds born
All night long—they will ride till dawn,
    And never a horse go lame.

Listen! I hear them chiming now,
    As hounds get on to the line,
And a Ghost Fox breaks from the cover,
    As white as the hoar-frost rime;
A great dog fox with a roving eye,
Who laughs at the hounds and the Huntsman's cry,
For he knows he's a ghost, and a ghost can't die,
Though hunted many a time,

From scent to view in the great grass fields
    They sweep like a scud of rain,
So the Ghosts of the Hunt of long ago
    Ride together again;
And I see the joy in their faces shine,
Ageless faces without a sign
Of the sadness of life, or the scares of time,
    Nor the shadow of tears and pain.

And many there be well known to me
    Amidst that ghostly throng,
Many with whom I used to ride
    In days now dead and gone;
And one amongst them who seems to say,
"We'll ride together again some day,"
And smiles at me ere he turns away,
    I have loved my whole life long.

One of them rode to the end of his day,
    And died, as his friend can tell,
The death that he would have wished to die–
    When hounds were running well.
Others are scattered far and wide;
Many of them like heroes died,
And, swept away on the War's flood tide,
    For their King and Country fell.

Now again they ride in glorious youth
    To the music of hound and horn;
I hear their laughter amongst the tree
    On wings of mystery borne;
Till all alone in the morning grey
I watch those horsemen fade away,
As they turn their horses at break of day,
    And ride into the Dawn.

[from The History of the Pyrchley Hunt, Guy Paget]

TRYING TO DO A DEAL
(Written after hearing a covert-side conversation in 1890)

He's a fine little hunter, you bet.
In fact, he's as good they make 'em;
In his stride all fences he'll get,
Where'er you may wish to take 'em.
Bounds off just in the right place,
Away in the next field he lands, sir.
And gallop, my word! Such a pace —
As fast as e'er man clapped his hands, sir.

Bill Tompkins can tell you a tale,
How I pounded the field at a yawner,
A hedge and a ditch and a rail,
Stuck high on a bank in a corner.
I was out with the ____ in a run
From Highwood they checked not a minute,
O'er the valley like demons they spun,
Only me and another was "in it."

How's he bred? Why, old Topthorn's his sire.
Believe me, there never was better.
His dam? Ah, my word, what a flyer!
If you'd seen her, you'd never forget her.
Is she sound? Yes, sound as a bell:
Just throw your leg over and try him.
My stable's so full, I must sell,
Or double the price wouldn't buy him.

Written by Tom Firr in 1890

THE QUORN PUPPY SHOW

"Well, Rattler, my boy, safe back from the show?"
"Yes, easily won the first prize, you know,
For the moment I came to the front
There was not another in the hunt!"
"Pooh! my dear boy, now don't be vain
It is deeds, not looks, that make a name,
And if your deeds should prove evil,
With all your good looks — you'll go to the devil!"

Written by Tom Firr of the Quorn about an imaginary conversation between two hounds after the Quorn Puppy Show which he instituted in 1870.

WATERLOO RUN

Tell me old chap, if acquainted you've been
    Of the doings they had t'other day;
How the hounds ran away and beat them all clean,
    Every man who took part in the fray.
Waterloo was the place where they put up their fox,
    And away they all scuttled like mad,
Till one and another had settled their crocks,
    Each man looking darnation sad.
Round Kelmarsh and Clipstone, where many got spilt;
    Lorks bless ye, to me 'tis a wonder
Over Oxendon fields there was none on 'em kilt
    O'er the oxers which rattled like thunder.
Right on past Farndon and Bowden Inn,
    With many a stile that was broken,
Until but a few of the best were left in,
    Not one with much go could betoken.
When down to the brook below Langton they went,
    I seed there was sport, for none feared it.
They rode like the de'il — on being over was bent —
    Harry Custance was all through as cleared it.
Then on towards Cranoe and Keythorpe like crows,
    The pack skid away o'er the pastures;
How the folk follows arter, the Lord only knows,
    Each and all meeting many disasters.
Past Hallaton Thorns, where some cove got a view,
    "Yoiks for'ard," he shouts, "tally-ho,"
Till the Captain* came up, and his whistle he blew,
    "Come tell me then, where did he go?"
"He's gone for the Welland, dead beat," cried the man;
    Like a genius, the Captain besought him.
Evening came on, and then darkness began —
    You bet, he'd like to have caught him.

*Colonel Anstruther Thomson.

The above is the shorter of two versions by Tom Firr of this famous run.

HUNTING TALES

THE WATERLOO RUN WITH THE PYTCHLEY

(From a meet at Arthingworth Hall, 2nd February 1866)

Yes, many good runs have I seen in my day,
Through woodland, o'er pasture and plough,
But none beats the one, I must candidly say,
Which I'll try to describe to you now.
Right well I remember the picturesque scene —
Dull, drizzling and damp was the morn.
No gayer assembly may ever have been
Than was seen on the Arthingworth lawn.
Though big was the field, yet their numbers were few
Who saw all the fun from the famed Waterloo.

Eventless the morning, no sign of a run
Worth calling by any such name;
A bad fox in covert persistently hung
For an hour or more, to his shame.
For over an hour he swung round and round,
Ere aught could induce him to go,
Then he managed to beat us, got safely to ground,
And in shelter we left him below.
Mid-day had fled; at a quarter to two
A good fox was found in the gorse Waterloo.

Miles sixteen or more by the flight of the crow,
And twenty, perhaps, as they ran;
Had fairly been crossed, but still onward they go,
As if they had only began.
Alas for the field! which was fast growing less,
No longer left by the score,
All beaten and blown, as they're bound to confess,
Save the Master and one or two more,
Who still to the pack are sticking like glue,
To finish the play from the famed Waterloo.

But every long lane has a turning, you know,
And runs they must all have an end;
Now past Slawston covert, yet onward they go
Where the banks of the deep Wellend bend.
But the dark shades of evening are closing too fast,
Of light there is left but a ray;
Hounds go near to Blaston are now stopped at last,
And a good fox has won him the day.
To him, then, we'll fill up a bumper or two,
And hurrah for more runs like the great Waterloo.

*A full version of Tom Firrs song may be found in Roy Heron's book
'Tom Firr of the Quorn' published by Nimrod Book Services 1984.*

THE MEET at BEEBY

Riders were fretting, their nags in a lather,
Blowing and stopping to left and to right.
Tails quickly shaking, each fence they were breaking,
While the keen, spotted beauties ran clean out of sight

Tom Firr c. 1881.

THE BURTON HUNT SONG

In seventeen hundred and sixty and three
The 3rd of December I think we agree,
At eight in the morning by most of the clocks
We rode out of Lincoln in search of a fox.

Old hunting song, author unknown.

CATCH US IF YOU CAN

For'ard on, for'ard on, there's a scent for a hundred,
The big 'uns are racing away for a lead,
A note from each throat is defiantly thundered
And threatens outpacing the fastest brave steed.
Come catch us who can, they seem to be calling,
While fences in front look black and appalling.

Tom Firr's notes, 8th December 1886.

THE QUORN, GT. DALBY, 1890

For an hour or more he led them a chase,
O'er the greenest of grass, and kept up the pace.
Through railroads and rivers, and villages too,
Came onto the line, he ran them clean through.
Till beaten and blown, and stiff as a post,
Still game, he reluctantly gave up the ghost!

Now standing erect, when placed on his feet,
In death as in life, his heart seemed to beat.
The country resounded with brightest of sounds,
The horn and the holloa, the baying of hounds;
All there to rejoice, bar one of the best
And truest of workers any kennel possess'd!

Now mangled and torn, flattened out on the rail,
Ne'er before was she known to be at the tail.
May he hear that shrill note full many a time,
The note which she uttered when crushed on the line.
And the heart beat high to the tune of "Remorse,"
Of the man who was riding the cursed iron horse.

(Written by Tom Firr after a train killed one of his best bitches)

THE QUORN

The air was soft as a morning in May
As I mounted my hack, and I galloped away
By hall and by cottage, by meadow and lawn,
To Baggrave to ride and to hunt with the Quorn.

It boots not to tell all the deeds that were done
By the lords and the ladies that rode in the run,
How a fox broke away when the Coplow was drawn,
And fast at his heels came Tom Firr and the Quorn.

How we sped o'er the pasture, o'er hill and o'er dale,
By Billesdon, and Norton, and Skeffington Vale,
O'er oxer and timber, through brake, bush and thorn,
In the first thirty minutes we rode with the Quorn.

Tell me not of the sport that the Meath can afford,
Of the walls of Kildare, or the runs with the Ward;
Till the Leicestershire pastures grow turnips and corn,
Still, still let me linger and ride with the Quorn.

Then high fill the bowl, let the bumper go round;
Here's a health to the horse, here's a health to the hound;
Here's a health to the huntsman, a health to the horn,
A toast to ourselves, and three cheers for the Quorn.

Verse by an unknown poet, first published in Baily's Magazine.
(A full version of the above is in Roy Heron's book,
Tom Firr of the Quorn, published by Nimrod Book Services 1984.)

THE HUNT as a SPECTACLE

The weary traveller forgets his road,
And climbs the adjacent hill; the ploughman leaves
Th' unfinished furrow; nor his bleating flocks
Are now the shepherd's joy; men, boys and girls
Desert th' unpeopled village; and wild crowds
Spread o'er the plain, by the sweet frenzy seiz'd.

Somerville

WILLIAM ABBEY

Reader, behold a genuine son of the Earth,
Like a true foxhound sportsman from his birth.
O'er hills and dales, o'er mountains, woods and rocks,
With dauntless courage he pursued the fox.
No danger stopt him and no fears dismayed,
He scoft at fear, and danger was his trade.

*An extract from an epitaph for William Abbey, huntsman
to the Earl of Gainsborough, who died aged 69 in 1772.*

THE OLD FOX

He waited not, he was not found,
No warning note from eager hound,
But echo of the distant horn
From outskirts of the covert borne,
Where Jack the whip in ambush lay,
Proclaimed that he was gone away.

An unknown writer in the early 1800's describe a wily old fox.

BACK TO 1946

In childhood days we'd watch the Hunt,
Me and brother Ned
We'd see the gleaming horses
And the beautiful coats of red.

We'd see the ladies in polished boots,
Many without their men;
They'd gone to fight in Europe
And would never hunt again.

We'd bonk off school on hunting days
And earn a shilling or two.
We'd hold the horses, shut the gates
Our mothers never knew.

There was sadness then in '46,
So many men had gone
But when you're only ten years old
Each day is a new dawn.

You see the world through childish eyes
The horses, the farms, the lane,
The hounds, the horn, the girls on ponies.
Those days won't come again.

For the fields and farms are a housing estate
The lanes dual carriageways
That's progress, but my heart is breaking
For my dream-like childhood days.

Written by an Anonymous poet, Brixworth, Northampton in 1983.

GET OUT OF TOWN

Hackneyed in business, wearied at that oar
Which thousands, once fast chained to, quit no more,
The statesman, lawyer, merchant, man of trade
Pants for the refuge of some rural shade.

R.S. Surtees: Hillingdon Hall (1844)

HUNTING TALES

WILLIAM, SECOND EARL OF LONSDALE

There's a noble Earl of ancient name,
Who hunts the fox but prefers him tame.
His father had mounted his thoroughbred horse.
And viewed the wild fox from his native gorse.
His son has come down by second-class train,
Worried the bagmen and home again.
Says the noble Earl to the elder Brown,
'Open the box and turn him down!'

A sardonic reference to the Earl's tame foxes which were bagged, taken out and released.
The verse is by William Reid in 1848.

THE CARBERY HUNT

In long years numbered with the things that were
Before the flood, a jolly pair,
Jack Beamish and his huntsman bold,
Jack Boing, man of slender mould,
With cheery sound of hound and horn
And with their dogs of Irish blood
The hare and fox alike pursued.

An unknown writer in 1730 recording the beginnings of The Carbery.

THE FINEST MUSIC

The finest music is to hear the hounds
Rend the thin air, and with a lusty cry
Awake the drowsy echoes and confound
Their perfect language in a mingled voice.

The above lines were engraved on a monument in Threlkeld Churchyard in the Cumberland Fells. Underneath the inscription are the lines: 'A few friends have contributed to raise this stone in loving memory of the undernamed, who in their generation were noted veterans of the chase, all of whom lie in this churchyard.' This is followed by a list of almost forty names of villagers and farmers, and is perhaps the clearest indication of the love of hunting in the Fell district.

A FAMOUS RACE

Two hours and a quarter I think was the time,
It was beautiful-great-indeed, 'twas sublime,
Not Meynell himself, the King of all men,
Ere saw such a chase, or will ere see again.
Tom Smith in the contest maintained a good place;
Tho' not first up, at last made a famous good race.

An anonymous singer around 1800 on the celebrated Billesden Coplow run.

The Smith referred to is Assheton Smith.

A PARTY IS HELD

When partying at Cobham, his Grace let it fall,
"Tell my friends I expect them at Knole's ancient Hall,
Tomorrow at seven and this understand,
Let each bring a neighbour, or friend in his hand.
For we mean to be gay, and that time shall give place
To the sweets of the bottle and charms of the chase."

A bugle was sounded the mirth to begin
When bounce went the corks as the punch was brought in.
All, all was true friendship that never beguiles
That springs from the heart, enlivened by smiles.
All, all was good humour till young squire Hoare
Fell back off his chair and could take in no more.

Now merry Frank Mackworth, a little afloat,
Emptied his glass down the young squire's throat.
Thus with high tales of sporting, the hunter's delight,
And libations to Bacchus we shortened the night.
Soon ended the meeting and foxhunters gay
Remounted their steeds and rode cheerfully away.

Adapted from Arminger's 'Sportsmen's Vocal Cabinet', 1830.

The banquet was given by Edward Sackville, Duke of Dorset, to celebrate a great run with Sir John Dyke's hounds in 1798 or thereabouts.

MAIDWELL HALL

Dear Master, as I could not leave
A pasteboard, slim, behind me,
I sent these lines that you may know
Your Althorp wine beguiled me.
And as I saw that noble Hall,
Those lovely views around me,
I could but think, what a lucky pink
Was he who joined the Pytchley.
But who am I to talk like this
My lectures are not Bampton
I'm nothing but a circuit judge
Whose circuits at Northampton.
Who having finished well his work
His crime and causes all,
Threw off his wig and donned his spurs
To hunt from Maidwell Hall.

Extract from verse written by Sir William Grantham and sent to Lord Spencer. Maidwell Hall was the home of Reginald Loder who instigated the 'History of the Althorp and Pytchley Hunt', written by Guy Paget.
Maidwell Hall is now a public school and the Pytchley Hunt still meet there.

THE VALE OF AYLESBURY MEET

Hunters are fretting and hocks in a lather,
Sportsmen arriving from left and from right;
Bridle roads bringing them, see how they gather,
Dotting the meadows in scarlet and white;
Foot people staring and horsemen preparing,
Now there's a murmur, a stir and a shout!
Fresh from his carriage as bridegroom on marriage
The Lord of the Valley leaps gallantly out.

Never stand dreaming while yonder they're streaming,
If ever you meant it, man, mean it today!
Bold ones are riding and fast ones are striding,
The Lord of the Valley is forward away!
There in the bottom, see, sluggish and idle,
Steals the dark stream where the willow tree grows,
Harden your heart and catch hold of the bridle,
Steady him! rouse him! and over he goes.

G. J. Whyte-Melville

LAY OF THE RANSTON BLOODHOUNDS

Pleasure that the most enchants us
    Seems the soonest done;
What is life with all it grants us
    But a hunting run!
Necks were stretched and mouths were deadened,
    Wind began to fail;
Sobbing sides and rowels reddened
    Told the usual tale . . .

G. J. Whyte-Melville

THANK GOD IT'S SEPTEMBER . . .

Now summer's dull season is over,
Once more we behold the glad pack,
And Wicksted appears at the cover
Once more on old Mercury's back;
And Wells in the saddle is seated,
Though with scarce a whole bone in his skin,
His cheer by the echo repeated
'Loo in, little dearies! Loo in!'

*An anonymous poet commemorating the start of the
North Staffordshire 1826 hunting season with Charles Wicksted
and his Huntsman William Wells.
The latter was thought to have broken every bone in his body
through countless falls from his horse, hence the reference.*

HAPPINESS IS . . .

The happiest he, who, far from public rage
Deep in the vale, with a choice few retired,
Drinks the pure pleasure of the rural life.
(And) You, who the sweets of rural life have known,
Despise the ungrateful luxury of the town.

R.S. Surtees: Hillingdon Hall (1844)

THE 45 MILE RUN

By the Royal Oak passed and through the known wood
That's called the Spring Coppy as far as they could;
So to Dunnington Woods on by Weston Park side
As hard as they could they continued to ride:

Crossed Durrant's Canal and so straight on to Tonge,
From thence quick proceeded, all halloaing along;
By Kilsal he ran and so through Gosford Wood
The horses and hounds went as hard as they could.

By Patty's Mill Rough, Hem Coppice and Audley,
From thence to Sturchley and so on to Dawley;
Through Gibbon's Coppice he passed like a buck
And over the Wrekin in Shropshire then struck.

His courage here did not serve him a rush
Twelve couple and Vernon lay hard at his brush;
Hard by to the Wrekin they run him in view,
Of forty good huntsman were here very few;

Back through Little Wenlock he seemed to run strong
Tho' they'd ran him forty-five miles that were long;
Through the Holbrook he passed to the Severn then flew
And plunged headlong in, tho' he'd broke from their view.

An anonymous poet in 1780 describing a long chase with the Meynell, led by Lord Vernon.

THE NEWBY FERRY INCIDENT

Eleven good men in the laden boat,
Eleven good steeds o'er the ferry float;
Alas! ere their ferryman's task was done
Two widows were weeping o'er father and son.

Let Yorkshire, while England re-echoes her wail,
Bereft of her bravest, record the sad tale;
How Slingsby of Scriven at Newby fell,
In the heat of the chase he loved so well.

Egerton Warburton on the York & Ainsty tragedy that killed Sir Charles Slingsby and five others in 1869, including his Huntsman and two boatman, due to an overcrowded ferry.

HUNTING TALES

THE BOLD DUKE

There, first in the burst see dashing away,
Taking all on his stride on Ralpho the grey,
With persuaders in flank comes Darlington's peer
With his chin sticking out, and his cap on one ear.

Badsworth Hunting Song c. 1810 about the deeds of the Duke of Cleveland.

The Earl kept a daily hunting diary and published
'The Operations of the Raby Pack' annually.
The hide of his horse Ralpho is said to be still at Raby.

TIMES CHANGE

All the world was there on Opening Day,
On chestnut, gelding, mare and bay.
I watched them come in Bedfords down the lane
And wished that I could be a youth again.

I saw the grocer coming with his girls
All paint and powder, not a trace of curls,
The Ifor Williams tail gate lowered and so
A few swigs from the hip-flask and ready to go.

Oh for the days of Jorrocks, lumpy squire
Of so little elegance, yet no-one went higher.
A master he? And they say the hunting sport
Is only for the rich and the upper-class sort!

Before my young days the carriages would show,
Disgorge the ladies in their finery and their beaux.
I imagined the Empress of Austria, riding hard,
Bay Middleton too, whom she would soon discard.

We watched the ladies and their fine young men
There was no ammonia – no antis then.
No swearing, placards or the painting sprays
Or any obscene threats in my young days.

Some say the world is better since my youth.
Old folk now are terrified – that's the truth –
Of being mugged or robbed or knocked about
By some foul, unwashed and low-class lout.

Now Opening Day is not the thrill it was
The Antis spit obscenely, flaunt the laws.
Oh for the days of ladies and their beaux
That cheered my youthful days, so very long ago.

An anonymous old foot follower written in 1990 in Market Harborough.

EARL FITZWILLIAM OF THE WENTWORTH

But hark upon the gentle gale is born
The note melodious of a huntsman's horn.
A foxhound's challenge floats upon the breeze,
And scarlet vestures flash among the trees,
While, like a torrent sparkling in its track,
Pours downward thro' the fern the eager pack.
A crash! a chorus bids the echoes wake
An answering harmony from hill and brake.
Now up the slope, swift o'er the russet mead
The hounds appear, each racing for the lead.

Extract from W. H. Hopkins tribute to Earl Fitzwilliam on his death in 1902.

HUNTING TALES

The Ballad of Missus Twee

One Monday night last October we were having a little chat
Over a drink at Les Pyke's place, about horses, and this and that.
We'd had a good day's cubbing, the weather had been kind,
The wine was flowing freely, we were starting to unwind.

The day had started poorly, we were all a bit on edge,
Till Bob Andrews, Mike and Charlie all jumped the Pytchley Hedge.
Then Mike Adams toppled off, and fell down with a thud,
The air was blue, his coat was ripped, his eyes were full of mud.

Then Bob fell off and, winded, lay, as three ladies came to his aid.
"I fancy the kiss of life," he moaned, and, suddenly afraid,
He saw Big Bertha riding up. " The kiss of life you need? "
Bob leapt to his feet and rode for his life on Jackson his trusty steed.

That evening Peter Jones piped up " Let's buy a racing horse"
We all nodded very wisely. We were in the best of spirits, of course.
" It won't take much effort, just a little bit of luck
So let's have a formal meeting and a little bit of tuck"

"We ought to buy a flat horse," the great Huntsman said
"One that's fast as lightning and a thoroughbred.
I know just the man- he'll see us all right,
He knows we're all brassic and that cash is a bit tight"

Then up spoke Gerald, a most canny lad,
"As ideas go, that's not really too bad.
I'll sell you a horse, it's out in my barn
Come and 'ave a look, it can't do any 'arm."

So we traipsed off to Hardwick, Oh Lord! What a sight-
The nag had three legs, and didn't look all that bright.
But Gerald said " It'll have some fair pace.
It'll be a dead cert in a three legged race"

Anyway, we all put a few quid in the pot,
And waited for all the offers -there should be a lot.
After six months there was a miserable three-
A stallion, a gelding and the mare, Missus Twee.

So we met at Peter's house, the lasagna was warm.
We looked at the photos and checked all the form.
Robert Percival told us he rated the mare,
Of stallions and geldings we ought to beware

So the die was cast, we bought Missus Twee
We found her a trainer and we did all agree.
We went down to Lambourne to see George Frost
He showed us around and he played mine host.

HUNTING TALES

After a dozen Lambruscos and a jug of beer
Mike Bletsoe-Brown said " Be of good cheer.
We'll have a little flutter and—let's be rational—
If she's good we'll run her in the next Grand National"

Her first time out at Warwick, the going was fine.
We all went to cheer her—and to have some red wine.
She finished a poor last but we didn't really care
We got tiddly again, and it was just nice to be there.

Then she ran down at Chepstow, bloody miles away,
Then Sandown, Towcester another day.
Southwell, Doncaster and Pontefract
Every time she finished at the back

By now we were desperate, feeling really low.
Gerald just said " I told you so,
You should have bought the stallion, that mare's a disgrace
All she does is come last every race"

But a last try at Warwick gave us all back our pride.
She looked beaten, but came up fast on the outside,
She lengthened her stride with a shake of her mane
And won by a nose, we all went insane.

We'd all been depressed, it made us all smile,
We'd make Gerald eat his words, she'd won by a mile.
The next race was at Ripon, she won by a head,
And we cleaned out the bookie, a fat Geordie called Fred.

Now our neighbours and friends were all desperate to know
Where she was running, they wanted to go.
After six wins, the trainer said, "Quick, hire a room
We've got an amazing offer from Sheik Mahommed Macktoum"

He offered us a million for old Missus Twee,
He said he admired her lightning speed.
He'd run her in the Derby, the Gold Cup and the Oaks.
We couldn't believe it , we thought it was a hoax.

But it wasn't a hoax, and we all met up at Pete's
With Monica, Lucy, Jeremy, our happiness complete
We split up the million, oh boy, what a sight,
And we toasted the Monday Club all through the night.

A Poetic piece of pipe-dreaming by Philip Kinell, Pitsford, 1994, in which any similarity to real events and people is purely imaginary.

HUNTING TALES

TOM RANCE

Tom Rance has got a single oie
    Worth many another's two;
He holds his cap above his head
    To show he'd got a view.
Tom's voice was loike the owd raven's
    When he shroiked his 'Tally-ho!'
For when the fox had seen Tom's face
    He thought it toime to go.

Tom Rance joined the Cheshire in 1830, acted as second whip for 31 years and never aspired to the rank of Huntsman. The poet is unknown.

A WARNING

Oh! gently, my young one. The fence we are nearing
    Is leaning towards – 'tis hairy and black,
The binders are strong and necessitate clearing,
    Or the wide ditch beyond will find room for your back.

Extract from a song by Bromley Davenport.

MY OLD HORN

Though toil hath somewhat worn thy frame
And time hath marred thy beauty,
Come forth! lone relic of my frame,
Thou well hast done thy duty!

Time was when other tongues would praise
Thy wavering notes of pleasure;
Now, miser-like, alone I gaze
On thee – a useless treasure.

And some who at thy call would wake,
Hath friendship long been weeping,
A shriller note than mine must break
Their deep and dreamless sleeping!

George Templer of Stover on giving up the Mastership of the South Devon to Sir Walter Carew.

HUNTING BEATS EVERYTHING . . .

Let statesmen on politics parley
    Let horses go fight for renown;
While I've health to go hunting with Charlie
    I envy no Monarch his crown.

G.J. Whyte-Melville

DAWN BREAKS

Oft listening how the hounds and horn
Cheerly rouse the slumbering morn,
From the side of some hoar hill,
Through the high wood echoing shrill.

John Milton.

KEEP YOUR TANK

Once I 'ad an 'orse
An' I 'ad a pair o' spurs.
They took away me 'orse
But they lef' me pair o' spurs.
Now I got a tank,
She runs a treat o' course,
But I look down at me spurs,
An' wish I 'ad me 'orse.

A poem by Walter Meade on wartime tank-driving.

THE CHASE

I remember how merry a start we got
When the red fox broke from the gorse,
In a country so deep, with scent so hot
That the hound could outpace the horse;
I remember how few on the front rank show'd,
How endless appeared the tail,
On the brow hill side, where we cross'd the road
And headed towards the vale.

Adam Lindsay Gordon.

ON RETIREMENT FROM HUNTING

What a grand thing 'twould be if I could go
Back to the kennels now and take my hounds
    For summer exercise; be riding out
With forty couple when the quiet skies
    Are streaked with sunrise, and the silly birds
Grown hoarse with singing, cobwebs on the furze
    Up on the hill, and all the country strange,
With no-one stirring; and the horses fresh,
    Sniffing the air I'll never breath again.

Siegfried Sassoon.

AND GOODNIGHT

"Oh goodnight, Brian and John and Tim
And thanks for a wonderful ride,
We couldn't have had more fun." we say
"It was one of the best, and with luck we may
Do it all again on another day."
And the daylight faded and died.

Joan Dunn from her poem 'Marsh Fever'.

LONG AFTER THE MEET

A warm glow came from the open fire,
The port was tasting fine.
We'd all had a great day's hunting,
Following the fox's line.

We'd lost him over near Sywell woods,
It didn't matter a bit.
The casserole was great at Jane's house
And the wine did flow like wit.

'Did you see that bloody Pytchley hedge?'
Said the Master, with a grin.
'I didn't' said Heather, and we all laughed
'Cos we'd seen her fall off and fall in.

'And Adrian Bracken, what a laugh,
His horse just seemed to peck'.
It got halfway over, changed its mind
And threw Adrian on his neck.

'That hedge has gotta be eight feet high'
Said Les Pyke on the right
'You're only exaggerating 'cos you leaped it
With over two feet of daylight'.

But Jane, Sallyann, Mon and Gaie
All waited at the rear.
The hedge was only FOUR feet high
By the time they jumped it clear.

'I've got the video, do you want to see?'
The all dashed from the room.
They watched it over and over again
The Master, field and groom.

'That isn't me', said a lady brunette,
'That's not my horse's stride.
And the rider's far too small in the bust
And much too large in the backside!'

Then the jokes started, and the stories,
Stretched long into the night.
'Did you see old Julian fall?' one said,
And they giggled with delight.

So on it went and the port was passed
'We must be on our way,'
Said Peter Jones the Huntsman
'Did you know its the break of day?'

He was right. And the dawn it slowly broke,
With bright streaks in the light.
The revelry was over as
They bade each other 'Goodnight'.

'Goodnight, Michael, Bob, Mon, and Anthea,
Leslie, Gerald, Jane and Gaie.
We'll see you all, God willing next week,
And thanks for a wonderful day'.

Philip Kinell, Pitsford, 1993.

NOSTALGIA

"I bet you miss it sometimes?" What should I miss of it?
Piles of manky sheep to skin and barrow loads of shit;
The endless hours in soggy clothes (whilst influenza pale)
Soothing feathers ruffled by what you did in the Vale.

A screaming midnight forest, all roaring in the storm,
And somewhere 7 couples, that just might hear your horn.
The telephone that never stops from early to late,
To have to stomach the abuse, whilst food dries on the plate.

Endless committee meetings that seem to stretch to dawn,
Because the folk of Hill and Vale are at daggers drawn.
The Chairman has "one of his turns" and swift for home departs;
Just guess which silly sod is left to keep the clans apart.

To stagger home exhausted to another scene of strife:
The whipper- has run off with the Stud Groom's new blonde wife.
There's piles of bills and more phone calls and bank statements in red
"What me miss being Master? you must be off your head!"

Then one summer morning, they brought hounds for me to see
They were happy with their huntsman and played and gambolled free.
I looked upon the waving sterns, the shining eyes and coats,
Then I felt a wet nose in my hand and something blocked my throat.

I gave the men some whisky (hoped they'd see nothing odd)
As I watched the hounds that once were mine and thought of me as God.
One word from Jack they gathered up and stood there in their pride
I smiled and thanked them as they left; then went indoors and cried.

R. W. F. Poole

ODE TO A CAP

The farmer's peaked cap is a wonderful thing
There are so many things you can do,
Like collecting the eggs that the hens have all laid
And removing the mess off your shoe.

You can cover the fence while you carefully stride
Over the wire that's electric and strung there;
It will save you a jolt if your stride is at fault
Or else you might well be just hung there.

You can shift sows from feeders or piglets to creep
Fend off bullock or boar or a horse.
It's as easy as pie, just like swatting a fly
Which you do with the cap off, of course.

You can mushroom at dawn at the edge of your lawn
(Carefully avoiding the lichen)
Secure in the knowledge it's quite safe to forage
Your cap will transport them to the kitchen.

Picking up broken glass is a pain in the leg
But with cap over hand it's so easy.
You can pick up all manner of sharp pointed things,
Or even a sheep if it's greasy.

You can kneel on it too, but with only one knee,
A secular low genuflection.
When you're working on tractors or lambing a ewe,
Or just when you're tired, on reflection.

You can grasp things quite hot, it won't matter a lot,
Your hands will remain in fine fettle;
We're thinking of bearings or motors or nettles
Or even a whistling kettle.

Its use as a frisbee is fun if you're bored,
When spun with great skill in the air,
To discourage stray tom cats who trespass at will
And leave with just seconds to spare.

In summer for picnics it could be a plate
Or else it's a nosebag for horse.
Then use it to clean up the country as well
To take home the litter of course!

These are some things can be done with a cap,
Simple list, but we're willing to share it.
Other suggestions? We really can't think.
Oh yes! We suppose you could wear it.

ANON
(Alterations and additions by Jenny and Brian Knight)

TRAITOR MAGPIE

The drips on the bracken sparkle and glisten
Where the old dog-fox awakes from his doze;
With uplifted pad, he pauses to listen,
As on the breeze comes a sound that he knows.

Quite calmly, he stretches, lazily yawning,
Sniffs, for a moment, the damp-laden air;
While, somewhere, a magpie cackles a warning,
Bidding him go, with the utmost of care.

Unruffled he trots to where the copse thickens,
Forcing his way through the bramble and thorn,
And out at the top, his pace – slightly quickens,
Catching a note of the querulous horn.

He drops to the ditch and runs it a quarter,
Doubles again where it touches the drain,
Then, easily jumping over the water,
Steals, like a shadow, away to the lane.

But ere he has gone a furlong from danger,
Over his mask flits a black and white shape,
Proclaiming the news to all, friend or stranger,
'Reynard is here, see, he cannot escape!'

Edric G. Roberts

OCTOBER MORNING

Horses tremble in the sunshine
    of a clear and crystal dawn
Riders waiting at the field edge
    listen for the vital horn.
Crack a whip to break the silence
    thump a boot with leather crop
Statue sentry at the ready
    waits controlled at covert top.
Scarlet huntsman in the woodland
    calling out blood-curdling cries
Men with terriers stand in gateways
    stamp their feet and strain their eyes.
Pretty girl in tight-filled jodhpurs
    leads a bonny 'Thelwell' tot
Follower nigh past his life-span
    finds himself a sheltered spot.
Takes a nip to warm his spirit
    feels the cold without a doubt.
Thinks 'I'll give it up next Season'
Then he hears those hounds sing out!

Rosemary Hankins

THE WHIP

As, still as a statue, he sits on his horse,
    Watching and waiting,
Or rounding up stragglers behind the gorse,
    Cursing and rating,
He's always the same, hard-bitten and game.

The voice of a hound, or the click of a hoof
    Tell him what's doing,
He knows, on the instant, alert and aloof,
    All that is brewing;
Lean- visaged and tanned, he's always at hand.

When hounds are at fault and are lifted in vain,
    Nothing resulting,
His musical holloa is heard through the rain,
    Faintly exulting;
He's sure to be right, whatever the plight.

And during a run, when the pack, in full cry,
    Goes hell-for-leather,
He sees, all the time, with his critical eye,
    Hounds are together;
No matter the pace, he's there in his place.

But after it's over we leave in our cars,
    Cosily weary,
While he collects hounds by the light of the stars,
    Placidly cheery,
Although it's hard work, there's nothing he'd shirk.

And if, every day, he's up with the dawn,
    Grooming and feeding,
There'll come a time, soon, when he'll carry the horn,
    True to his breeding;
The salt of the earth, he'll show what he's worth.

Edric G. Roberts

A FOX'S TALE

Oh Joy it's November and hunting has started,
There's a frost on the ground and swallows departed,
I'll leave my deep earth long before man arises,
To plan my escape route (I don't like surprises).
Now where is the meet – ah yes Farmer Biggs,
It's always a laugh how those horses hate pigs,
I've only to run through the field near their sty,
One grunt from a sow and some riders will fly.
And how I shall laugh for there is always one,
Who lands upside down with his face in the dung.

The field is assembled I watch from afar,
The followers come by foot and by car,
The more the merrier I chuckle with glee,
For they get in the way when I'm ready to flee,
Some block up the gateways and cut up the lane,
While fumes from the cars drive the hounds quite insane.

Now we run through the field where I know a great way
To put paid to that cocky chap up on the bay,
It looks such a nice fence, a hedge and a rail,
But the drop on landing would make Red Rum quail.

Now it's way past midday and we've had some fun,
I've taken the pack on a fifteen mile run,
The field has caught up, the master will soon,
At least he did last time (by the light of the moon),
It's time to go home and I just have to pray,
That those silly anti's don't get in the way,
I like to get home while there's still lots of light,
So I'll just wish you all a "Goodnight sir , goodnight".

Linda Pestell

THE LOST HOUND

Whenever the moon and the stars are set
Whenever the wind is high,
All night in the dark and lonely rain
A man goes riding by.
Late at night when the fires are out,
'Who is he, mummy? And why does he shout?'

'It's alright darling, he's lost a hound,
Old Annie is missing and can't be found.
Let's call him over, offer him sloe gin,
For it's Jeremy Reed, the whipper-in!'

So whenever the moon and stars are set
Whenever the wind is high,
All night in the dark and lonely rain
If a man goes riding by.
You'll know the kennels have lost a hound,
It's Annie again and she must be found.

And when the whipper-in is tired
And makes his weary way home.
He longs for a scotch, a coffee
He's soaked through to the bone.
Who greets him at the Kennel gate?
It's Annie, she's been home since eight!

Philip Kinell, Pitsford 1994
with apologies to Robert Louis Stevenson

HUNTING TALES

THE EARL OF LEICESTER

Now Billy Coke, who never lost a chance,
Down the hillside came rattling on 'Advance',
And though he saw the willows, still he took
His line, and crammed him straight at Langton Brook.

From 'Melton in 1830', The New Sporting Magazine, Vol. 13

SKITTLES

In Liverpool in days gone by,
For ha'pence and her vittles,
A little girl by no means shy
Was setting up the Skittles.

A popular ditty about the early life of Catherine Walters

HUNTING HILL

Jesse Russel, a Pennsylvania farmer, asked to be buried in Hunting Hill.

I've marked the place. They call it Hunting Hill.
Sound wood! I've jumped my foxes there past thirty year.
The sweetest find, I say, on Ridley still.
Rare scent for hounds to work at. Good spot, too, to hear
Them push him up, once he leaves the white oak side
It's grass there – open honest grass to ride!

What more to ask? I'll rest there year by year,
Content enough till corn is in and harvest through.
Then maybe – some way – fall by fall I'll hear
Once more the music of those sweet notes on dew!
Gods, will I wake a while and feel the thrill
When hounds score true to cry on Hunting Hill!

Extract from Hunting Hill by Clifton Lisle

GHOST HEATH

There they went
Across the brook and up the bent,
Past Primrose Wood, past Brady Ride,
Along Ghost Heath to covert side.
The bobbing scarlet, trotting pack,
Some horses blowing with a whinny,
A jam of horses in the spinney,
Close to the ride-gate; leather straining,
Saddles creaking, men complaining,
Chaffing each other as they passed,
On Ghost Heath turf they trotted fast.

John Masefield
From 'Reynard the Fox'

HUNTING TALES

DON'T BE A THRUSTER

Green grows the grass
O'er a sporting old stager
Who overrode hounds
Of an ex-Army Major.

*Written anonymously
but attributed to an American Master in the 1920's*

THE MUCK HEAP

Old grass and sound going, sweet country to ride,
A few post and rails that we take in our stride.
We wouldn't miss hunting for thousands of pounds
These hours of enjoyment, out with the hounds.

And the farmers, they're mostly all smiles and good fun,
Except for one we called Attila the Hun.
He'd glower and glare, not a smile as we passed.
Though we privately thought him a bit of an ass,

We'd still smile sweetly and raise our hats as we rode
Past his farm and his fields and his unwelcome abode.
Then one day he smiled, not a sign of distress,
So, steaming past Pitsford, onward we pressed.

Now the buttons were shining, the scarlet divine,
The joddies spotless, the boots gleaming with shine.
Across a wide ditch, then a fine field of grass,
We aimed for a bullfinch – the next fence to pass.

First over was Master and blue was the air,
Two thrusters, three ladies of complexion fair.
My horse pecked. Oh shame! How well I had ridden
As I flew through the fence into Attila's midden.

The Master was upside down in the heap.
'Ware dung heap!' I yelled as they started to leap.
Too late! Two more riders came over the fence,
You can imagine the sight, and the smell was immense.

We finally freed the Master, his breeches all torn
His face flushed with anger, his features forlorn.
The rest of the field were well down in the pasture.
Laughing their socks off at our smelly disaster.

Our scarlet was brown, our hats were a mess
We pulled out the ladies in obvious distress.
The horses stumbled out and were watching us sadly,
From a safe distance as we brushed ourselves madly.

Then came Attila, rode up on his horse.
Peered over the bullfinch, his laughter was coarse.
He roared and he laughed, he coughed and he cried.
'I've never seen anything like this', he sighed.

'Oh shit', said the Master, and we all dissolved
Into laughter, and even the farmer resolved
To clean all our clothes, as he saw our distress
And offered his house for a drink and a rest.

So the day ended well, against all the odds.
We drank Attila's sloe gin as he cleaned up our jods.
He promised to move his whole muck heap away
And we'd be welcome on his land on another day.

Philip Kinell, Pitsford, 1994
Based on an incident with the Oakley in the 1800's described by S. C. Whitbread in Book Seven.

HERE WE GO AGAIN

Summer is over, Autumn Chill draws near,
A season close to my heart, one I hold dear,
Horses will now be brought in from grass,
Preparations begin so they may perform their task,

Very gently we will exercise them at walk,
At this point no rushing, we'll just walk and talk,
Talk of the exciting days soon to come,
When the pace gets fast, and hounds really run,

It's five o'clock and all around appears so still,
You shiver, rub your hands from the morning chill,
The horses tacked up, the stables all clean,
We move off to the hunting scene.

As a new September day is dawning,
We settle with friends for a cubbing morning,
Hounds alert noses close to the ground,
Horses hooves, our low voices the only sounds,

November's now here we really begin,
The dressing up, the meet at the Inn,
The scarlet coats mingle with black,
Shining black boots, horses gleaming tack,

After several drinks at the Inn with friends,
We will anticipate our day, all the twists and bends,
To jump high gates also hedges low,
The thrill is not knowing where we will go,

Its been an exhilarating day for all,
Fortunately no one hurt in a fall,
We rode the land, breathed in clean air,
Our minds relaxed without a care,

Its late and time to return to the yard,
A hot feed for my horse who has worked so hard,
A deep bed, a welcome net of hay,
Thank you my lad for my safe hunting day.

Carol Nicholls

AND WOMEN . . .

Fox hunting was the first sport that men allowed women to participate in, surprisingly. There were, naturally, objections, including John Thomson's poetic effort in 1730.

To spring the fence, to reign the prancing stead,
The cap, the whip, the masculine attire
In which the roughen to the sense and all
The winning softness of their sex is lost.

A LAMENT

If falls that blow we first begin to dread
When the foul primrose reared its monstrous head,
When first uprose from bank and mossy dell
The flaunting violet's disagreeable smell
When vicious lambs commenced their savage bleat.
Oh! when they're roasted, won't revenge be sweet?

The season's over, we have heard this morn
The last sweet note of gallant Percy's horn;
And sweeter still, the last melodious sound
Of deep-toned music from the eager hound.
All now is mute save one word whispered low
To horse and man alike, and that is 'Woe'.

From 'A Lament to the Rufford Hunt'. (April 1861)

ODE TO A COURTESAN

Here lies Skittles
A woman of deep feelings,
An authority on the ceilings
Of the rich.
The courtesan of the century
A great beauty, a major force.
Now she's dead, and rests
On her back, of course.

(with apologies to Graham Lord, Daily Telegraph)

HUNTING TALES

HOW MUCH WOULD WE MISS

Out beagling the other day
I had a chance to talk
To other followers about the way
We all enjoyed our sport.

How strange our Saturdays would be
If hunting was to end,
No walking thrills, no hounds to see
What would we do instead?

Shop, play golf, a day trip out
Or just a ramble round,
So boring, dull, there is no doubt
Without a pack of hounds.

We'd miss the gathering at the meets,
The friends we'd see that day,
The atmosphere, the drinks and the eats
To help us on our way.

We'd miss that thrill when hounds first find,
The holla, horn, the cry,
The whimper of puppies left behind,
Uncertain, nervous, shy.

The test of strength and stamina
To keep us with the few
Who last the day, who run so far
To keep the hound in view.

That satisfaction walking back
With hounds, as darkness comes
To join the tea, and warm and chat
In steamy farmhouse homes.

And personally, for me I know
I'd miss that hunting cure
For weekly worries, tales of woe
That gradually mount in store.

I dwell on these, my frets and fears
And then they fade and disappear
Absorbed by hunting sounds.

This natural hunting country scene
Has been part of life for years,
But times have changed, and know it seems
We've enemies to fear.

The "anties" want all hunting banned,
And rallying up support,
They're sure they have the upper hand
To end our country sport.

But surely they have overlooked
That threats are not enough
The British hunting folk
Are made of sterner stuff.

Though numbers small, we must unite
And show our strength and powers,
We yet have time to plan our fight
Defending what's rightfully ours.

Angela Heaton

INDECISION

The forecast is dreadful, strong winds, heavy rain,
Go hunting today, I must be insane
A victim of comfort, warm in my bed
Perhaps after all, I'll stay home instead.

The hallway needs painting, there's shopping to do
Tasks such as washing, to name one of a few.
Surely more sense on a day such as this
Yes that's what I'll do, I'll give hunting a miss.

But as daylight strengthens, some courage returns
Somewhere inside me that eager spark burns
The scent could be good, hounds could run well
The rain might blow over, one can never tell.

That lure is too strong, I cannot resist
The challenge, excitement, sheer fun I would miss
By chickening out of fear of the cold,
What comparable thrill would the day otherwise hold?

So grab up the barbour, pull wellies on feet,
Drive off in the car to where hounds will meet,
Where that electrical thrill of what lies ahead
Dissolves all those worries I had in my bed.

And when the day's over and I'm back in the warm,
That relaxed Happy feeling having weathered the storm,
And enjoyed every minute as I strode after hounds.
What alternative pleasure could ever be found?

Angela Heaton

A TRIBUTE TO MY FATHER

They catch the eye whilst standing there,
To start the hunting day,
A well turned out distinguished pair,
My father on his bay.

As people meet and gather round,
To chat, he moves apart,
His mood reflects the restless hounds,
He's keen to make a start.

A hunting man he's always been,
With passion rarely found,
His top hat, green coat, part of the scene,
Out with the Dumfries hounds.

At last they're off, the eager field,
Respond to huntsman's horn,
Alert to what the day will yield,
They wait, as covert's drawn.

A fox is stirred, and hurries on,
Across the woodland ride,
With stealth he moves, and soon has gone
Leaving the covert side.

My father waits on his patient horse,
Until the rush has gone,
Observes the foxes likely route,
And then sets off alone.

He knows the countryside around,
Is not for the unwary,
Unseen ditches, marshy ground
Will hinder those who hurry.

The field, too keen to gallop on,
Have lost all sight of hounds,
And notice not the backtrack run
As fox seeks sheltered ground.

My father's independent line,
Today has served him right,
As hounds swing back, check, and re-find,
Their fox within his sight.

All those who've ridden blindly on,
No doubt have had their fun,
But for him who rides with care and plan,
What satisfactions won!

Contributed by Angela Heaton, whose father was Master of the Vale of Lune Harriers in the 1960's. He eventually moved to Scotland, near Lockerbie where he is now 79 and a distinguished member of the Dumfriesshire Foxhounds.

HUNTING TALES

THE ANTIS

The hunting horn was high and clear,
The scarlet coats were grand.
The Anti hid behind the hedge,
Ammonia in his hand.

He squirted it over near the hounds
Just so they'd lose the scents.
He turned away quite satisfied
He'd spoiled the sport of gents.

"I say, good sir," the Master said,
"Why exactly do you come?
The fox is vermin, we kill him quick,
Yet you treat us like scum."

"You come out here and protest
As is your democratic right.
But you disrupt our pleasure
From Scotland to the Isle of Wight."

"And furthermore you insult our girls
With rude and foul abuse.
You block our cars, take photographs,
Please tell me, what's the use?"

The anti spoke, "You stupid prat,
You think you own the land.
You sit upon your bleedin' horse
And sneer at the anti band."

"You think you're God's gift to the human race,
And your Lady Muck as well.
You look down your royal nose at us
And tell your friends we smell."

"Just look at you, all dressed in red,
And your pals in bowler hats.
You consider you're a class apart,
But we just think you're prats."

"Well, we won't stop till you're all gone,
And we'll get the anglers too.
We'll hound them from the rivers
Just like we've hounded you."

"We'll go to every single meet,
It is our legal right.
We've got your number and your name
And we'll harrass you day and night."

The Master slowly shook his head,
His astonishment sublime.
"Why do you hound us in this way?
How do you get the time?"

The anti said, "I don't have to work.
The Pop Stars pay the bills.
Linda says we've got to drive you
From the valleys and the hills."

"I get my dole, I don't need a job.
In fact life is really grand.
Every day I hound you poofs
I get sixty quid in my hand."

He raised his hand, a throng appeared,
With dirty jeans and banners.
They swore and spat and blew on whistles,
Unworried about their manners.

They squirted ammonia at the hounds,
Insulted all the footies.
Then very calmly stopped for lunch-
Diet Pepsi and chip butties.

The hunt moved off, the Master rode
Quite proudly at the head.
The chase was on, but he couldn't forget
What the protester had said.

But there was nothing he could think of
And little he could do.
And nothing he could ever say
Would change the anti's point of view.

For the antis see the hunting field
As a difference in class.
They see the sport as a chasm
Over which they cannot not pass

"If we can't join let's wreck it,"
That's what the antis say.
So they go and disrupt hunt meetings
Virtually every day.

They don't really care about the fox,
The horses or the hounds.
All they see is class warfare,
And the hunt is the battleground.

"Ban hunting!" they cry, and the newspapers
Want an angle for the news.
They would love to see an anti die
Under a horse's hooves.

So the hunter on his day of sport
Is harrassed and hounded still
By the unabashed and the great unwashed
Of little social skill.

Now the hunters work and pay their tax
And the antis are full of hate.
They get their dole and readies too,
Supported by the state.

For they swear, they curse, they shout and spit
Uncaring who hears the oath.
It's a strange and a lenient society
That hounds sportsmen and then rewards sloth.

Bedale hounds - 1842 (British Hunts & Huntsmen 1911)

The wrong way? (British Hunts & Huntsmen, Vol.3)

Book Five

The Emerald Isle

Several of the stories that first attracted me to begin writing this book were told by some horsemen just returned from hunting in Ireland. The fun they had, the lies they were told (which passed as blarney), and the long wet evenings in the pub form vital parts of any Irish story I've heard. One man hired a car with a group of hunting friends, drove home suitably "well-oiled", got lost innumerable times and finally ran off the road and halfway up a stone wall. It was their last night and as far as he knows the car is still atop the wall. But it was the sheer terror they felt that made me wonder — the fear at going across strange country on an unpredictable horse across a strange set of wild banks and hedges, not knowing if there's a deep bog on the other side.

So in this little section, we present a few tips on how to translate Irish speak into English, what to say when you're offered a horse in Ireland, and a few stories to warn you – or attract you.

UNDERSTANDING THE LINGO
by Cooky McClung

You don't have to be in Ireland long to realise that the Irish love their horses with a vengeance. So much so that they often treat them like family, only in some instances, better.

My grandfather, Sean Patrick McMahon, held the firm view that his horses were superior to most people he knew. Master of his own pack of hounds, Sean Patrick revelled in the joy of foxchasing. Hounds roamed freely in his house (until he married my grandmother), and he was known to bring an ailing foal into the kitchen near the big cookstove, where it would be warm and he could keep an eye on its progress.

Like many of the Irish who foxhunt, Sean Patrick learned to sit a horse as a toddler. His theory as to why the Irish are so at ease on a horse early in life is that so many of them learn their good seat before they're born. Bizarre as this theory may seem, Sean Patrick included several women each season in his own hunting field who were in various stages of pregnancy. The fact that they had to tie baling twine through the loops to hold their riding habits over their protruding tummies in no way deterred them from their sport.

FEARLESS

The problem with the Irish becoming so competent as riders at such a tender age is that they believe everyone shares their fearless ability. They have adapted a language all their own in dealing with horses and hunting. None of these phrases are explained in guidebooks, so it's best if you understand them before you join the field.

The first and most important thing you must understand is that when asked how well you ride, never, never reply: (a) I'm a very experienced rider; (b) I've hunted since I was a child; or (c) I don't want a horse that's too quiet. If you say you're experienced the Irish will test you. Believe me, you may not want to ride their version of a horse suited to an experienced adult who's hunted since childhood.

And rest assured that when you're a guest hunting in Ireland, you'll be offered a mount that knows where he's going and the quickest way to get there. Long gone are the days when the Irish (my grandfather included) would bring out a rank, unschooled youngster to "see if the Yank can ride."

NICE MOUTH

Your safest reply when asked how you ride is: "I've ridden some, but I prefer a horse with a nice mouth." This will separate you from the steeplechase variety of rider who really enjoys hunting something that's 18 hands and breathes fire.

One year, when I took eight of my friends pony trekking in Ireland, I had prepped them on how to answer when asked about their riding experience. You can imagine the puzzlement of our guide wondering why nine relatively inexperienced people would want to spend eight hours a day in the saddle. We were all arguing over who was the least experienced so that we could get the most docile horse.

Often the stable where you're hiring a horse will allow you choose your own mount. Obviously, it's difficult to pick a horse by peeking in the stall, so hop on for a few spins around the arena and listen carefully to what is said about the horse.

LAMB LIKE

For example, one of my friends, a most timid rider, spied a small gelding wandering around the paddock with his tack on, reins looped over his big lop-ears. She was taken with his benign, lamb-like expression and said to the owner, "Oh, I think I'll take that one."

"Oh indeed!" the Irishman beamed. "And he's a fine ride he is." Red flag! When the Irish say "he's a fine ride," they mean he's a fine ride for someone on the Olympic three day team. "A fine ride" means just that, only better.

My friend swung up in the saddle and instantly disappeared. Our host, waiting for the rest of us to mount, gazed unperturbed as he watched her dust cloud evaporate over the horizon.

"Ah faith!" he remarked. "So she favoured the old event horse did she. Well now, at least she's going in the right direction," he finished, ambling off to her belated rescue.

WARE BOG

Beware also of the Irish use of the words "a bit" or "soft," If they encompass both words in a sentence, as "Careful now, the going up ahead might be a bit soft," prepare yourself. Hunting in Ireland often includes going through bog. Unlike our mud, bog is far deeper and more treacherous.

While Irish horses find it old hat to step into this deep going, you may panic when your horse's tail disappears. Pulling horses and riders out of several feet of wet bog is as common in Ireland as crossing deep streams in the States, the only difference being we don't need front-end loaders.

If the Irish say. "This horse is a bit plain, now," don't be concerned. I was once mounted on a short, stocky cob that would have been laughed out of the hunting field in the United States. But for all his homely appearance, this honest little fellow jumped effortlessly and helped me overcome my terror at facing unaccustomed ditches and banks. He even forgave my ill-fated forward seat, which sent me nearly into the next country over the first gaping ditch. With a long-suffering sigh, the gelding merely waited for me to extract myself from the bog and remount.

If you hear, "This horse gets up in the air a bit over a fence," wear your parachute. If you hear, "This horse gets a bit peevish," you want to keep him in the jolliest of moods, even if it means never leaving the stableyard.

Be honest. If your hosts asks if you mind riding a horse that "pulls a wee bit or takes a wee bit to hold," say yes, unless you do a lot of bench pressing.

WEATHER

Bad weather rarely deters the Irish foxhunter. Although they often have crisp, beautifully sunny days, it isn't called "The Emerald Isle" because it's so dry. When you hear the phrase, "It's a fine soft day for the sport!" you'd better reach for your flippers and snorkel. The amount of rain encountered can be anything from a drizzling mist blown in from the sea to a full-blown gale with rain or sleet slanting sideways so powerfully that you can't tell where you're going or what you're jumping (sometimes an advantage.)

Though the Irish tend to exaggerate (under the guise of blarney), they will be truthful in telling you that foxhunting in their country will provide you with the most exhilarating, spectacular and sometimes frightening experience you can ever have. You may, as we did, crawl off your horse at the end of the day, swearing you'll never go over another ditch or wall, risking life and limb and sanity.

Then you'll be led into a pub, enjoy a hearty dinner and perhaps a pint, with wonderful company who will convince you that you had the time of your life. And sure enough, you'll be up and out with the hounds the very next morning. Just remember to hang on tightly and let your horse do his job.

THE ENGLISH/IRISH HUNTING DICTIONARY

WHAT THE IRISH SAY

The horse gets up in the air a bit
This horse is a bit Peevish
He pulls a wee bit
It's a fine soft day
He's a fine ride
He's a bit plain
The going's a bit soft
Do you want a quiet ride?
He takes a wee bit to hold
Do you fancy a couple of pints?
Let the horse guide you
It's a bit of a drizzle
There's a few stone walls about
There's a bit of a frost
There's a little bit of wind
He's full of character
He'll run like a Christian

WHAT THE IRISH MEAN

Wear your parachute!
He's bloody mad!
It'd take Hulk Hogan to hold him!
It's piddling with rain!
He's an Olympic 3-day eventer!
We'll soon see if this Yank can ride!
There's a bog ahead!
We'll give you the mad gelding!
You'll never stop him!
You'll be too drunk to hunt in the morning!
Hang on for your life!
It's coming down in buckets!
Every wall is 6 feet high!
There's 3 feet of snow!
It's a full blown gale!
He's bloody-minded!
But only God knows how!

SHAKEN, NOT STIRRED

The standard of Irish hotels – low! – astounds the parties of English foxhunters who flock there to ride every year. Staying in a one-horse town hotel near Dublin, a Mr. Jones tells us of his mistake in ordering morning tea. Just before seven-thirty, a girl knocked and threw open his bedroom door.
'Sugar in your tea, sir?' she shouted.
'No thank you,' he replied
Before she banged the door shut, she said 'Don't stir it, then!'

ONLY IN IRELAND

Sign seen in Galway hotel:
> To Call Room Service
> Please open door and Call '**ROOM SERVICE**'

MISSING AT FUNERAL

Two Irish farmers were discussing the good and bad points of an old horse dealer who had just died. One of them asked the other if he'd be going to the funeral.
'No,' he replied, 'He's not coming to mine, so I'm not going to his!'

QUAYSIDE CHOICE

Sir Henry Tate recalls hunting with the United in Cork many years ago. Finding horses wasn't too difficult, he recalls. 'They used to line the horses up on the quay for us to look over as we docked. We'd be told 'Have a ride on this one sir. He's sure to carry you well,' even though he was only three and just broken!

SEND PICTURE

An Irish farmer who hunted with the Galway, widowed some years before, advertised in the Farmers Weekly for a wife. 'I am 60 years old with 40 acres. Would like to marry a woman of 40 who has a tractor. Please send photo of the tractor.'

LEPPERS-TOWN?

Overheard while on a hunting trip to Ireland, a conversation between a horse dealer and his victim. 'He's a grand wee lepper, he is. Mind you, I haven't seen him jump meself!'

JUMPING HOUSES

A friend from Bicester was on a hunting trip to Ireland. He was offered a horse by a man who claimed the horse would 'jump houses.' It fell at the first fence. 'Sorry, sir,' apologised the owner who witnessed the fall. 'He just tripped over the xxxxxxx chimney pot!'

HUNTING TALES

LEFT FOR DEAD

At a point to point in Ireland, an old horse called Creggan Heights fell at the last and lay as if dead. The vet was summoned from the bar, examined the horse, and told the lady owner who was comforting the horse that it was no use, he'd have to use the humane killer. In an advanced state of inebriation, the vet promptly shot the owner in the foot. The startled horse got up and trotted back to the stables.

LECTURE BOUND

Police in Cork stopped a car in the early hours of the morning and asked the driver – still in full hunting gear – where he was going.
'I'm going to a lecture.'
The Garda were suspicious and asked where the lecture was. The driver gave an address identical to the one on his driving license.
'And who's giving this lecture?'
'My wife,' replied the man sadly.

NO AMBITION

A hunting man wanted to show his new-found friends in Dublin that he was proud of his heritage.
'I was born an Englishman. I live as an Englishman. And I'll die an Englishman.'
A voice piped up from the corner. 'To be sure, sir, have you no ambition in you at all, at all?'

DON'T COME WITHOUT THE GUINNESS!

'You'll come to our house later for a party?' The question was put by a local Irish Master to a visiting horseman from the Quorn. The horseman readily agreed.
'Do you know how to get there?'
Directions were given, then 'Be careful when you come to the garden gate. Push it open with your elbow and be careful not to tear your coat.' The horseman nodded, somewhat puzzled.
'Now when you get to the front door, press the bell with your nose'.
My friend was now even more puzzled. He'd been told to open a gate with his elbow, and press a doorbell with his nose.
'But why,' he asked, 'do I have to open the gate with my elbow and press the doorbell with my nose?'
'Ah, well, sir, how else could you do it with a case of Guinness under each arm?'

NO WATER, PLEASE

Rebecca Linville tells the story of an Irish groom in Kilkenny who used to fall off horses, and lie dazed, in the hope of being revived with a swig of something from a hip flask. On one occasion he did his usual trick and was shocked to hear a visiting English Master shout 'Quick get him a drink of water!'
'To be sure,' he said indignantly, 'how far do I have to fall to get a glass of whiskey?'

NO CRITICISM

Sometimes visitors to an Irish hunt can be critical. They moan about the jumps, the horses, the weather, anything at all. But the Irish hosts are very generous, even to the carpers. One moaner from Leicester almost drove the host Master to distraction. I commented on what a moaner he was. But the Master refused to condemn him. All he would say was 'Ah, sure the man was upsetting to himself with his moans but wasn't he great at it?'

DRINKING & DRIVING

Mick Adams tells of a trip to Ireland a few years ago. They hired a car and after the hunting party, much alcohol was consumed. His friend the driver was more than inebriated when a policeman came up as they reached their hotel.
'To be sure,' he said, 'you're too drunk to be driving.'
'To be sure,' said the driver, 'can't you see I'm in condition no to walk?'

CLOSING TIME

A few friends from the Pytchley were in a pub in Galway on their first hunting trip to Ireland. As everyone knows, closing time is fairly flexible. They sat around drinking as midnight approached. 'When does this pub close?' asked one. 'Around the middle of next week,' replied the owner.

SEX

Bob Andrews reports that SEX in Ireland is an eight letter word called MARRIAGE. On hunting trips there, he has been at post-hunt parties and when the band strikes up, the girls mysteriously line up on one side of the room, the men on the other. Even the celebrated Frank Harris complained 'How do the Irish have this insane belief in the necessity of chastity?'

ANCESTORS

Another hunting man counsels the unwary about Irish taxis. Never, never, admit to being from New York.
'Do you know my cousin, Seamus, from the Bronx?' 'No'.
'Do you know my sister's nephew, he lives in Brooklyn?' 'No'.
'I suppose you've got a few Irish ancestors?' 'No'.
'Well, you can't be 100% American then!'

SWEATING UP

The legendary Lady Mollie Cusack-Smith was hacking back from hunting one day when she was hailed by a local farmer.
'That old horse is sweating up a bit , 'Mollie', he shouted.
'To be sure,' she shouted back, 'you'd be sweating up a bit yourself if you'd been between my legs for five hours!'

EMERGENCY

During the Second World War, the Galway Blazers were kept going after their three male Masters went off to war, and Mollie Cusack-Smith took on the sole Mastership. The wartime years were known in Ireland as 'The Emergency', primarily because alcohol was difficult to get hold of, according to Lady Cusack-Smith.

IRISH PROVERB

A good crack and a drink are three parts of an Irish horse deal.

BIG BOSOMS

Big bosoms are fine on a hen turkey or a woman, but no bloody good on a horse.
Malachy Phelan, famous Irish Vet

ALL INNOCENCE

There was in the Galway field a notorious thruster on his first visit to Ireland. For an hour he rode in the Huntsman's pocket, on occasions being actually ahead of him. At one thick hedge he almost rode over the huntsman. The next fence unseated the thruster and the Huntsman approached the next rather high jump which happened to be hiding a wide stream. He slowed as he approached, calling to the thruster, who had now caught up, 'Take it nice and fast, sir.' He gathered his horse for a mighty leap and into the middle of the stream he went. The Huntsman went on to where the stream was narrower, jumped safely over and continued on his way.
After the Hunt, the field all gathered and the Huntsman passed around the welcome drinks. He pressed one on the thruster, who declined saying he'd have to get back to his hotel, as he was soaked to the skin.
'Soaked, sir? To be sure, how did you get wet?' asked the Huntsman innocently.

WINE TASTER

The bar in Galway was crowded with revellers after a fine day's hunting. One of the visiting English foxhunters pompously announced that – even blindfolded – he could identify any wine they could produce.
The Irish Master glanced at him dubiously but took up the challenge for £10. A dark handkerchief was placed over his eyes and glasses of wine were poured and lined up on the table.
'Chateau Neuf de Pape 1978.' he announced.
'Neirstiener 1982. Cotes de Rhone 1985.' And he was always right.
Finally someone handed him a glass he couldn't identify.
He sipped, sipped, then sipped again. Then, with an oath, he spat it out and pulled off the blindfold.
'Dammit, Master. This isn't wine – This is urine. Just plain old pee!'
'Yes,' said the Master with a smile. 'But WHOSE is it?'

THICK

The Irish foxhunter came home early one day from hunting and found his wife in bed with his best friend.
'Hey, Sean, what do you think you're doing?' he asked.
'See,' the wife said to the man beside her. 'I told you he was thick!'

LOST LIMB

A well-known Master in Limerick was justly famous for his hospitality towards visiting English foxhunters. Unfortunately he also suffered from two afflictions – a wooden leg and an unfortunate thirst. He would often awake after a days hunting and a night of revelry and be unable to recall where he had left his leg the previous evening.

OLD IRISH SAYING

Fear runs down the reins.

LOST.........

The late and much missed Monty Shine once took a party of friends to Ireland. He was well known for his ability to get himself lost, and this trip was no exception. Having gone down the same lane three times, his wife Jo suggested they ask someone for directions. Eventually they found an old Irishman.
" Which way to Eniscorthy?" he was asked. " I'm not sure, sir," he replied.
" Well, how do we get there?" " I'm not all that sure," replied the old man. " You see, sir, if I was going to Eniscorthy, I wouldn't be starting out from here!"

GOOD IN TRAFFIC?

On one of my frequent visits to Ireland, I was staying with Boodley, the late Lady Daresbury. We were out riding two 4-year olds who had been broken only a few days before and we came to a stationary donkey-cart. We managed to persuade our horses to sidle gingerly past the empty cart. I could see they were both nervous but Boodley turned to me proudly and exclaimed: 'See, they're fine in traffic!'

Contributed by Ulrica Murray Smith, the Quorn.

BANKING RIGHTS

One day out hunting in the bank country of Limerick, I told Boodley I didn't know how to cope with banks. She said, 'Leave the horse alone. He knows what to do. Hold on to his mane.'
I did as I was told and the horse jumped the ditch on to the bank beautifully but then went sideways across on to the bank, knocking Lord Harrington, the Field Master, off his mount! He took it very well but suggested I jump the next bank on my own!

Contributed by Ulrica Murray Smith, the Quorn

HUNTING TALES

The Whissendine from a painting by H. Alken

Book Six

Around the World

Cissy Dove

BOAR HUNTING IN FRANCE

"Zey do not, 'ow you say, canter. Zey are trotters from racing". We looked at each other, Nigel Peel and I, and I detected in his eye a certain gleam which boded ill for ze trotters. In fact, it was a miracle I could detect anything in his eye following the previous night's inspection of the Parisienne night life. Nigel, who was then Joint-Master of the ponderously named Chiddingfold, Leconfield & Cowdray and hunted hounds, had insisted on taking a deep, lengthy and, as he insisted, objective inspection of the delights on offer. The result the next morning as we drove north to the Foret de Compiegne was a trifle unpleasant. I'm sure the oysters were off, though Nigel blamed it on the moules.

The object of our boy's own excursion was to hunt le sanglier, the wild boar, with a certain Rallye whose precise name need not concern us now. I had shot driven boar on numerous occasions and had more than healthy respect for their size, teeth and ability to use them. This, I told Nigel, could be a fascinating day's sport.

We were both kitted out in decent English foxhunter's plumage. Red coats, Nigel in a cap and myself in a topper. The Masters and the field, when we eventually cast up, having lost ourselves in a maze of forest rides, were almost indistinguishable. All wore very long 18th century blue coats, the men were in caps and two ladies wore tricorne hats whilst everyone seemed to carry a hunting horn wrapped round their bodies.

The huntsman, a squat, swarthy individual, was carrying, I observed, a short sword or a rather long bayonet. Either way it looked warlike and impressive.

We discovered that nearly all the horses were ex-trotters from the race tracks and none, quite literally, knew how to canter. As to jumping! We eventually managed by some brilliant horsemanship i.e. whacking them, to get them into a shambling gait which could pass for a canter if you were not too fussy and once or twice we even jumped, or rather fell over, a tiny fallen tree. "Ah, you Engleesh, you are such crazy jumpers," cried our Gallic companions, and we felt frightfully bucked.

The hounds were a fairly motley crew whose main features seemed to be length of limb which seemed inordinate and a tendency to wander off and do their own thing. The first hour was spent rounding up stray hounds and a litter of piglets which seemed determined to become bacon sandwiches, but at last a boar of huntable proportions was roused and with a wild cry from the hounds and the huntsman we were off.

For the next 45 minutes we trotted flat out to keep up with the fleeing pig and its pursuers. Fortunately the forest is well provided with tracks and the only hazard was to keep in touch. However, as the field would stop from time to time to perform a short concerto on the horns this presented little difficulty.

At last hounds brought the wretched boar to bay, the huntsman leapt off his sweating horse and strode amongst the baying pack, whacking them aside as he drew his sword with a flourish. With no hesitation he drove the blade between the boar's shoulder blades. In theory the pig should have keeled over; in practice it squealed and took off with the bayonet sticking out of it.

I will not go into details. Suffice to say that for the next minute or so the air was filled with Gallic oaths, the howling of hounds and shrieking of the pig. At last the final rites were delivered and we stood back and glanced at each other in some wonder. After this, we agreed, foxhunting will never be quite the same!

Contributed by Tony Jackson, publisher of The Hunting Handbook

GETTING AWAY

We turned the bend of the wood, to see the hunt streaming down a long slope. I had a glimpse of blue distances before I turned my attention to the curbing of my mare. I had made up my mind to follow Mr. Coalville as best as I could, but it was with difficulty I could keep Cantilever from getting ahead. My arms ached; my fingers were numb. The mare made that noise that the Bible translates as "Ha, ha!" and bounded on. It was downhill, and all were converging towards a single gateway. I could no longer hold Cantilever. I saw disaster ahead, and resigned myself. I understood then the intoxication of the Gadarene swine in rushing down a steep place into the sea. I did not care what happened.

The gateway was a stampede of horses. Somebody in a pink coat went crashing through the hedge to the right with a catastrophic din. Horses squeezed me on either side. Stirrups clanked against mine. Hosts were behind, indicated by fierce panting breath and squelching mud. Cantilever's nose was against the warning red ribbon on another's tail; but that was nothing to me know. Somebody said, "Big dog fox, going like smoke." Suddenly the pressure on either side of me relaxed. We were through the gateway. Cantilever started to gallop again. Where now? I looked round, but saw no sign of Mr. Coalville. I was careering along a tarred road. I had been taught that one should never canter on a hard road, and tried to pull Cantilever to a trot. In vain. At least half the Hunt was galloping ahead; others were mounting a slope to the right. A man in front of me swerved his horse to the hedge and jumped it cleanly. I wondered, should I do that? I thought, not yet. So many were keeping to the road that there could be no dishonour in it.

We dashed through a village street with a terrific clatter. Women stood in doorways, children clung to mothers' skirts; at the inn, mugs paused half-way to mouths. The good news from Ghent to Aix; yes, that was it. Cantilever's hoofs between the houses begot echoes of a more heroic purpose than the chasing of a fox.

Ahead, a gate was being held open by a yokel, and the hunt was streaming through. A man in a pink coat paused in passing to press money into his hand. Sign of hounds and huntsmen there was none, but I was surprised to see Mr. Coalville standing just inside the gateway watching the others go through, as though they were so many sheep he was counting. I thought he was far behind. His face lit up on the sight of me, and he cantered on alongside.

"I was wondering if you were all right," he said.

Extracted from 'Corduroy' by Adrian Bell

HUNTING DOWN UNDER

Having just returned from three wonderful years in Australia, nailed my Akubra and Drizabone to the shed, dusted off my English hunting coat and rejoined the Pytchley, I shouldn't have been surprised by the number of questions I've been asked . . . "Do they really hunt out there?" . . . is a typical starter, quickly followed by "What?" and "How?" I will try to give a flavour of the hunting scene "Down Under", which has, incidentally, more similarities with our own sport than differences – so settle down, pour yourself a coffee or something stronger, and I'll try to make this painless.

Let me begin . . . . . Yes, they do hunt in Australia, primarily around Sydney, Melbourne and Victoria. As I spent my three years in the Sydney area I was fortunate enough to hunt with three of the five Sydney packs. We hunt foxes and there are lots of them. They were introduced from England at the turn of the century and Charlie has clearly relished the sea, sand and sun, and has bred accordingly.

A major difference in the hunting in Australia is that no earths are 'stopped' for the simple reason that the countryside is too big and it would take too long. So Charlie tends to run us around for a while, and then, once bored, heads for safety. The odds are definitely in his favour, except when he heads away from the protection of coverts and finds he's heading into open territory. The chase is then often long and furious. Kangaroos are occasionally 'put up' but must be left alone and Hounds are considered to be "rioting" if they do anything but allow the surprised Roo to disappear over the horizon at a great rate of knots.

Our hunts take place on Sundays and Wednesdays and the season runs from late March to early September, the Aussie winter. A typical 'field' will consist of about 60 followers, although opening and closing meets attract over a hundred. Hounds are all from British stock and are similar in conformation to our own.

The typical horse seen out hunting is an Australian thoroughbred. He is around 15.3 - 16hh, light boned and in all other ways similar to our own thoroughbreds. The racing industry provides the large percentage of Australian horses and they are inexpensive if bought 'off the track'. Additionally, the Australian stock horse can be seen; he is of similar height to the thoroughbred but tougher and wirier – what he loses in speed he makes up in stamina, and is normally a "real good sort'.

The field, in the Aussie fashion, is much more relaxed than our own, but they are encouraged to follow correct dress patterns. Whilst to many Australians this is difficult to comprehend, the majority comply. Each hunt has a nucleus of committed hunt enthusiasts who work hard at setting an example and introducing more people to the sport. Collars are awarded in a similar manner to the Pytchley, so red coats add colour and character to the Australian hunting scene. Horses are plaited and shined, and typically we would hunt nine or ten couple of Hounds. There will be a huntsman and whipper-in to show Hounds to their best advantage and, of course, the master to organise the field.

The meet is at 8.30 am with the master calling for Hounds at 9.00 am and with no second horses we will say G'Night (the opposite of G'Day) around 1.00 pm, it is then that Australian hunting comes into its own, and they beat us hands down. Because we all finish together, we all head back to the lorries - hose and feed the horses - turn them out in nearby paddocks and the Barbie (Australian for Bar-B-Q) takes over. A significant part of everyone's hunting gear is the Esky. This is a mobile fridge to keep the beer cold and the steaks in good shape. By the time the horses are looked after, the Barbies are alight, the first ice cold golden nectar slips easily over the tonsils, meat begins to cook and, at that point, as the Aussies would say, "You wouldn't be dead for quids". It's a chance to sit around talking about every fox put up, every jump, every horse and especially about every fall! A great way to end the day.

There are five Hunt Clubs in the Sydney area, varying in size, and typically they would hunt a 10,000 acre property. If the property has been hunted for a number of years it will have been "capped" (not the sort that makes our secretary smile), but a wooden cap that allows the wire to be jumped. (In New Zealand they don't bother to "cap" and jump wire, but Australians find that as hard to believe as you do). Wooden fences will have been built and the field master will do his best to keep the field amused, moving and under control (with respect to my Australian friends, that, as they say "ain't always easy").

Whilst we hunt in winter, the weather is invariably good, clear blue skies and not dissimilar to a pleasant English summer day. There will be a chill as we prepare for the day, the stirrup cup will be welcomed and the day will get warmer throughout the morning and by mid-day, with the sun at its highest, we will have developed that wonderful thirst already mentioned.

Having hunted with three packs, all different in styles and objectives, it is difficult to generalise. The McArthy Hunt, south of Sydney in the Narellen area, is small and is all about Hounds working. Small fields, never more than 20, follow Hounds closely and the day is about them and Charlie. The Sydney Hunt Club, the founder and largest of the Sydney hunts, has the biggest 'field', the most relaxed approach and the largest pack of Hounds, hunting with between twelve and fifteen couple. There are lots of jumps and a well established central committee. The third is Hunter Valley, situated two and a half hours north of Sydney in the wine production centre of New South Wales. Here we hunt in glorious, lush countryside, where we hunt around and through vineyards which lie over every hill. On a tired horse you are sure you are never more than twenty minutes from a cool Chardonnay.

Because of the early start on Sunday and the lengthy drive (well, lengthy to us Poms, its "just down the road" to the Aussie), most of the Sydney-siders head for the Hunt Bungalow situated in the heart of the Hunter Valley on the Saturday afternoon. The "Bungie" is a small, single storied house with about 10 acres which becomes the central point for the weekend. Horse floats (trailers to us Poms) surround the area and the paddocks fill up with horses. As it's only 400 yards from the kennels it is the perfect meeting point for everyone. Overnight the adventurous camp, in and around the Bungalow, whilst the rest of us check into local motels. Everyone, however, turns up to burn steaks, drink beer and tell stories until the small hours, a good start for the day's hunting that will soon follow.

The Australian hunt scene is about more than a day's hunting. This is taken seriously - but to the Aussie hunt enthusiast you can't separate the fun and the beer from the hunt. They are all part of 'the day'. To a newcomer, the fields are friendly, curious about you and very anxious that everyone has a good day, enjoys it and returns.

It is great to be back with the Pytchley, the lush grounds, beautiful countryside, great jumps and magnificent Hounds, but I do miss that raging thirst and that first . . . wonderful . . . not-to-be-hurried . . . . . glorious . . . . . ice-cold beer.

Derek Loud - Pytchley, 1992
Reprinted with kind permission of the 'Pytchley Echo'.

A DINNER GIVEN TO COLONEL J. G. LOWTHER BY 'THE GENTLEMEN OF THE WHITE COLLAR' AT ALTHORP ON APRIL 22ND 1960 ON HIS RETIREMENT FROM THE JOINT MASTERSHIP OF THE PYTCHLEY HOUNDS (1923-40, 1949-60).

1. Colonel J. G. Lowther, CBE, DSO, MC, MFH
2. Earl Spencer
3. Major R. N. Macdonald-Buchanan, CVO, MBE, MC
4. Captain G. H. Lowther, MFH
5. Lord Cromwell, DSO, MC
6. Viscount Wimborne
7. Lt.-Colonel T. A. Thornton, CVO
8. Lord Braye
9. ? Lionel Ho... E. F. Wyndham, MC

21. T. P. D. Spens, Esq.
22. D. L. Barratt, Esq.
23. W. V. Cross, Esq.
24. T. Gibbs, Esq.
25. G. H. Spencer, Esq.
26. Major J. K. Maxwell, MC
27. Lt.-Colonel T. G. Boardman, MC
28. Major P. W. Cripps
29. Major P. Blet... Brown

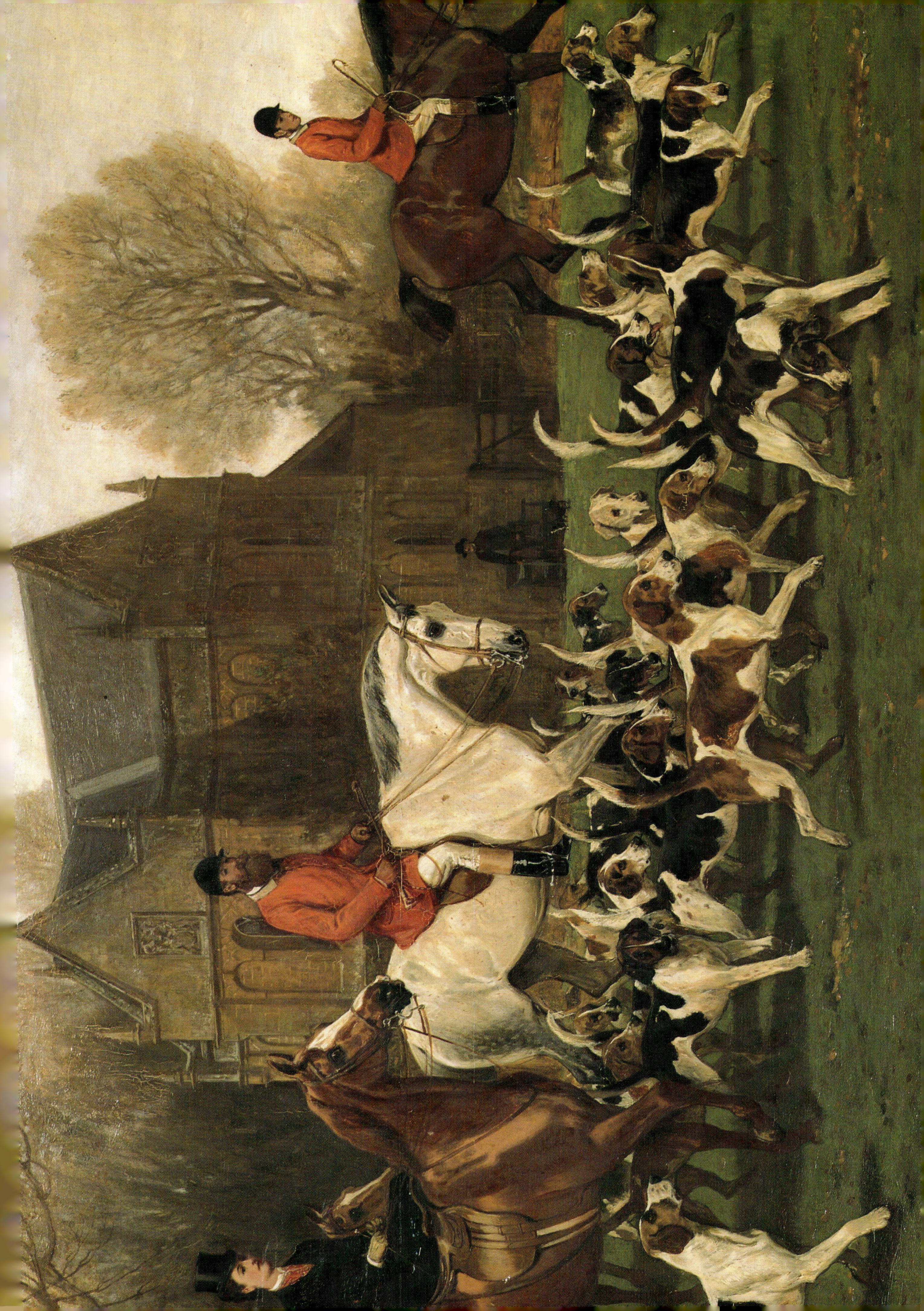

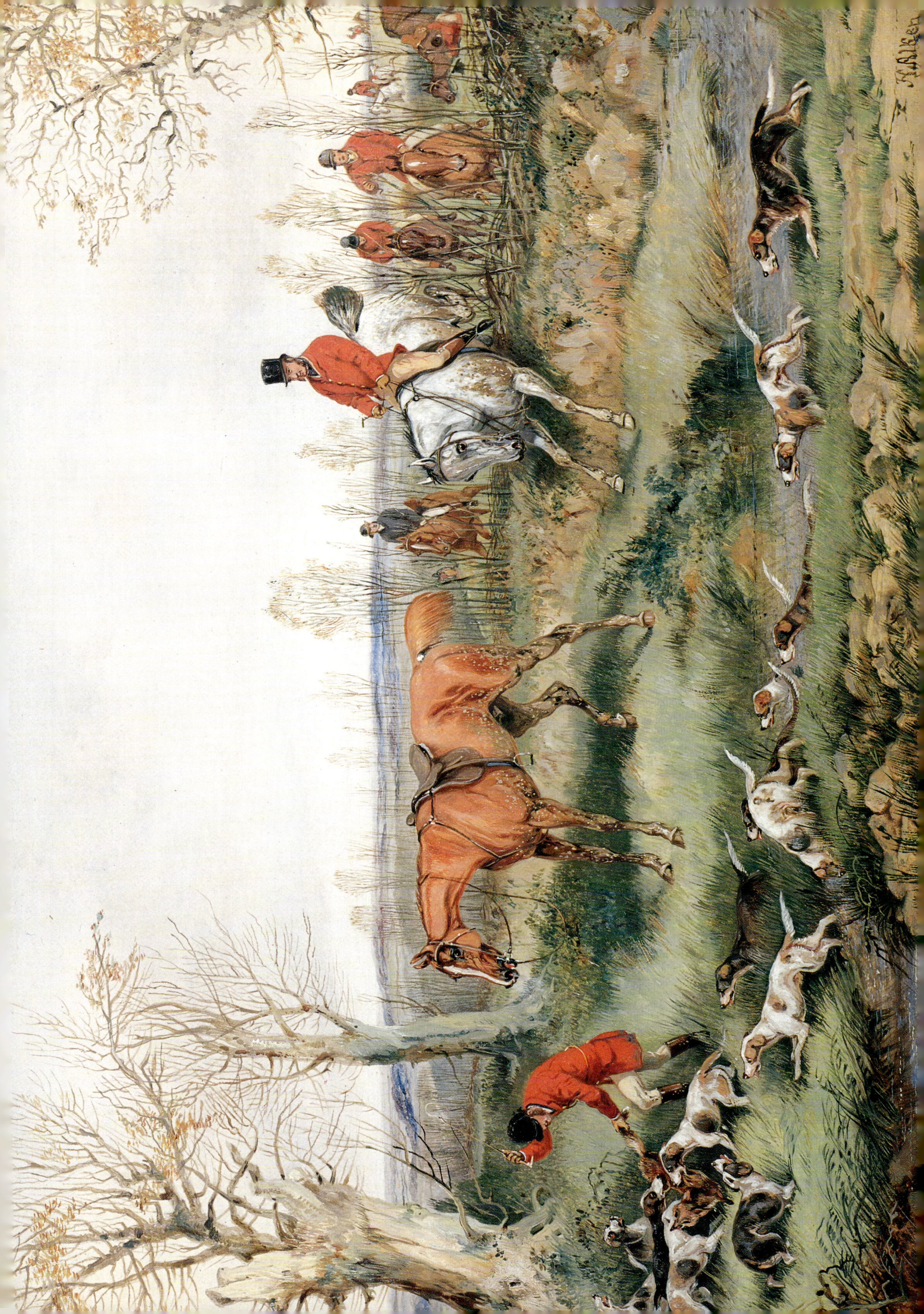

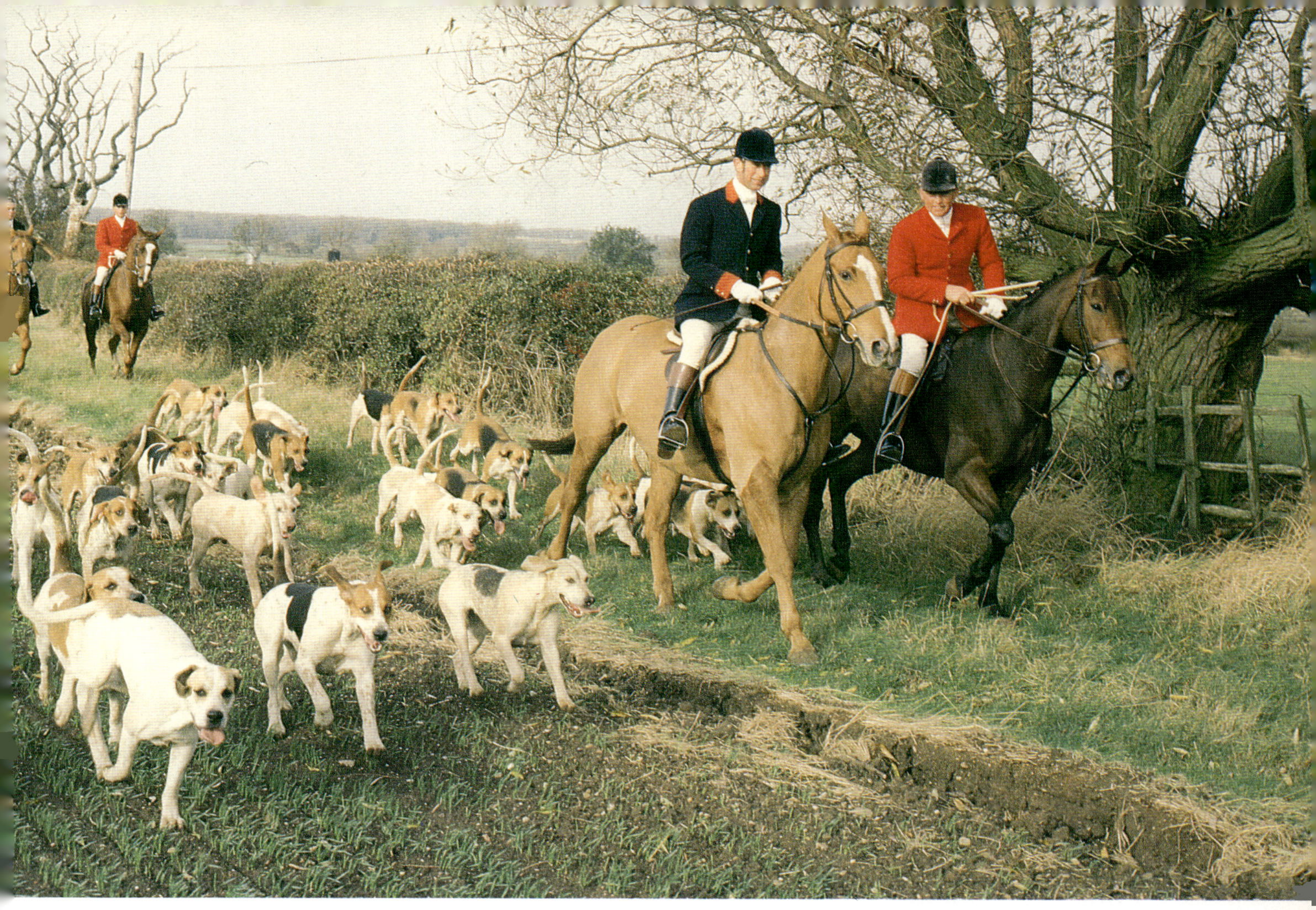

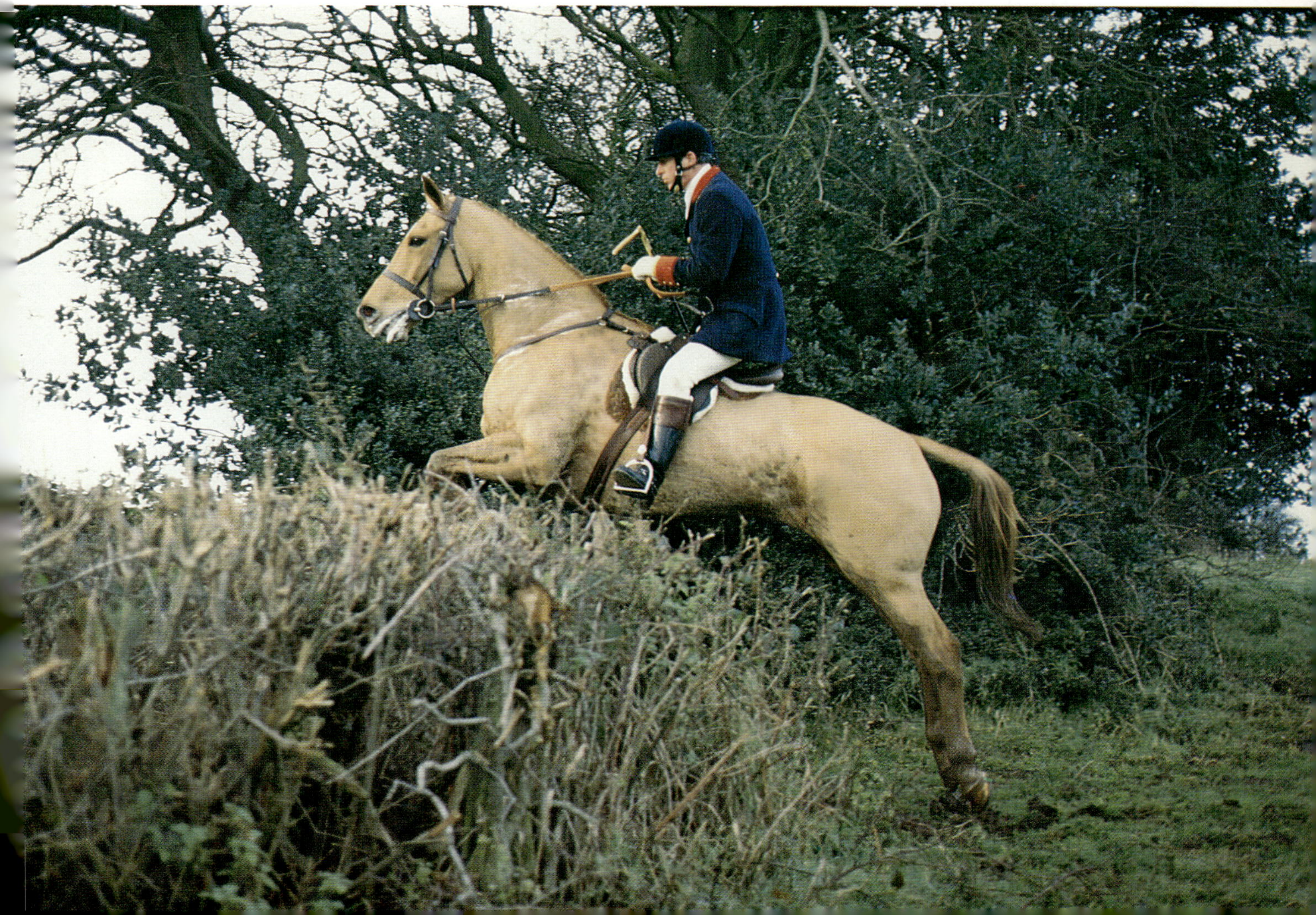

HUNTING TALES

ROMAN FOXHOUNDS

On a warm November morning of last year, bedecked in a heavy black hunting coat with whip and bowler on lap, I watched my host for the weekend negotiate the heavy Saturday morning traffic that clogged the Piazza Venezia. Lumbering on past the Coliseum, cars hooting, my silly preconceived notions that a large horse box was not an ideal city conveyance were fast evaporating. It held a certain weight of authority on the seemingly lawless Roman roads.

My host and driver, the Conte Cavazza-Borghese, Master of Roman Foxhounds, was explaining the past history of his unique pack. They were started in 1850 by an Englishman, Lord Petersfield, while in attendance to his wife who was convalescing in the mild climate. Infuriated to be missing a season's sport in the Shires, Lord Petersfield on casting his eyes over the rolling Roman hills realised its potential as good hunting country. Being a man of action and fortune, he immediately imported from England one pack of foxhounds, one huntsman and one whipper-in. Setting up kennels on the Appian Way, his sole remaining need was for a field to admire the sport he would undoubtedly show.

Initially viewed with much skepticism and probably even distaste by the young Roman aristocracy, they soon started coming out for a laugh. By the end of the season they were hooked on the sport and the clothes that it entailed. On Lord Peterfield's return to England and the Mastership of the Pytchley, the hunt continued under the auspices of the Romans themselves. Despite various setbacks, it has flourished ever since. Pope Pius IX actually tried to ban the hunt due to a spate of accidents culminating in the death of a young English visitor. The hunt committee solved the difficulty by knocking a hole in every single hedge or wall that would be conceivably jumped that season.

As we approached the meet I asked my host what sort of a day we could expect. Formello, I was told, was awkward, thickly wooded country, difficult to get "Charlie" to break cover. Added to the warm weather and prevailing drought which had wrecked havoc not only on the scenting conditions, but also on the crops, he suspected that the days sport would not be memorable. I, on the other hand, was really too consumed with interest to worry over such trifling matters. (Secretly, indeed perhaps relieved that my own sporting skills were not going to be called into too much question).

The meet itself was a singular affair by British standards. No village children to welcome the hounds, or foot followers knowing better than any mounted follower in which direction the hounds would run. It was a strictly private affair. But then hunting operates in a very different manner from the British hunts, in so much as it remains extremely elitist. There are no Hunt Supporters' Associations, no foot or car followers and this is undoubtedly to its detriment. It remains a perfectly preserved example of what the small privately owned hunts in England must have been like a hundred years ago. An inconvenience to the local farmer and beyond the aspirations of many would be followers. Perhaps it lacks the tradition and the satisfactory sense of continuity and conservation that a village meet provides here. But how could it? This is not a traditional Italian sport, merely an isolated import that has changed and evolved to suit its own needs and requirements.

We moved off promptly at eleven, across the Rome-Formello road and down a track to the first covert. With the field nearly chocking to death in the dust I was told there had been no serious rain for two years. Count Cavazza-Borghese was absolutely correct in his prediction. It was not a good day. Absolutely beautiful woodland to ride through, but without the merest trace of scent. Home was blown at 3.30 for which I was quite thankful. Feeling dirty and sweaty and with a badly sunburnt face we returned to Formello for the serious business of the day – Lunch.

My second day out was very different. Being the closing meet of the season, it was traditionally held at Pantone-Borghese. I was lent a horse by the Marchese Vicenzo Lepri (an ex-master) and was warned that things would hot up considerably. We drew the banks of an ancient Roman aqueduct, from which a fox broke immediately. With hounds in hot pursuit, the speed was ferocious. With my arms being tugged out of their sockets and leaping obstacles I would sooner have avoided, we crossed the length of Pantone-Borghese before the fox went to ground. From there we moved onto an archaeological dig and drew a recently excavated Roman village. Again, we found a fox and took a line of a tributary road to the Old Appian Way. He went to ground after a good run of about half an hour.

The physical difficulties they face are so much more pressing than our own. The beautiful countryside surrounding Rome is being lost daily by indiscriminate building that ignores all planning regulations. Foxes themselves are in short supply due to the "Rights of the Hunter" (poacher's rights? EC take note) that allows anyone to carry a gun for hunting purposes, to go wherever he likes and to shoot whatever he likes. But, however difficult the circumstances, the Roman Hunt sure do know how to enjoy themselves and I fervently hope that they continue to flourish. "Buona Caccia"!

Hugh Jolly

OPENING MEET GEORGIA STYLE

For the past 44 seasons I have travelled the world, photographing and writing about hunting and believing that I had seen just about everything! However on one trip to the confederate states of America, a friend said to me in a rich Southern drawl," Boy, until you've been to the opening meet of the Belle Meade Hunt near Augusta, Georgia, you ain't seen nuttin'"

With my interest thus aroused, I quickly made plans with the joint Master and Huntsman, Epp Wilson, in an endeavour to fill this huge gap in my hunting education! Friday departure day dawned and Delta Flight 65 wafted me effortlessly and smoothly from Manchester to Atlanta in Georgia. The fact that the airline kindly upgraded me to Club class only added to the enjoyment.

Swiftly clearing customs and immigration at this most modern of airports, I walked in to the arrivals area where I was met by Jimmy Scherer whose Cadillac saloon covered the 100 or so miles to Epp Wilson's home and horse barn complex in under two hours. Following a quick drink, my host said," Hurry up and get changed as we are expected at a barn dance down the road, the first function of the weekend of the opening meet."

Within 30 minutes of arriving I was at the barn dance, cavorting round the floor with glamorous Southern belles. However this provided me with another first, for the evening had turned so cold that the barn was freezing, and my dance partners wore long coats and gloves! Still, the steaks and barbecue sauce were terrific and the dancing soon warmed us up. Even so it was nice to eventually sit down by a crackling log fire in Epp's lounge and partake of a drink or two, before retiring to bed, 24 hours after leaving my own bed 4000 miles away, back in the Welsh hills!

Next morning was warm and sunny and the first event to attend was a really extravagant Hunt breakfast at the Belle Meade country club. Here hunt members could indulge themselves in any number of delicious goodies, both hot and cold, with waitress service and linen tablecloths. I settled for grits, crispy bacon, kidneys and mushrooms, washed down by that most popular of soft drinks, iced tea. Then it was time to drive to the splendid home of Joint Master Peter Knox, where the opening meet was to be held. Althought we were an hour early, a large crowd had already gathered and the local sheriff and his men were busy controlling both cars and pedestrians. More and more people arrived until there were around 130 mounted riders gathered around the house in its splendid setting amidst a grove of trees which provide shade during the long hot summers.

At the appointed hour, hounds arrived, led by Joint Master and Huntsman Epp Wilson, his wife Sharon and several red-coated whippers-in. A hush descended on the huge gathering as Belle Meade's hunt Chaplain, the Rev. Father Ed Frank, immaculately attired in Hunt uniform, began by blessing the hounds. Then everyone who was to ride to hounds that day came forward to receive a St. Hubert medal, a tradition which began many years ago. I was greatly honoured and delighted to accept one for myself, although I was to hunt on foot.

Once everyone had remounted, hounds moved off, followed by the 130 horses and, what I found absolutely fascinating, more than 25 Tally-Ho wagons,each carrying around 20 people. These Tally-Ho wagons are farm trailers on which have been installed bench seats with cushions and are drawn by tractors or 4WD vehicles, although one was pulled by a traditional pair of heavy horses. Needless to say, everyone on board had brought picnics and drinks, for these Americans just love the outdoor life with a few home comforts thrown in!

Leading this massive convoy was the hunt Founder Master and Huntsman, James Wilson, a much revered foxhunter, who no longer rides but whose son Epp has taken over the horn. Bringing up the rear was one extra large trailer which, to my utter amazement, contained not bench seats, but 12 smart PortaLoos, so that the lady followers could spend a penny in comfort when hounds checked!

It wasn't long before hounds were running and the mounted field were in action jumping coops, which are similar to our " Tiger traps", but are filled with panels. During this hunt I was lucky enough to take a picture of hounds crossing a river below a waterfall, and althought it meant getting wet to the knees, it was well worth while. The country was a mix of open grassland and woods, in fact I don't recall seeing one field of arable all day. Scent was moderate as the ground was very dry, with the winter rains not having started, yet these cross-bred hounds kept things moving fast enough to delight all the followers. At one check, veteran whipper-in Charles Lewis, with the touch of a circus artiste, stood up on his horse's quarters and explained what was happening to the Tally-Ho wagon followers. At another, riders dismounted and champagne was handed round, whilst overhead a passing light aircraft, seeing this vast gathering in the middle of nowhere, put on an impromptu aerobatic display!

Finally it was time to hack back to the kennels. Here, in what I thought was a particularly nice touch, all those riders who were still out, formed an avenue through which passed the Huntsman and hounds, to the cries of "Thanks for a super day's hunting" from the happy field. However the entertainment was by no means over, although it was by now almost dark. Without changing, we all hastened to the Halfway House, a really old place set in its own gardens, and here we indulged in a barbecue party, both in the house and outside. Eventually no-one could eat another burger, hot dog, sausage or chop, to name but a few of the assortment of foods on offer. I for one was pleased to adjourn to Epp Wilson's home where another party was soon under way!

Apart from being a hugely successful PR exercise for the hunt, it is a tremendous way to raise money. For each of these functions, ranging from the Friday night barn dance through to the breakfast; to the riders on the Tally-Ho wagons at $25 each; to the evening barbecue, tickets are sold in advance and money collected. At the end of the Opening meet weekend, the hunt funds were better off by a sum reported to be in excess of $15,000- very different to here in the UK.

Contributed by Jim Meads, one of the world's leading sporting photographers.

HUNTING TALES

THE FIRST FOXHUNT IN URUGUAY

Before separating after "John Peel" had been sung with great enthusiasm, someone proposed that we should get up a foxhunt, in real English style. Everyone agreed, glad of anything, I suppose, to break the monotony of such an existence, and next day we rode out, followed by about twenty dogs, of various breeds and sizes, brought together from all the houses. After some searching about in the most likely places, we at length started a fox from a bed of dark-leafed Mio-mio bushes. He made straight away for a range of hills about three miles distant, and over a beautifully smooth plain, so that we had a very good prospect of running him down. Two of the hunters had provided themselves with horns, which they blew incessantly, while the others all shouted at the top of their lungs, so that our chase was a very noisy one. The fox appeared to understand his danger and to know that his only chance of escape lay in keeping up his strength till refuge of the hills was reached. Suddenly, however, he changed his course, this giving us a great advantage, for by making a short cut we were all soon at his heels, with only the wide level plain before us. But Reynard had his reasons for what he did; he had spied a herd of cattle, and in a very few moments had overtaken and mixed with them. The herd, struck with terror at our shouts and horn blowing, instantly scattered and flew in all directions, so that we were able still to keep our quarry in sight. Far in advance of us the panic in the cattle ran on from herd to herd, swift as light, and we could see them miles away fleeing from us, while their hoarse bellowings and thundering tread came borne by the wind faintly to our ears. Our fat lazy dogs ran no faster than our horses, but still they laboured on, cheered by incessant shouts, and at last ran into the first fox ever properly hunted in the Banda Oriental.

Extracted from 'The Purple Land' by W. H. Hudson (1901)

RUSSIA
1807 – 1812

The count, still smiling over Sémione's last speech, sat gazing into the distance with his snuff-box open in his hand, without thinking of taking a pinch. Danilo's horn warned them that they had caught sight of a wolf; the packs followed close to the three bloodhounds, and all gave tongue in the manner peculiar to a wolf hunt. The dog-keepers now only shouted encouragement. Above all other voices and cries Danilo's was distinctly heard, passing from the deepest bass to the shrillest yell, and loud enough by itself to ring through the wood and far across the country with its cheering call.

The count and his squire soon perceived that the pack had been divided; one half, barking vociferously, was becoming more distant and the others, driven by Danilo, were breaking through the wood at a few paces from where they were posted; presently the direction of the noise told them that the hunt was moving further afield. Sémione sighed and slipped one of the dogs; the count, too, sighed, and his attention reverting to his snuff-box, he opened it and took a pinch.

"Back!" cried Sémione at this instant to one of the dogs that was struggling to make for the open. The count was startled and let his snuff-box fall. Nastacia dismounted and picked it up.

Suddenly—as will happen occasionally—the hunt was coming their way; all those yelping, baying throats seemed to be close in front of them—upon them!

The count looked to the right and caught sight of Mitka, who, with his eyes starting out of his head, was signalling to him with his cap to look at something in the opposite direction. "Your game!" he shouted in a voice that was all the louder for long suppression; and slipping the dogs, he rode up at full gallop.

The count and Sémione rushed out of the wood, and, on their left, saw the wolf coming towards them at a swinging trot, with easy bounds and no appearance of hurry. The excited dogs tore themselves free, and flung themselves on his track.

The brute paused, turned his heavy head to look at them, with the deliberate awkwardness of a man suffering from angina, then, cocking his tail, went on his way and in two leaps vanished in the thicket. At the same moment, from the opposite skirt of the plantation, out came a dog, then another; then the whole pack, astray and puzzled, crossed the clearing in pursuit of the game, and Danilo's chestnut, covered in foam, came pushing his way between the nut-trees. The rider, bending as low as he could, and bareheaded, his grey hair all on end, his face red and streaming, was shouting till his voice cracked to rally the dogs. But when he saw the count his eyes flashed fire. He threatened him with his whip, roaring out a thundering oath: "Devil take such hunters. . . . To have let the game slip! . . ."

Judging, no doubt, that his master, who looked quite scared, was unworthy of further comment, he let the blow that had been meant for the count fall on the quivering and steaming flank of his innocent steed, and disappeared among the trees after the hounds. The count, taken aback by this audacious scolding, tried to smile, and turned to Sémione with a look of pathetic appeal. But Sémione was gone too. Riding in and out of the brushwood he was trying to start the wolf again, and the greyhounds, too, were working right and left; but the beast sneaked off through the cover and was soon lost to their ken.

Nicholas, expecting every minute to see the wolf pass, had not left his post; and as he heard the cry—sometimes near and sometimes far—and the different bark of the hounds under various circumstances, when the shouts and yelping were at their height, he could form a good idea of what was happening. He understood that there must be two old wolves in the plantation with their cubs; and he instinctively felt that some bad luck had come in the way. Then he invented a thousand theories, and tried to calculate which side the game would come from, and how he would finish it—but nothing came. His hopes turned to despair; he even found himself praying—entreating providence—as we do under stress of some feeling, even while owning to ourselves the triviality of the object prayed for.

He strained his eyes to mark the slightest movement, and his ear to catch the faintest change of tone in the dogs' cry. Presently, as he glanced again to the right, he saw something come leaping towards him, across the open ground. "Is it possible!"—he could scarcely breathe in the agitation of seeing his hopes on the eve of fulfilment; and this piece of good fortune, so hoped for and despaired of, was coming straight down upon him, noiselessly, with no preliminary fuss or warning. He could hardly believe his eyes, but soon it was beyond a doubt. It was the wolf, and no mistake—an old wolf, with a grey coat and russet belly, trotting at his ease, safe from pursuit, striding heavily across ridge and furrow.

Rostow, holding his breath, looked at his dogs: some were lying down, others standing by, but none had seen the game—not even old Karaë, who, with his head thrown back and his muzzle half-open, showing his yellow teeth, clattered his jaws while he hunted the fleas on his hind-leg. "Up, dogs! Wolf!" said Rostow in a low voice. The dogs pricked up their ears, and Karaë, ceasing his search, started up as if he moved by a spring, wagging his tail, and shedding a few tufts of hair.

"Shall I slip the leash?" said Nicholas to himself.

The wolf, quitting the cover, was coming on a direct line, suspecting nothing. Suddenly he checked himself: He had just seen a man's eyes fixed on him, no doubt—a sight hitherto unknown to his experience. He stood hesitating and seemed to reflect: should he turn back, or go on? "Beware," he seemed to think. He started again with apparent indifference, but at a round pace, and went off with long leaps, and without looking behind him.

"At him! Wolf!" shouted Nicholas. His clever bay went off like an arrow, over hedge and rut, to reach the open after the wolf. The hounds, swift as lightning, soon out-stripped him. Nicholas, perfectly unconscious of all minor details—of his own shout, of the terrific pace at which he was riding over—saw nothing but the wolf. The brute, without turning to the right or left, went faster and faster, straight for the hollow. Milka, the large brindled hound, was the first to overtake him; nearer and nearer; she was on the point of gripping him when he just cast a side glance at the foe, and Milka, instead of setting her teeth in him, as usual, cocked her tail and stood pointing.

"At him! Wolf!" yelled Nicholas. Liubime, a large red-haired dog, close on Milka's heels, flew at the brute and gripped his haunch, but shrunk off again in alarm. The wolf crouched for an instant, and showed his teeth, then he galloped on again, followed, within a couple of feet, by the dogs who dared not attack him.

"He will escape to a certainty!" thought Nicholas, and he tried to incite the dogs, but his voice was husky; he looked around for his staunch old hound, his only hope, and shouted to him with a vigorous call: "Karaë—Wolf! At him!"

Karaë, with every muscle strained to the utmost his age allowed, was keeping pace side by side with the terrible brute, evidently intending to outrun him, and attack him in front; but Nicholas could see from the swift wiry action of the wild beast, and heavier pace of the dog, that this manœuvre would be frustrated. He saw with horror that the space between the animals and the copse, which would be the salvation of the wolf, was diminishing rapidly; but in a moment his hopes revived, for, beyond the wolf and coming towards him, a huntsman and several dogs were now approaching. One, a dark-coloured hound, unknown to Nicholas, and belonging, no doubt, to a strange pack, flew at the brute, and nearly overthrew him; but he recovered his balance, and attacked the dog with amazing nimbleness, setting his teeth in his flesh; and the hapless aggressor, with a gash in his loins, beat his head on the earth with howls of anguish.

"Karaë! oh, merciful Heaven!" cried Nicholas, in despair.

The wolf, scenting fresh danger from old Karaë—who, now that his foe was checked, barred his way—tucked his tail between his legs, and went off with a bound at a tremendous pace;

but, wonder of wonders! Nicholas saw Karaë suddenly leap on the brute's back and set his teeth in his throat, and then wolf and dog rolled over together, and down into the dell beyond.

The whole pack rushed after them. The sight of the struggling wolf down in the hollow, in the midst of that chaos of heads, where all that appeared of the prey was now and then his dull fur or a kicking hind leg, or his panting muzzle with ears laid back—for Karaë still gripped him by the throat—was one of the keenest delights Rostow had ever known. He laid his hand on his saddle, and was about to dismount and go down to dispatch the foe, when the brute, shaking his great head free above the dogs, sat upon his haunches; then, showing his teeth, with a whisk of his tail, he leaped up and was out of reach in an instant. Karaë, either wounded or bruised, and with his hair on end, dragged himself with difficulty out of the ravine into which he had fallen with the wolf.

"Oh! what a grievous pity!" cried Nicholas in despair.

Fortunately the little uncle's huntsman, followed by his dogs, was ready to fly off at a gallop after the fugitive and intercept him in time. He was again surrounded; Nicholas, his groom, and the little uncle with his huntsman, all prancing round him, shouting: "At him! Wolf!" prepared, whenever he crouched, to jump off their horses, and riding forward to circumvent him each time he pulled himself together to make a rush for the thicket, which was his last and only chance for life.

At the very beginning Danilo had come tearing out of the plantation, and, looking on at the struggle, had taken the victory for granted; but seeing the brute make good his escape, he rode off in a straight line to the copse to cut off his retreat, and, thanks to this manœuvre, came up with him just as the little uncle's pack once more held him at bay. Danilo rode up without a word, his bare knife in his left hand, while he flogged his bay with his huntsman's whip as if it had been a flail, till the foam lay in streaks on his reeking flanks. He flew past Nicholas, and the next instant Rostow heard a heavy fall; it was Danilo, who had thrown himself on the wolf's haunches and seized him by the ears. They all— even the wolf—knew this was the finish. The foe made a final effort to free himself, but the dogs held him fast. Danilo rose and then again dropped with all his weight on the brute, still gripping him by the ears. Nicholas went forward to stab the panting beast.

"No need for that," said Danilo. "We will put a bit between his teeth!" He set foot on the wolf's throat, and forced a short thick stake between his tightly-set jaws; then the men tied his legs, and Danilo took the brute on his broad shoulders.

Tired, but triumphant, all helped to tie the wolf on the back of Danilo's horse, which stood quivering with alarm, and he was carried off to the rendezvous of the hunt, followed by all the dogs in full cry. Everyone came up to examine the victim, whose great, square head hung down from the weight of the stake in his jaws, while his glassy eyes glared at the crowd of dogs and men. His limbs trembled at every touch. Count Ilia Andréïévitch came up with the rest: "Ah! an old one! It is an old one, is not it?" he said to Danilo.

"Certainly, an old one," said Danilo, taking his cap off respectfully.

"Do you know you were in a terrible rage just now?"

Danilo did not reply, but he smiled with the embarrassed shy look of a spoilt child.

Extract from 'War and Peace' by Leo Tolstoy (1828-1910)

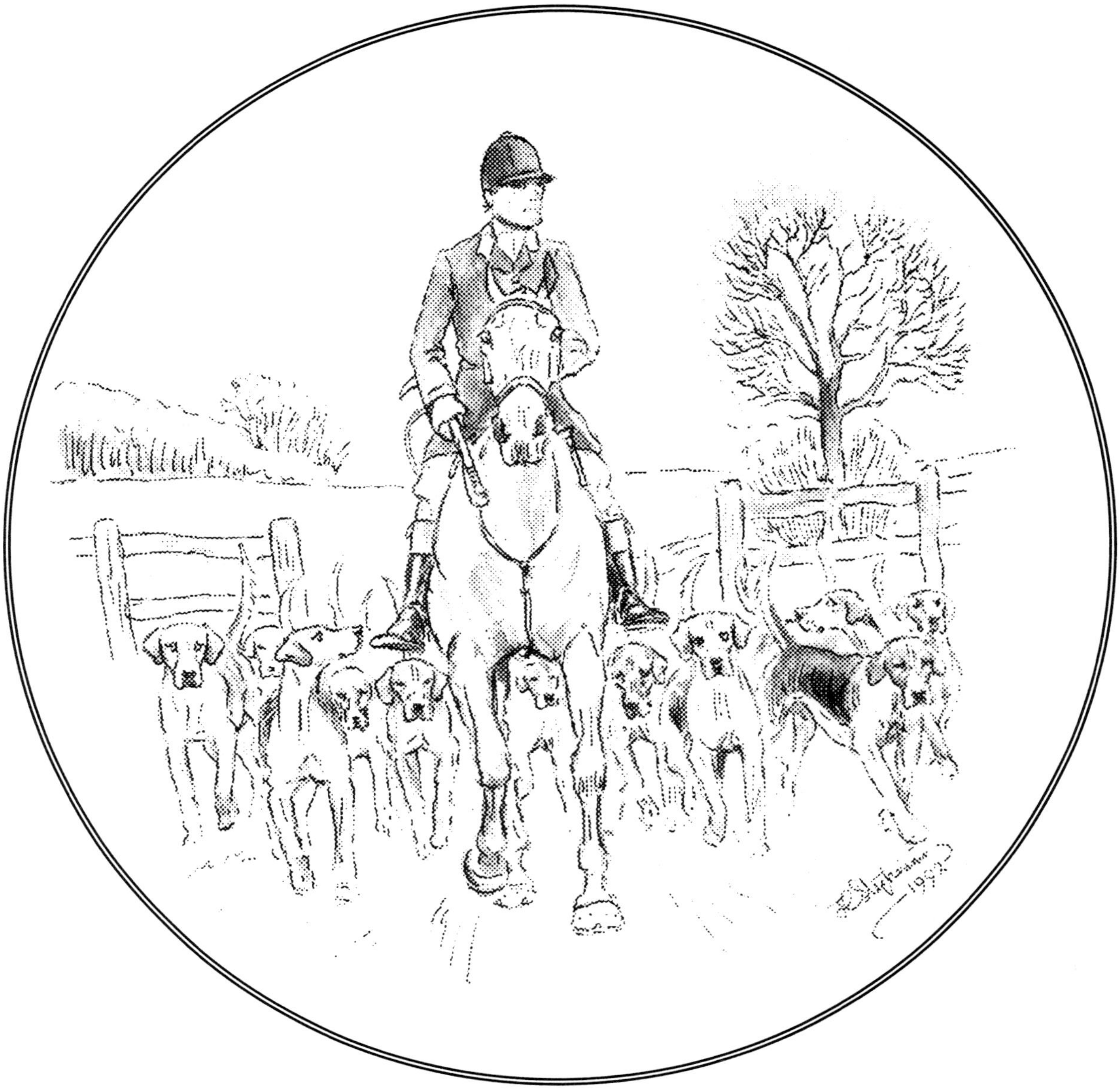

Emma Ann Mortimer

Book Seven

Tail-end pieces

Selected writings on riding and hunting

HUNTING ADVICE FROM "FOXDITCH"
(Correspondent with the "HORSE AND HUNTING DOG".)

So you have made your pile, and you want to hunt with the Pytchley (pronounced Pie-jelly after I believe a well known baking powder benefactor in the hunt).

First of all look down the housing and land columns for sale in the local papers. Find preferably fifty or more acres in the hunt area which can be found out by ringing up the foot follower's secretary and purchasing a hunt map. Fifty acres plus is a magic figure, as now you are retiring from business you can do what everyone else does and become a farmer. In so doing a subscription does not have to be paid, so it's a good form of investment, although you must join B.U.P.A. as broken bones are sure to follow, (contact Mrs. Christina McKenzie for advice on this score).

I don't expect your land will have a house on it as farmers are selling off all their houses, barns and cottages to pay off their overdrafts, Lloyds debts, falling share prices and mistresses. But don't despair, all you have to do is shove up a few sheds, fill them with rabbits, chickens, calves, goats or llamas, dig a hole and stick a few trout in and before you know it the planning officer will be round to see where you want to build your palatial home and stables.

Now you are a Country Gentleman, all the benefits will follow. The Tories are gradually stopping the loopholes but you can still reclaim the VAT on your Land Rover that is going to pull your horse trailer, and if you can convince the taxman that your gelding is used for business, numerous allowances follow.

Grants and subsidies have really been jumped on but if you play your cards right you can get help with the swimming pool, just remember to call it a slurry lagoon. Another good idea is the government scheme to help hunting called "set aside", where a farmer is paid to grow ragwort and thistles which are getting very popular in Northamptonshire.

The next step is a horse. A Mr. Dick Saunders may be able to help you, but beware of ex-racehorses as they are usually clapped out or flatten out when jumping barbed wire. So go for something with a bit of bone to deal with some of the wet clay you will come across. You won't be hunting the wilds of Wales or Exmoor so dress is quite important. This means a visit to a reputable horsey store, where you and the wife will be fitted with everything needed from a no bounce bra to a Kite Standard hat, with or without the new fangled attachments.

The big day arrives and you are off to your first meet. Being new to the area you are going to have problems where to go, as on your meet card you will just have the name of a farm or public house, and that is part of the fun, to discover where it is. It is a cardinal sin to park within a mile of the meet – so beware. A piece of advice is to look out for cars and lorries with unusual registration numbers such as 3BIX, SEX1E, MFH4, MCNZI, W1SKE and BOR1C. You must know who is who in the hunting field. For starters, there are four masters. After bidding them good day, avoid like the plague because being a new boy you will most likely be blamed for everything from letting cattle out, breaking rails, or parking on someone's lawn. So make sure that when you say "good night" you have your check book in your pocket.

In charge of the dogs, who you will now call hounds, is the huntsman, a cheerful fellow called Peter Jones who is bound to be on good behaviour because he is after a long service gold watch. Don't worry too much about him as you will most probably only see his backview in the distance and hear him blow his top or trumpet. He's usually helped by two whipper-ins who will keep coming up to you and say "where's he gone"? meaning the huntsman or fox, so make sure you get your facts right or the day's hunting will be confusion. Hunting is a stop and go affair, so brush up your facts such as the stock market, property developing, page three girls, latest cattle and sheep prices to keep conversation going during one of these stops.

Next on the list are the foot followers who come out for a number of reasons – walking their dogs, bird watching (both sorts), see how many foxes they can head in a day (I think the record is seven), getting away from the wife (I should know) – but they really do a great job supporting the hunt and raising a great amount of much needed cash.

Enjoy your hunting and remember when you are galloping over someone's freshly planted corn that they could be over your acres in the near future. If the huntsman approaches you and says "would you like to walk a couple of puppies" be warned, it is the quickest way to divorce, the little varmints have washing off the line, chase the neighbours cat and pinch the Sunday joint; on the other hand you are not plagued by commercial travellers as they have only to jump up and scratch their cars once and they won't call again. You will make a lot of friends (and a few enemies) out hunting, hear a great deal of gossip, no doubt some about yourself, and take care, there is usually a baby boom the following summer after the hunt ball. If you survive the season's hunting and still want to cash in on your medical insurance, there is always the point-to-point in the Spring.

Good hunting.

Foxditch

THE COMMANDMENTS

according to

A WELL KNOWN HUNT SUPPORTERS ASSOCIATION 1994

1. Thou shalt not follow the Field Master, this is dangerous and hypocritical.

2. Thou shalt not gallop in an irresponsible manner through stock or over sown land except on hunting days.

3. Thou shalt never go first; this is the prerogative of the fox.

4. Thou shalt always wear clean underwear and endeavour to go home in the same condition.

5. Thou shalt not let thine horse kick out at other horses or hounds. If this should happen, please dismount, cut of the offending hoof and feed it to hounds.

6. Thou shalt endeavour to attend all cancelled Meets. This is an old tradition of the Hunt and enjoyed by many members. Bring hip-flask with Sloe Gin at all times.

7. Thou shalt not use abusive, insulting or obscene language; selected officials in Padua Red are the only people allowed to do this.

8. Thou shalt not leer, drool or dribble when ladies are straining to open gates; fantasy is not part of the sport.

9. Thou shalt not expose thyself to females while pretending to have a pee, this privilege is strictly reserved for Masters only.

10. Thou shalt remind thyself that Joint Masters are a religion unto themselves and are above God at all times.

NOTES ON THE OAKLEY

These are extracted from a manuscript in the handwriting of Samuel Charles Whitbread, and dated 1876. Club Secretary of the Oakley 1824-1845, Whitbread frequently clashed with G. C. G. Berkeley, Master from 1829 to 1834 and their lack of accord almost resulted in a duel on more than one occasion. Berkeley's own term is described vividly in his 'Life and Reminiscences' written around 1854.

The following stories, reports and anecdotes have been kindly provided by the Oakley Hunt from a collection of Harold Bowley and published with their permission. As far as we can tell, they have never been published anywhere until now.

February 16th 1876

(These notes are) dedicated to my old friend William Higgins, a straightforward honest rider, afraid of nothing, yet never getting into scrapes. I ought to have no love for him. For three seasons I was an acknowledged leader, but when Bill Higgins appeared, I was nowhere.

1876. February 16th.

On this day I have completed my eightieth year, and have taken a fancy to put upon record some of the events which I witnessed many years ago with the Oakley Hounds.

My father was a perfect horseman, and the best judge of a horse I have ever known. He took great pains to teach me to be a good horseman, and I may say that I was a very apt scholar. From the time I was twelve years old my father trusted me to ride all his magnificent horses and as they were all fit to carry 16 stone and I weighed 8 or 9 stone, I was completely spoiled and never could ride an indifferent horse in after life.

I will not be answerable for correct dates, even if I venture to give one, as unfortunately I never kept a Hunting Book.

HUNTING TALES

THE LONG RUN

The greatest run on record with any Pack of Fox Hounds took place on Jan. 31st 1815. After a six weeks frost and deep snow the hounds met at Colworth. I was standing at the corner of Lousy-Acre, with Wells and Short the surgeon, when a fine fox came out of the covert and stood quietly before us. He shook himself and Wells said, 'If ever I saw a fox likely to give a run that is the one'.

It was exactly 12 o'clock, and after running 4 hours and 36 miles the hounds ran into him in the middle of Rothwell open field exactly at 4 o'clock when the sun was setting. The first burst was over the best part of Lord Fitzwilliam's country, Stanwick Raunds Meadow. They then turned to Wellingborough when the hounds were taken over a bridge, they were soon on him again and skirted Ingwell Wood and hunting slower and slower came to check in the middle of a wide open field near Market Harboro. Lord Tavistock who thought it was all over trotted by me to tell Wells to give it up and take the hounds home. At that moment there was a halloo in a great distance, and Wells, without waiting for the arrival of his Lordship, went off as fast as his horse could carry him and I after him. We came down to a small Osier bed and the shepherd said the fox went in there 10 minutes ago. Wells put the hounds in and the poor tired fox jumped up in the middle of them, but to his surprise the fox got clear of the hounds and went away again.

He gave the hounds a very sharp burst for 20 minutes, no one really rode this last burst except Charles Hoare, on a chestnut mare, for which Chester offered him 365 guineas the next day, and a man of the name of Scott from London said to be a Tape Dealer and a friend of Newland's. This last burst was a ring which enabled a few of us to get up. The whole party who were in at the death, were Lord Tavistock, Wells, Tom Ball, my brother William on Coppice, myself on Becket, Charles Hoare and Scott, old Monk, old Newland and Short. During the earlier part of the run, Wells upon his famous black horse was galloping up the middle of a large turnip field at Wellingborough, when his horse stood still, Tom Ball was obliged to go to him, and with much grumbling gave up his chestnut horse to him. Later in the day the chestnut stood still, and Tom Ball came up with the black horse quite fresh upon which Wells finished the day. Dick Perkins who was second whip had been sent home on a young horse in the middle of the day. We all left our hunters at Market Harboro, under the care of Tom Ball and rode Post Horses home. Wells took the horses home to Oakley with a post boy as Whipper in. No one doubted that it was the same fox we found at Lousy-Acre. We had no opportunity of changing.

THE FOX AND THE CARTER

I once went away from Hanger Wood, upon Coppice, with a capital scent, and the fox took a new line through a number of small enclosures which even I did not know. Wells was a hundred yards to my left upon his celebrated Timber Jumper, George, (who could not stretch over a moderate ditch). I rode down a steep ploughed field with a small brook at the bottom, which I got safely over. I looked to my left and saw Wells horse jump high in the air, and come straight down in to the bottom of the brook which he exactly fitted. I saw Wells roll over like a ball and jump up, so of course I never stopped. In going up the opposite field, I could not see my way out anywhere and I came to a thick Ash Plantation.

Coppice stepped over the little ditch, and then I dropped my reigns and pulled the tall ash stems wide, and he went through like a cat. The hounds were but a little way before me and away I went with no soul in sight for more than a mile down to the Bedford and Woburn Road when the hounds checked. In three minutes Wells came up, both horse and man blown, and before he attempted to cast the hounds he rode up to me and said "How did you ever get out of that field". The Ash Plantation had pounded him. It was a long time before any of the field came up and when they did Wells had given up all hope of hitting off the line, and well he might, for what do you think became of the fox?

A carter from Emery of Kempston Hardwick (Christ's Hospital Farm) had been early in the morning with a load of corn to Woburn, and was returning with his empty wagon and three horses. The carter was sitting as usual in front, his attention was attracted by the cry of the hounds, and on looking back he saw the fox coming along the road and in one bound he jumped into the tail of the wagon. Much to his credit, the following are his own words, "Oh if you have come to me for protection, I will take care of you". He got back into his wagon and threw some empty sacks over the fox and went on three miles till he came opposite to Kempston Wood when he addressed the fox again. "Now I have saved your life and it is time for you to get out" and kicked him out of the wagon. This is a true story.

THE FOX AND THE LABOURER

The next anecdote may very well follow the preceding one as the finish was equally remarkable.

Major Weyland, a fine horseman and really hard rider who lived at Ickwell Bury called as usual at Cardington on a bitter cold morning, and there Simpson and I joined him. As we were riding through Bedford I remember Weyland saying "What fools we are to come out in this blustering east wind, it is impossible we should have any sport". A fox was found directly in Kempston Wood and the body of the field got away from the eastern end.

Weyland, Fred Hogg, Phillimore, Wells and myself were in the farthest western end. I led them down a good foot path in sight, fully a quarter of a mile on our left, when to our great delight the hounds turned at right angles in a large ploughed field straight to us, we had nothing to do but to wait. The hounds came on at a racing pace, crossed the Kempston and Marston Road and ran inside the hedge of the road that led up to Emery's Farm at Kempston Hardwick.

Then they turned sharp to the left pointing for the Race Course. As soon as we were in the first field out of the road, I saw the hounds running for a very high stile. Weyland and Fred Hogg charged it. I was on Jacob (a horse I brought from that very great swindler Jacob Wardle) and I knew he could not and would not do it, so I rode straight in the moat, plunged out into the middle of the moat, my horse began to crawl out and I was on him again in a moment. Phillimore took advantage of the great hole I had made in the hedge, and his horse did exactly the same as mine and landed in the middle of the moat shooting Phillimore on to the bank, his horse began to crawl out and we began to ride away. I called out to him to catch hold of his bridle, but Phillimore stood shaking all over, allowing his horse to walk by him and then to gallop off, and he never saw the horse again for an hour. In the meantime, Wells who did not like the look of the stile or the moat had galloped off to a gate wide on the right, and we never saw him again.

On coming to the Kempston road there was a deep brook into which I forced my horse, and walked out into the road, there I found Weyland and Hogg high up in the air on this raised stem causeway flogging and I am afraid swearing at Phillimore's horse which stood broadside across a low stile. I could not help laughing at them and finished my ride up to Kempston Wood alone. A great portion of the original field joined us. The fox did not dwell a moment in the Wood but went away on the other side, he took us a good hunting pace over Mount Pleasant to Great Oaks. Fox was dying and could not face the covert, he ran down the last side, and I was the first to get over the hedge at the bottom along with Tom Ball. The hounds who had run down savagely to the hedge flashed into the next field for 50 yards and threw up. I have never forgiven myself for what happened afterwards, and I blame Wells and Tom Ball particularly for of course they had much more experience than myself. We all three ought to have known that the fox was in the hedge and could not possibly be anywhere else. Instead of looking for him there, Wells in this intensely bitter evening went on casting all over the country down to Radwell and Felmersham for two hours till a deep snow came on and the horses feet were balled so that we had the greatest difficulty in getting home. What then really happened was this.

As I rode through the hedge, I nearly rode against a tall old labourer leaning upon a three pronged fork with which he ought to have been swishing. He heard a rustle at his feet, looked down and saw the poor fox creeping through. He up with his fork and with one blow on the head killed him dead. He immediately heard the hounds, got frightened and with his fork pitched the fox on the top of a Pollard Tree.

A QUICK SALE

Having mentioned the name of the great swindler Jacob Wardle in a previous anecdote, I will now relate a story about him which old Monk told me. Jacob was a very strong man of undoubted nerve, or rather had no nerves at all, and he was out in the Vale of Belvoir when the hounds had a very fast thing for 30 minutes, ran into the fox in the open. Jacob had led throughout over very stiff fences which when the field came up one man offered to buy his horse. Jacob said it was an extraordinary horse and he did not want to part with him, but if the man were to take him as he was, and pay a large sum on the spot he should have him. The man closed with him and sent the horse home to his own stable. The horse was found to be completely blind.

A JEALOUS RIDER

The first time I ever rode Coppice to my own satisfaction in a fast run was one afternoon from Great Oaks. I got away well with the hounds and came down to a very nasty place in the Turvey Road. Coppice was managing it very cleverly when Dick Maxey (a hard rider but a most jealous and disagreeable companion in the field) came behind me on his celebrated grey horse and shouted out at me "You will never be able to do it, let me come". I took no notice but got through into the Turvey Road and up the nasty bank opposite into a nice grass field. I was ridding close to the hounds and making for a stile in a narrow corner, when Maxey came from behind with his thundering large horse, knocked me on one side and got over the stile first. We ran over the best part of the country towards Mount Pleasant, and riding over a very large field with a very small fence in the middle when down came Maxey's grey like a dead horse.

I did not stop to pick him up but went on at the best pace, and on jumping into a field just before we got to Kempston Wood, I saw the fox quite clear close before the hounds. The fox got into the road and into a drain, and when Lord Tavistock came up he decided that it was contrary to fox hunting law to dig up a public road so that the good fox saved his life. The only man that I recollect as riding with me after Dick Maxey fell was his own brother who was also a good rider and not so disagreeably jealous.

TOO YOUNG TO TRADE

One word about Dick Maxey's celebrated grey horse. It was an immense animal, 16 hands high or more. On starting, Maxey would ride him over some tremendous fences, but I never recollect seeing the horse shine in a real run, he was soon blown and I thought him worthless as a hunter. I would not have accepted him as a gift if the condition was that I should ride him. This horse was the cause of the first scrape which George Payne (of racing celebrity) got into. He had agreed to give Maxey 700 guineas for him. Payne was under age and his trustees would not hear of such extravagance. Maxey was disappointed and angry and told me that he meant to bring an action against him. I never heard any more about it and I do not know what became of the horse, he disappeared from our field.

A GREAT JUMP

One fine morning we found a fox in Weston Wood and ran at a racing pace down to Paxton Brook opposite to Duberley's house. The brook was brim full, a small river. Wells did not like the look of it and cast his hounds along the brook towards Kimbolton but of course was obliged to come back. In the meantime two or three of us were standing on the edge of the brook looking in this formidable piece of water and George Mumford said "What a pretty leap". I did not say anything but observed that the landing place on the other side was 2 or 3 feet lower than where we were standing. I knew that my horse could do it and would do it. I was on Wolsey, when Wells came back and put his hounds over they took up the scent directly. There were 200 red-coats out. I drew back 100 yards or more and hallooed out "make way", they saw what I was at and made a line on each side. Poor old Monk screamed out "For God's sake, Sam, don't attempt it, you will lose yourself and your horse". I merely replied "Make way". When I set Wolsey to it, he turned short round. There was no whipping or spurring I merely put my whip on his neck, turned him straight and spoke a word of encouragement, and pressed him with my knees. I shall never forget his going at it in a sturdy canter, measuring his steps like a man who is going to take a wide leap, and carrying me over without a jolt. There was more than a murmur of applause when I rode away up the opposite field after the hounds. There was not much courage in doing this because I knew that Wolsey could, and would do it.

The field were to go half a mile down to a bad ford through the swollen brook and come up to me at Agden Green. When Joe Leeds (a very hard rider and very jealous) heard of it afterwards he said it was nothing, that he had often jumped Paxton Brook.

Unfortunately for him there is no record of his ever having done it once. I was pleased to hear lately that my performance is still kept in memory among the inhabitants of Great Staughton.

CLEVER HORSE

The hounds went away from Hanger Wood with a good scent pointing for Wootton Wood one fine morning and being first I came to a very nasty stile in a corner with a drop of 4 feet, into the next field.

Joe Leeds came pressing behind with a large horse of Naton's the dealer which he was riding for sale and as usual hallooing out, "get out of the way". I did get out of the way. I was on Rowland. I got his chest against the stile, pulled his head up, pressed him with my knees and he sprang from his hind legs, never hit the stile and landed with all his four feet at once in the field below. It was one of the cleverest things I ever saw a horse do. I rode away leaving half a dozen men fighting at the stile. We ran across the Stagsden Road, and they did not catch me until we were going into Wootton Wood.

COPPICE

Another instance of beating a jealous hard rider was, I was sorry to say, the last time I ever rode Coppice after three seasons of real enjoyment on horse-back. We came away from Moulsoe Wood, ran without a check for some miles and were riding up a nice grass bank toward for Bromham. I was close to the tail of the hounds when Lorain Smith who had been quite out of it all this time rushed by me with his one-eyed horse into the middle of the hounds (and he boasted of being a sportsman). I saw that the fence we were coming to was an impenetrable high hedge, on my left hand was a low fence into a nice grass meadow. Without stopping Coppice in his stride I pulled him to the left and took this low fence in a slanting direction and he did it most cleverly. The field I had left Smith and others in gradually rose higher and higher from my meadow, and I had the satisfaction of seeing them all pounded at their thick hedge and of riding on eight feet below them when they could not get at me. We ran on to the rising ground at Bromham overlooking the town of Oakley and came to a check. There was a halloo at Oakley Mill, and away went Wells, myself and Pearce and Tom Ball on Hyena. The hounds hit the scent at Oakley Mill, ran fast across the Park and over the fields to Milton Mill, and straight up to Twin Wood. They killed a fox as they jumped over the hedge into the wood. I own that I was always under the impression that it was not the hunted fox but a fresh fox that the hounds accidentally met.

When the hounds had disposed of the fox, Lord Tavistock, old Sam Ongley, old Monk and Smith came up, and Lord Tavistock came to me and said that he should never be happy unless I sold Coppice to him. He offered me three horses which he had just bought off Col. Pack for 400 guineas. I was most unwillingly obliged to part with Coppice and rode home upon him with a very heavy heart. The three horses turned out all screws, they could do nothing, and I sold them at Tattersalls for nothing.

In the beginning of this run I came away with all the hounds, over all the fences while the whole field rode down the well known large grass field a quarter of a mile to my right. Wells had joined me and we came down to Chicheley Brook which was fully swollen, and in fact a torrent, I thought I was more clever than I turned out to be, I thought I knew the fence which I had often crossed when the brook was low and I put Coppice in. He swam across most gallantly and tried hard to get up the opposite bank, he could get no footing, and I found I had made a mistake I was obliged to swim back again. Wells who stood on the bank meaning to follow me if I succeeded said "that horse swims as fast as he gallops". We were obliged to go down to the bridge a long way off and luckily found the hounds in a check at Chicheley House.

Lord Tavistock rode Coppice two or three seasons, and when his legs began to fail sent him back to my Brother according to his promise. He went beautifully in harness for some years and at last fell down dead in his stall at Southill, without any previous symptoms of illness.

Nobody could find out how he was bred, my father bought him off Wood the Vicar of Cranfield, and therefore named him Coppice. This horse objected to eat his corn out of his manger. Old John Ainsworth used to take off his headstall and turn him loose, when he walked quietly up to the large cornbin, threw the cover up with his nose and ate where he liked. Coppice's picture now hangs before me while I write.

THE EAGLE-EYED LAWYER

A friendly farmer at Stagsden persecuted Lord Tavistock to come and hunt his pet fox which laid among some haulm shocks in a large wild field on the left hand of the Newport Pagnell Road. He wanted to carry his haulm but would not disturb the field till the hounds had been there. At last Lord Tavistock met at Stagsden, he went to this field and every man with the farmer at their head took a separate row of haulm shocks and beat them close up this rising field, it was quite a sight. Wells in the middle of the field came to a large deep old pond with very thick bushes growing in it. He stood on the bank, cracked his whip, and most of the hounds went through it. No find; much to the chagrin of the friendly farmer who said the fox ought to have been there. Wells went on with the hounds out of the hand gate, and the whole field had disappeared.

I was riding up this field with old Kidman the lawyer (a keen old poacher) and he was just telling me that at 85 years old he could still see a fly upon a church steeple, when, at a hundred yards before we got to the pond he screamed out "Tally-ho! I see his eye". I did not see his eye or anything else. The fox in the pond thinking all danger was over, had put his head out of the thick bushes to reconnoitre, and this keen sighted old man had seen it. We two galloped up to the pond, the fox broke on the other side in the direction of the hand gate and the hounds having heard the first halloo rushed back through the gate one over the other with their heads up in the air staring at us. The fox ran straight to the middle of the pack and then turned to the right close under the breasts of the whole of them and not one hound saw him. They soon settled to the scent and we had a sharp thing up to Moulsoe Wood where he turned back to his own country and was killed in the neighbourhood of the field where we had found him.

If I had not seen it for myself I could not have believed that a whole pack of hounds going through this pond, and Wells cheering them and cracking his whip this fox could have been missed.

The friendly farmer was more than overjoyed.

TIT FOR TAT

A story about the above Lawyer Kidman. He was always poaching, either with gun or greyhounds. One day I was out shooting at Cardington and found Kidman two or three fields within our boundary with his gun and dogs, he told me that he was following a hen pheasant. I expressed surprise at his impudence and he said that he knew the Law, that the pheasant had got up on his own ground and that he had a right to follow it wherever it went. I told him that I did not know the Law, but that I was quite certain I should not allow him to trespass any further into the Manor. Old Kidman was very indignant, talked very big, and a good deal about Law, but I walked him off. He was no more after a pheasant than I was in the open country where not a pheasant existed. This produced a nice little quarrel, and soon after while I was riding after the hounds in the cold splash country, old Kidman rode after me and said "This is my property (a field of 8 acres) and I warn you off" I said "I shall soon be out of it, and for the future I will ride round it".

THE POND

We came away from Weston Wood with a capital scent, and I was leading on Wolsey much to my own satisfaction, when within one field of Bushmead I charged a moderate looking fence and landed in a deep pond full of water, such a splash, Wolsey never lost his legs, and walked out comfortably. I lost the remainder of the run, because Wolsey had unfortunately left one of his fore-shoes in the bottom of the pond, and as he was lame in the fore-feet I dare not ride him a yard without a shoe, and I had to walk full two miles in the wild country before I could find a blacksmith. As I never forgot a field I had once been in, or a fence I had once been over, I was never found in the bottom of that pond again.

THE SAW PIT

We went away close to the fox from Thurleigh Park over the wild grass field there and came to a small farm house, by the outside of which the hounds ran. I rode at a low fence and saw when it was too late a saw pit, made under the hedge. I was fortunately upon Reprobate, a firm, strong, well-bred horse that I had bought off Lord Robert Manners, a little slow but very sure, he saw the scrape we were in, checked himself in his spring, popped his hind legs down on this side of the saw pit and strode over it.

At the same time I heard a terrible chitter on my right, and there was Peter Payne who had jumped into the whole collection of the farmers implements, ploughs, harrows etc. He made a great noise but horse and man came out unwounded. I never got into that saw pit again.

THE DEATH OF MONK

We found a fox at Moulsoe Wood. A very large field out. The hounds ran very hard through Salford Wood, crossed the road and there we saw the great brook, brim full.

Monk, myself and Palmer of Goldington faced the brook. This Palmer was a regular nuisance in the field. He had a quick horse but never could see his own way when hounds ran, but watched the leading man and when he saw what he had made up his mind to, would try to cut him off. On this occasion Monk, on his large one-eyed horse, rode hard at the brook calling out "Come along Sam, don't look at it". This was the last cheer he ever gave in the hunting field. I was a few yards on the right on Monk, and when I was within two strides of this wide brook Palmer cut right across my horse's nose and if he had fallen I must have killed him, for I could not stop my horse.

As it was, we all three got safe over. Monk who was a first rate leader saw at once the weak place in the fence before us and I rode behind him with my horse well in hand to let him get safely over when Palmer came round me and charged Monk while he and his horse were actually in the air, hit him on the right shoulder and knocked him over and over horse and all some distance into the next field.

There they lay as if they were dead. Of course I had stopped my horse, and as it was an awkward fence with a considerable drop in the next field, I took my horse back to give him a run, jumped the fence and pulled him up before I got to them groaning on the ground. There we were alone all three, nobody to help, as Wells was the only man who attempted the brook, and we had left him as usual with his great omnibus horse, Banker, swimming about in it. The hounds had been in full cry close before us, and I shall never forget the desolate feeling as the cry of the hounds vanished in the distance, of being left alone with as I believed, a dead man, and a dead horse, and nobody to help me but this scoundrel Palmer.

After some time we got Monk on his legs and got his horse up. After abusing Palmer I sent him to lead both our horses to Woburn, full three miles and to bring back a chaise and pair. I found that Monk's right arm was broken close to the shoulder, and with great difficulty I managed to walk him to Salford Mill not far off. There we waited two hours till the Post Chaise arrived, and propping him with pillows I took him all the way to Holm near Biggleswade full 20 miles. I never had a more distressing task. He was in great pain and the jolting of the chaise made him worse. As we at length drove up to his own door we met Mr. Grath (the old surgeon of Biggleswade). We got him into the house, got his clothes off and examined his arm, it was broken in two places close to the shoulder-blade. Unfortunately Mr. Grath did not discover that the shoulder was also out of joint and after weeks of suffering Monk was obliged to go up to London when the surgeons put him in fresh torture in trying to get the shoulder in which I believe they never did.

In a year's time Monk came out once or twice to the meet upon a pony, but of course he was miserable when the hounds went away and he could not follow them. He lived in pain about two years and then ended his life himself miserably. Monk was a man about 50, when this happened, a strong stout man and must have ridden 16 stone.

An excellent horseman and a most determined rider. He had hunted nearly 30 seasons with the Oakley Hounds and never had a serious accident. He had resided all that time in a small farm belonging to Lord Spencer. This was afterwards sold and is now in the possession of Charles Lindsell. I went back in the chaise and tired horses to Woburn Abbey where I was staying for a few days, and at 11 o'clock at night had to relate all this to Lord Tavistock.

This story would not be complete without the following anecdote about that scoundrel Palmer. After this day of misfortune a very severe frost set in and lasted several weeks. When it broke up, Lord Tavistock sent the hounds over to Cardington for exercise in Warden Wood. A very few people were there, but among them Palmer. As we were walking along the road up to the Wood quietly, Palmer came alongside of my horse with his whip up in a threatening attitude, and in a loud voice demanded immediate satisfaction for blaming him when he rode over Monk. He said "If you had not been there nobody would have known anything about it". I said "most likely not". He raised his whip to strike me but turned coward immediately. If he had touched me, I should have repaid him with interest, and sent him home with such sore shoulders that he would have been very uncomfortable for a week. In addition to this, 4 or 5 good friends had closed round us when the row began, each of whom were prepared to pitch into him if he touched me. In that case he would have had sore shoulders for a fortnight. If I am not mistaken, this happened in the year of 1823.

CHARLES BASSETT IN A DITCH

Having found in Clapham Park one afternoon, the fox gave us a capital run and very straight over the best part of Thurleigh Country, and when we were within a mile of Bushmead we came to a deep double ditch with a slight fence on the top of the bank. Bassett's favourite black mare had had enough of it, she cleared the first ditch, and then turned over and landed him in the second ditch, and herself with all her four legs in the air, the saddle and all her weight across Bassett's thighs. We summoned two labourers who were going home with spades upon their shoulders and attempted to dig behind his back, but the clay was so stiff that it was evident that our object could not be accomplished in less than a long day's work. I then took command, pulled off my own stirrup leathers, put the irons in my pocket and told Bennett (Peter Latour's groom) to do the same thing. The mare laid quiet, and having buckled the four leathers round her fetlocks, I gave the word to pull together, and the first attempt the two labourers who had got tight hold of Bassett by the cuff of his neck dragged him clean out. I expected to find both his thighs broken, but he had suffered no real damage. We then pulled the mare head over heels and righted her upon her legs in the bottom of this deep ditch from which she soon found her way out, and Bassett rode her home to Stratton Park, full twelve miles away. This operation had taken full twenty minutes, and Bassett who was in a fix if ever a man was behaved most gallantly, till at the last he began to give way from pain. We fortunately had some strong men out, among others, Simpson of Cardington and the young Duke of Manchester, who were very useful in lifting the mare. The only man who did not stop to help his friend was Fred Hogg, who rode on with the hounds and killed the fox in Bushmead.

DEATH ON THE CAUSEWAY

Mr. Edwards drowned at Brayfield. Mr. Edwards was a waggoner in a large way of business at Silsoe, and frequently came out with the hounds. We had found at Clifton Spinneys and run to Norton. The fox had evidently crossed the river altho' it was in a high state of flood at least a furlong wide. Between Norton and Brayfield there was a raised causeway over these low meadows, with a bridge in the middle over the river. Pinfold of Chicheley (frequently out of his mind) went in first. Then Wells, Bundett, Hobhouse, and Simpson all of whom got safe over. Tom Polhill followed next with Edward Pratt (his brother-in-law), Campbell and three more. Tom Polhill was a very nervous man, and I was just going upon Reprobate when I saw Polhill allow his horse to sidle off the causeway into the flood and the whole of the horses following him went off as if they had been tied to him. There were 7 horses, 7 men and 7 hats all swimming in this tearing flood and it looked like 50. I saw Edwards swimming and holding his great chestnut by the bridle. The horse found his legs and reared up and came bang down with his fore foot upon Edwards head. Nothing more was seen of poor Edwards. Polhill, Campbell and the others swam against the stream, till they were exhausted and gave themselves up for lost, and then found themselves standing on the meadow with the water not much higher than their knees. With a little help they were all landed on the bridge. The horses swam down the river but were all rescued in different places on the banks below. I myself saved Campbell's horse a mile below this teem. Two or three days afterwards Edwards' body was found at Turvey Mill doubled up. On this same day two men were drowned with two different packs of hounds in the North of England. The hounds followed the fox but when we had got round by Turvey Bridge and told them what had happened they gave it up. It seems indescribable but Pinfold (the madman) went back home by himself in the dusk over this causeway.

THE OLD VIXEN

Weston Wood was always a favourite Covert of mine. For 3 or 4 seasons a famous Vixen Fox dwelt there, and the moment she heard the horn she was off at the north end of the Wood, and ran a splendid run across Stagsden and Astwood towards Great Oaks where she escaped we never could make out.

She always had a litter of cubs. The last season she had only one cub, and her coat had become very ragged. We found her as usual and she went away as usual. There was a burning scent and the hounds ran her for two miles into a small wood, killed her and eat her before anyone could get up, she was quite worn out with old age.

HUNTING TALES

THE OAKLEY HUNT SONG

This was written in 1828 by Frederick Delme Ratcliffe, and in 1875 a sporting Parson the Rev. Powney of Hampshire produced a verbatim copy of it, with merely a change of the names of the performers, as a song written by himself in honour of the Tedworth Hunt. Someone recollected the old Oakley Song of nearly 50 years ago and taxed him with piracy.

The Parson denied most solemnly that he had ever seen or heard of the old song, but when they printed the two songs side by side in the newspaper he was obliged to confess. He was an eccentric old man, very fond of writing verses on sporting matters, who died recently at the age of 80. Ratcliffe had sent his cloths to the Swan at Bedford on the day of the Oakley Club dinner. He arrived there at 4 o'clock and before dinner at 6 o'clock he composed this song, which to our surprise he sang after dinner. To make the song intelligible, I will here give the names of the persons alluded to. In the second verse, Tom Ball, First Whip. A heavy weight, but a capital sportsman. He always turned up at the right moment, in the right place.

In the fourth verse, George; George Mumford, huntsman. He succeeded Wells. A light weight, a good sportsman and a cheery fellow.

In the fifth verse, the Critic, a young man who came down to Bedford with two horses without any introduction. His name was Perry. I believe he was the son or nephew of old Perry the famous Editor of the Morning Chronicle. He could not ride a yard, but was constantly putting paragraphs in the newspapers sneering at the Oakley Hounds, the consequence was, that he made no friends, and we all avoided him in the field. His last performance was an article abusing the Oakley Hounds, and saying that they never had a fine slanting run. What that meant I do not exactly know. The same man is now the well known Jim Erskine Perry.

In the sixth verse, The Marquis, The Marquis of Tavistock, the best Master of a Pack of Hounds that ever lived. Whitbread, myself, who could ride a good horse, and could not ride a bad one. In the eleventh verse, Fred Hogg, a light weight never missed a day with the hounds, and never knew where he was, always riding neck or nothing, and getting into everlasting scrapes. He is still living at Girtford Bridge, and must be older than I am. Lord Gardner, a very hard rider. As a boy he was put under my protection by his Uncle Bob Smith (afterwards Lord Carrington). In the twelfth verse, The Rev. Daniel Crofts, Rector of Shelton and sole manager of the covert Shelton Gorse, which he did preserve in good earnest, an excellent man and a good rider. Frederick Delme Ratcliffe, the Author of the Song, died in 1875.

I have overlooked the name of Squire Peter Payne in the twelfth verse. A man whose name will always be remembered by every English Gentleman and Foxhunter, who were fortunate enough to know him. Peter Payne, (afterwards Sir Peter Payne, bart., and Member for the County of Bedford) had been an enthusiastic lover of horses and hounds from his earliest days. He never could afford to mount himself on splendid horses but he always had two good ones which he knew how to ride, and wherever the hounds were Peter was sure not to be far off. At this time he was above sixty, and always told me that he was riding on sufferance. I shall never forget a County Election when Peter Payne and old Dick Orlebar undertook to propose and second the Candidate. They were both furious stutterers, and the fun was enormous.

THE MUCK HEAP

Dick Maginnis, with one arm and stone deaf, was a first rate horseman. He is dead now poor fellow, but when he happened to meet me on the Platform of a Railway, he always roared out in a loud voice before a crowd of passengers "Sam, do you remember the muck heap?". This made the passengers stare at me. The story is this:

We went away very fast from Galsey Wood down hill pointing for Keysoe. There was only one light place in the first hedge, which looked like a tempting leap. Dick Maginnis was first, and landed up to his girths in the largest and highest muck heap you ever saw. With his Irish mare which was used to Irish Bogs he waded into it beautifully, and it was some time before he saw the other side of it. I allowed Tom Ball to go next, and he got well into it. I shall never forget his fighting and floundering and at every plunge halloing out "Come up" as if it was the fault of his poor weak mare with a curb bit on half a foot long. Nobody else had come up in that moment though there were plenty in the distance, and I got my steady horse Reprobate close up to the fence, made him jump standing and as his fore-feet touched the ground I pulled his head to the left enough to break his neck, and walked him round the heap. As I rode away across the next field I looked back, and to my great amusement saw the muck heap full. The Farmer who was a great enemy to fox-hunting had placed it there on purpose to catch us, and I only hope he was watching to see his wonderful success.

A SHARP BURST

We met at Marston Thrift in a dripling morning, found a fox immediately which took a line to the south side of Cranfield Parish at a slow pace in the direction of Moulsoe Wood, when suddenly the hounds took up a scent at the bottom of Cranfield open field, and ran one of the sharpest bursts on record, being without check over the whole of the open field, very deep about a mile and a half and on to North Crawley. Most of the field were left behind, but those in luck were Lord Tavistock on Coppice (I believe the first time he rode him after I sold it to him), Bill Higgins on Maximilian, Newbigin, Lord Lynedoch, mad Palmer (who afterwards killed Monk) and Wells.

These few had it all to themselves and at the second fence beyond the open field, Bill Higgins mastered a very stiff stile in the middle of an impracticable bullfinch at the time when his companions thought that his horse must have been fatally blown. This gave him a great advantage. Lord Tavistock was the first to catch him riding hard throughout. I was riding a fair hunter (Stingo) and having lost the start rode quietly after them and met the hounds running back to the country where they had found, and my horse being fresh I had a pleasant ride with the leading hounds who were then running soberly without a check. We came to a thin hedge through which the leading hounds dashed as if the fox were close before them, but unfortunately the tail hounds took up the scent of a disturbed fox on this side of the hedge, at right angles to the true line. Wells made a sad mistake, and I saw it, but could not interfere. From that time we went on slowly all over the country for two hours till we came to Marston Thrift. It was then getting dark, and every horse and hound was dead tired.

THE POINT-TO-POINT

I study the lists of runners and try to decide which meeting to go to, as my mare is entered in races at at least two meetings. Based on the likely going at the courses and the probable runners, I make the decision as to where we shall race, fairly sure that in the light of events, that decision will prove to be the wrong one and go to bed early on the Friday evening.

Saturday dawns bright and promising. I wish that wind had blown a bit more as the going is likely to be a shade too soft for the mare. An early hack at the walk may kid her that this is just another ordinary day, for as soon as she senses the preparations the mare will be shaking with anticipation. We used to plait her mane to keep it out of my fingers when I changed my grip on the reins, but we don't any more as it only upsets her.

We arrive at the course a couple of hours before her race. As we neared the course the nervous tension had started me yawning and I walk the course in the wake of my Irish Wolfhound, our lucky mascot, yawning still. The jumps look terrifying - I kid myself they will not look so bad when I am 16 hands high.

Jockeys, some nervously chatty, others silent, change under cold canvas, nylon breeches, paper thin boots and chattering teeth. To weigh out for the race I take my saddle, breast plate, weight cloth and lead weights. The scales, sometimes the real McCoy with a little seat for the jockey and a mammoth circular face, but more normally a set of old farm scales, hover over 12 stone 7. I drop a 1lb weight on the grass and the clerk of the scales nods "That's O.K. no. 7" he says.

To the horse-box lines where the mare is already bridled and ready to come out of our trailer. She is sweating slightly but stands head nodding as we saddle her. Breastplate over the head, then number cloth, weight cloth, wither pad, and that mean bit of leather which is an apology for a saddle. Girth-up not too tight – we shall have to check them in the paddock.

As the mare is walked round to warm up, I return to the dressing tent, suddenly lonely, for all the rush is now over and it is only the interminable wait. Another visit to the screened off bucket in the corner and then a seat on the bench next to the others in gay jerseys and grey faces. The desire for that last cigarette overcomes the knowledge that it will only thicken the wind.

The bell jangles "jockeys out please". This is it, no turning back now, and I walk to the paddock hoping I look the gay sportsman, with not a care but not feeling it. At sight of the mare I am heartened for she looks good striding round the paddock with my wife in tow. The old adage "a head like the lady's maid and a bottom like the cook" is an apt description of the mare as, ears pricked she surveys the competition and her rounded rump is barely covered by the blue and white paddock sheet.

The second bell "jockeys up". I beckon my wife to the quietest corner of the paddock. Off with the surcingle and rug and then tighten the girths. I vault into the saddle and as we are walking round I adjust my stirrups. Whip under the arm as I tie a knot at the buckle of my rubber covered reigns. I feel better already as this is where I belong and pray for no speedy departure from this powerful beast. I say to my wife – nonchalantly, I hope – "O.K. darling" and she unbuckles the leading rein. Immediately the mare dances a few steps as I run a hand down her long brown neck and talk gently to her. The huntsman blows his horn to signal our departure from the paddock and the mare bucks and prances as we fly out onto the course. I sit low with my weight against her pull as we settle to a swinging canter down to the post. We pull up gradually and turn to trot into the first fence to have a look. Invariably the mare takes a mouthful of gorse from the fence as if to express her contempt and then drops it as it prickles her lip.

Back to the start where I check my girths as we circle round, summing up the competition and weighing our chances. As the starter calls the roll, I pull down my goggles –

not before, or they may steam up. He is calling us into line and I jockey for a position on the inside rail. As there are plenty of runners I want a good view of the first.

"They're off" and with a great surge of power she is galloping with me crouched low over her withers. We seem to be going fast and yet I know I must boot her even faster into the fence. Kick, kick, kick and she stands back for a courageous leap. Within a stride I am up her neck again as we swing on to the next lying about third.

Horses seem to crowd in on me from each side, we are squeezed for room but push our way forward for a view of the next which she jumps fluently. There's a faller beside me, but I don't know who – hope he's O.K. As the pace steadies we are back in about 5th place but going easily. We are approaching the open ditch – a fearsome obstacle with a cavernous ditch on the take-off side – and yet most horses jump it well. Accepting the generalisation the mare flies it gaining a length on the horse on our inside.

The fences flick by. I take a pull here to avoid the horse jumping left-handed. We surge on there to get ahead of that loose horse. The mare takes one fence "by the roots" – perhaps that will make her pick her feet up – but she hardly checks in her stride. We must have done two miles and jumped a dozen fences and now the serious business is upon us. With a mile to go we must shape up for our challenge. Stragglers are dropping out behind us and yet there are still five or six good horses ahead and they are really galloping.

"Come on girl, where's that turn of foot I know you possess?" we fly the next, four from home, jumping past the fifth horse. The one in front is tiring and we are with him at the next – plenty of daylight at each fence now. "Come on" I pull my whip through and give her a couple of sharp ones. Half a mile to run, two fences to jump and three horses to beat. We forge on close to the rails. The going has been testing and she is tired – but so are the others . My God how tired I feel – kick, kick, kick.

It's too late, but go on, they may all fall at the last. They don't but the mare gets a stride too close and "fiddles it". What a mess, but the third one's had it. We could be in the money. I can hear the roar of the crowd as they cheer home the first two battling it out on the run in. The mare hears it too and responds to the rising noise. We are having our own battle with that big chestnut, gradually closing the gap. Head down, crouched low, hands and heels, hands and heels, hands and heels. As the post approaches we storm past the chestnut into third place, about 5 lengths behind the winner. I stand in the stirrups and gulp down air as we pull up and the mare breaks into a trot. I pat her shining neck as she walks head low, sides heaving back to the paddock.

As we walk into the unsaddling enclosure I pull up my stirrups and unbuckle the breastplate. I slip to the ground and my knees crumple under me. I unbuckle the girths and pull the saddle onto my arm. Another pat for a plucky horse and thanks for a super ride. I return to the scales to weigh in, probably a pound lighter than when I weighed out. As I sit again on that friendless bench, I feel tired but elated. The chatter is animated, the tea is sweet and the atmosphere relaxed except perhaps for those who ride in the next as well.

There is not much money in it and its amateur status is wearing a bit thin, so why do we race in point-to-points? Because we love it, all of it, the tension, the speed, the spice of danger, the crowds and above all we love that proud thoroughbred aristocrat who makes it all possible – the mare.

David Spilman

HUNTING TALES

ONCE UPON A TIME

When I was twenty four and running my own riding school and pony trekking centre in Cumbria, I went to the John Peel Centenary celebrations at Caldbeck. Five packs of hounds met there on that day, all except one being foot packs. I looked for the horses and found a field of about thirty, ranging from an immaculate young man in swallow tails on a thoroughbred horse, to boy of twelve, wearing a bowler hat so big that it rotated on his head and carrying a walking stick, as he sat bareback on a little carthorse with blinkers, bridle and rope reins.

Hounds moved off and I followed on foot. After about fifteen minutes I saw the immaculate young man standing beside his horse, holding a stirrup iron minus leather. He was very good looking, so I thought I would see if I could do anything to help! He said the leather had broken and if only someone would take his horse he could go off in the car with his friends. I said I would take the horse if I could go on hunting it. He said "Can you ride?", I said "Yes'. We removed the remaining iron and leather and as he legged me up he said "Come home with the whipper-in, he's on our other horse". then as an after thought "Look out - he bucks".

The rest of the field were at the bottom of a grassy hill down which we proceeded, with bucks. Almost immediately they found a fox and we were off. I was glad to find I could hold the horse and that he jumped the five or six fences we met willingly but somewhat 'greenly'. When we checked I went to the young whipper-in and told him what had happened. He said "How did you get over those fences?" Thinking he meant because I had no stirrups, I told him I had held onto the mane. He said "He's only a four year old, he's never jumped before!"

Later on, I was nearly falling off with exhaustion so I took the leathers from the saddle and caught up with the others. I had to get to the whipper-in because I did not know whose horse I was riding, where it lived, or where I was! I hacked home with the hounds after a truly memorable day, corduroy trousers, no hat – but what a horse.

Over twenty years later I was teaching in Cumbria and was offered a days hunting and invited to a hunt 'NeetOot'. There at the supper table I told the story of my John Peel Centenary day, the slim good looking young man and the young boy whipper-in. The plump and portly master said "I was that young man", and the wizened, weather beaten huntsman said "I was the young whipper-in you rode home with"!

Josephine Knowles F.B.H.S.

THE WANDERER RETURNS

There is a little lodge/gate-house that used to stand by a bend on the road between Daventry & Staverton. The house is still there but now stands well back from the new road and the area of course is very built-up. But whenever I go past, I always think of Dasher!

Dasher was 'left out' after a days hunting in the Daventry area. During the three weeks that followed, I went with my father on several occasions to 'blow' for him – very often to the field by the lodge. The phone at The Kennels rang regularly – he had been spotted again. Back we would go, but it was always the same old story. There was never any sign of Dasher!

Then one day, after about three weeks, he walked casually into the kennel yard, no doubt pleased to be home after a nice holiday well fed and none the worse for his escapades (whatever they might have been!). I think everyone was pleased to see him – he was a great favourite.

And who knows what stories he would have to tell the others that night as they snuggled down in the straw on their benches!

Susan Rogers

HUNTING IN A RECESSION

When one's first love is hunting, (don't tell the wife), what do you do in times of recession – losing money in Lloyd's, thrown out of tenanted farms, having your house re-possessed or having funds drained by greedy land agents, solicitors and accountants. One must learn to cut your garment according to the cloth. If you lose everything else make sure you hang on to the hunter.

You can't afford any more livery stables and huge weekly bills. Just park the car out in the road and convert the garage into a stable, up and over doors are a problem but you can train a horse to do most things. Just get him to roll in and out under it.

Exercising the poor beast is a must, you cannot expect a full day's hunting on no work so let me recommend a gadget invented in Surrey called a treadmill. With a bit of ingenuity one can usually fit one in the hall, so all one does is shove the animal on while you have your breakfast and the 'Mrs' can get the garage cleaned out and littered up again. Which brings us to bedding. Collect all the paper, magazines, bank statements etc from the office and get round the local boy scouts and girl guides and put all through the garden shredder (the scouts and guides could be a bit messy though!) The end result is masses and masses of bedding, sell what you don't need for mulching gardens which knocks a bit off the feed bill.

Another thought, feeding the darned animal. One has to be a bit careful here as horses are prone to a problem called colic so always have some Epsom Salts handy in the bathroom cupboard. Hay is essential, dried lawn cuttings have been tried but avoid unless you want to dig a large grave in the vegetable garden. So let your dearest go and chat up a farmer (let her wear those frilly bits you gave her for Christmas), not only will she come back with a load of hay but his unsown oats as well. Make sure the housekeeping stretches to a few packets of All-bran and the horse has a diet good enough to win the Grand National.

The biggest hurdle is going to be the subscription, unless you can get round the local Hunt Secretary - tough luck if male and you are not in to that sort of thing but if a member of the opposite sex go for it. Although it will be quite a challenge as most Hon Secs have a huge waiting list and can only manage about ten affairs per season. The last resort is to rob the kids money boxes throughout the year and hope come October there will be enough in the kitty.

Hunting dress is very important and unfortunately doesn't very often crop up at jumble sales. The only items from this source are outgrown children's jodhpurs and out of date kite standard hats, but at least better than nothing. You certainly need a good day's hunting when looking and feeling like a ballet dancer all day (tight jods do help when holloaing a fox away). Some foxhunters have been known to be buried in their hunting kit, but I think that is going to extremes especially with the digging involved, unless of course you are on good terms with the terrier man. Finding a pink coat is quite a problem unless you can find a member about your size who hunts during the week and do a fifty - fifty deal.

Lets pray that after all this, business picks up or you find a wealthy widow in the hunting field.

*Note that garages used as stables do get a rebate under the new rating system provided they are not connected to main drainage.

Good luck and good hunting, remember where there's a will there is a way!!!

Contributed by Robert Myram

BUYING A CHILD'S PONY

So the kids want a pony - a good talking point on the train or bus to the office or work place on Monday mornings, to boast about the little brats' achievements over the weekend. But beware, it certainly has its pitfalls and draw backs - only a small minority win the points cup at the pony club show or get a rosette for apple bobbing at a gymkhana, and as much chance of qualifying for the Horse of the Year show as winning the pools.

After seeing the bank manager for a loan, start looking down the horses for sale columns of the local rags, and putting in an order for the Horse and Hound (a must as once you have a hay burning little monster, you need to know where all the shows and events are, cut price insurances, tee shirt offers etc). On reading down the pages of adverts, all of which seem suitable, "no vices, good to shoe, easy to catch, good to load" and so on. Believe ten percent and you won't be far off course!

A brief guide on breeds is necessary starting at the small end of the scale. The toy horse is only suitable as a pet or for extra small children. Next we have the Shetland which will do anything except the right thing and guarantee bow legs in latter life, the only good point is that you can cart them around in the estate car.

The native ponies follow such as the Welsh which usually has an unpronounceable name and has an A, B, C, or D rating not on looks or performance, but size. The Exmoor and Dartmoor are very hardy and tough, but make sure the fences are in good order. The New Forest does most things and is very partial to apple trees so keep out of the orchard! So eventually you finish up with something with four legs a feeding end and a kicking end, parked in your newly erected stable, or eating its head off in your expensively fenced ex vegetable garden or tennis court.

The headaches and problems should now fall into place. Don't ask any advice from any so called horsey person as every answer will be different; 'Try a snaffle', 'You want a double bridle', 'Put a grackle on', 'Use brushing boots', 'Knee pads'. You name it, you will get told to use it!

So, you have got the pony, sorted out the harness - now you need some petrol in the tank. Start off on a low octane - grass and water, not too much lush grass though, otherwise you will be getting plenty of visits from the vet, to deal with a complaint called laminitis. You have to feed to the childs ability or your nervous wife's, if she is to exercise the monster on school days. Good hay is a must, try a local farmer. Get him to throw bales down from the top of the barn and when you find one that doesn't bellow out clouds of dust and mould, grab it. Horses and ponies are very prone to dust allergies so take care. You will have to supplement the diet with non-heating cubes and mixes, (no you don't have to cook the stuff, it's just lower in oats and protein) and some chopped up hay or straw called chaff.

Now off to the riding school where your child will be instructed in the finer points of horsemanship, usually by a bossy, busty woman in very tight breeches claiming to be an A.I. (incidently, nothing to do with artificial insemination) but an exam passed by the B.H.S. (British Horse Society, not to be confused with British Home Stores) You will soon learn a lot of new words and phrases if you stay and watch the proceedings. If you shut your eyes you could be listening to a sex tape; 'Lower leg back, bottom up, bottom down, toes up, heels down. Turn at K, rise at H'. After an hour your child will most probably be in floods of tears and not wanting to attend again, but persevere, bribe with sweets, trips to the cinema etc, and their riding education will take off.

Many happy days and years will ensue until the magical age of fifteen or so, when the poor pony after years of loyal service will be sadly neglected in its paddock, and the boy and girl friends appear to charm your child. Let's hope all the instructors words of wisdom are forgotten!!!

Contributed by Robert Myram

LONG, LONG AGO

It is a cold damp Friday morning in late November 1935. Shortly before eleven o'clock many horses converge on Newnham Village. The Pytchley Hounds are meeting and every lane entering the village is congested with second horsemen and their mounts. They have all hacked there, riding one and leading one and are busy with sponge and stable rubber removing any mud splashes as well as polishing the bits and stirrups ready for their master to mount his first horse. He will arrive in a chauffeur driven car.

Tom had started work in the stable yard at six, mucked out two horses, quartered one of them, breakfasted in the stable mess room, dressed in his hunting kit, and collected his sandwiches from the big house kitchen before he hacked the twelve miles to the meet.

Hounds move off, followed by over two hundred subscribers, some hunting farmers and a hundred second horseman. Young Tom, the General's second horseman is amongst them, riding along side George, the terrier boy from the kennels. Sailor the terrier rides safe inside a leather bag on George's lap. Tom glances admiringly at George "I do like your scarlet, it makes my black look very dull". "You'll have to get work at the kennels Tom". "That's my ambition but father is very strict and says I mustn't get ideas above my station. How's that new strapper getting on?". "Only lasted a day! He pulled his horse out for exercise with a tail full of straw, hadn't even quartered it properly. Mr. Hawk soon had him down the road, the man shouldn't have said he was experienced".

Hounds run fast and Tom follows the kennel second horsemen. As they cross a grass ridge and furrow, one horse gets his head down and bucks furiously, the second horseman sits several but eventually they part company. Tom catches the horse, and leading him back to his rider is amazed to see him placing his bowler on the ground and putting his horses foot right through it. "There, they'll have to buy me a new bowler now!."

When the huntsman changes horses, most of the others do the same. To save time, the huntsman does what's called a flying change, leaping from one horse to the other without dismounting.

Now riding the weary first horse, Tom jogs homeward amongst a large throng of second horsemen. One by one they turn off until he is left alone. Hounds run straight and Tom is not really sure where he is, but at each cross roads he drops his reins and old Duchess knows exactly which way to go. Fifteen weary miles later, Tom is glad to see the stable gates, and quickly dismounting he gives Duchess to a strapper and hurries to the mess room. He has little time to waste before the chauffeur arrives to take him to fetch the second horse, he doesn't want to miss his meal. Today he is lucky, and he gets two cups of tea as well, before the car comes. Before long he is mounted on the lathered, tired second horse, it is nearly dark and he has at least ten miles to jog home. When he arrives, a strapper takes the horse and Tom just has his saddle to clean before starting on his hunting clothes.

Quite a heavy day for a fourteen year old and he'll have to be off to the meet again at eight thirty in the morning.

Isobel Williams

HUNTING TALES

MEMORIES OF STANLEY BARKER

The first time I ever set eyes on Stanley Barker the huntsman, my mind goes back over 50 years, October, November 1943 to be precise, to those drab miserable mid years of the war. My own dear brother had been a prisoner of war for over two years, his prolonged absence seemed long, as the tide of war had finally turned in our favour.

Being apprenticed to T. Wilson Builders (now the Wilcon Giant), I was engaged in building farm workers cottages at Kelmarsh, Arthingworth, Clipston and Sibbertoft. One of those strange war time orders, when suddenly the labour and materials were found to build 3,000 farm workers cottages all over the country to ease the chronic shortage of accommodation. The cottages were unusual in the method of roofing, they had traditional pitched tiled rooves from outside but in fact, the only timber involved the tile battens and wood roof slabs that lay between the "concrete rafters". I've often wondered why this system did not continue after the war, of course it was very heavy and labour intensive and took a 4 man team to do the roof. The hours were long, 10 hours a day, 8 hours on Saturday, Sunday off. In winter we worked alternate Sundays until 4 o'clock. The Saturday before a working Sunday we finished work at 1 o'clock. It was on such a Saturday that I viewed Stanley Barker and his hounds for the first time, and what a splendid sight they made on that drab wartime day.

It happened like this. We were returning to Northampton from a site at Kelmarsh, on the approach to the Hanging Houghton turn, our transport slowed down, and suddenly there they were, the huntsman resplendent in hunting attire, and his hounds. My first impression was the superb colour tones, red coat, white breeches, black riding boots, the black, white and tan of the hounds, which the huntsman had under superb control. The pack appeared to ripple over the wide grass verge. This scene, so typically English, left an indelible impression, it still shines like a bright star in my memory of the distant past 50 years ago. Little did I realise at the time, some 17 years later would be the last time I saw him, an even more memorable day, (but later).

Two years after first seeing huntsman and hounds, I was to don a 'red beret' and sail away to Palestine as a proud young member of 6th Airborne division for three years. The division was engaged in a most disagreeable job of maintaining law and order. In off-duty moments in lonely and remote places with strange sounding names, I read such classics as "Tarka the Otter" by Henry Williamson, "Amateur Poacher" by Richard Jefferies, and of course, Siegfried Sassoon's immortal "Memories of a Foxhunting Man", Stanley having kindled the spirit.

We eventually sailed home on the "Samaria" docking in Liverpool. We boarded a troop train for Andover. Travelling down through my beloved England in all her midsummer glory it was like returning to a garden (from a desert). I remember when we arrived at Camp Barton Stacey, the sheer joy of walking through knee high rye grass, looking at the strange wave-like patterns as the wind sighs through the grass. Little things in the country we take for granted, the delightful scents and sounds of a wood after rain, a blackbird singing of a spring evening. To stand under a lime tree in full bloom, that delightful scent, and the drone of a honey bee working and the blossom so evocative of England in high summer.

This is what I missed by going to foreign places. Once settled in to our camp, we all went home on leave for seven weeks, the longest holiday I have ever had. I bought my first motorbike (the sheer joy of independent transport), the second week I helped a local farmer hay making. After a day's work in the hay field, I would go to the local mill on my motorbike with a friend to swim. The mill race still ran clear with green fronds of weed waving in the current, with shoals of elusive silver chub (now regrettably a dirty brown stain and certainly unfit to swim in). In the three years I had been away change was in the skies of 1948. No longer the great bomber fleets daily and nightly bombarding

Germany, but unusual aeroplanes in the form of the AW flying wing and former Lancaster bombers with two piston engines and two of the new jet engines.

In the hay fields of 1948 within two or three years, the swath turners, tedders and buck rakes were to become museum pieces, and give way to the low density pick-up balers. The age of the combine was just around the corner, the reaper and binder were about to take their place in the museum. Progress it is called, but I think we lose something, each time we take a step forward. On that hayfield of 1948, was the last time I was to see a corncrake, that shy elusive bird with its laboured, undulating flight, it is hard to accept this bird undertakes long migratory flights to warmer climes. Sadly now at the point of extinction in this sceptred isle.

Now for the last time I was to see Stanley Barker not knowing at the time it was also his last day hunting hounds before his retirement. It was like this. It was opening day at Hollowell Reservoir for the brown trout season, (no rainbows then), and I had arranged to go fishing with my uncle and cousin. It was also the closing meet of the season for the Pytchley.

The day dawned fine and calm, with that magical scent of spring in the air. Having first obtained our permits from Cliftonville, (5/- per day then) and motored out to Hollowell Reservoir, we exchanged the normal pleasantries with Charles Dickens who lived in the keeper's house in that idyllic position overlooking the reservoir. Then we made our way to our favourite fishing spots, mine being on the point by Guilsborough Bay.

After the morning warmed up a little, the trout started moving and I caught a fine brown trout of about 2lbs. At about mid-day I thought I heard the sound of a horn. Then a scene unfolded before me which I found hard to believe. There was I, knee deep in water fly-fishing, when on the far bank appeared huntsman and hounds who commenced to draw the hedge bordering the reservoir (no trees then) in the direction of the Guilsborough/Welford Road. Suddenly the hounds spoke, and there before me unfolded that unforgettable scene, "Charles James Esq," that red flash streaking for Hollowell with the hounds not far behind in full cry and the huntsman taking fences so beautifully. I realised at once the rare situation I happened to be in, enjoying two totally different field sports simultaneously. Hounds lost their fox in Hollowell village but appeared yet again later in the day from the direction of the Welford road. As the sun went down on what was to me a red letter day in my life's interest in field sports, I walked back to the fishing hut with a brace of fine brown trout in my bag with that undefinable scent of spring in the air. So ended a wonderful day in my life, so ended the wonderful career of Stanley Barker, huntsman to the Pytchley Hounds.

Charles Fox, 1993

SUMMER MONTHS

The beginning of spring is always an unsettling time for the ardent foot-follower of Hounds. All through the autumn and winter months, life for us revolves around the days that we are out hunting. Sometimes as many days as we can possibly pack in during the week.

For many of us, holidays are used up in the days out hunting and while others spend their time on foreign beaches, we are quite content to spend our time following Hounds. The sighting of a fox at close quarters can make our day complete and remain a subject of conversation with fellow companions for many hours later. (Of course the fox always increasing in stature as the tale is passed on). Often we foot followers have many advantages over the mounted field, we walk great distances and often happen to be in the right place at the right time, thus we frequently see many more foxes.

Many hunt followers, especially those who are mounted may sometimes get aggravated by our presence, but many of them realise how fortunate they are to have a dedicated bunch of men and sometimes women, who spend many weeks throughout the summer months working in the coverts, clearing the ridings and dropping thorns to enable more growth and cover, also shelter not only for the foxes but for birds and other wildlife. This is very hard work, especially if the weather becomes hot, but for the few who participate in this work, they are rewarded when the hunting season resumes, the covert is drawn and a fox is found!

This is reward enough for their hard work during the summer months.

Foot Follower, Pytchley

George Templer of Stover complete with mounted Charlie.

HUNTING TALES

LONG SERVING HUNTSMEN
(ACTIVE)

(Extracted from Jackson's Hunting Handbook 1993/94)

VIVIAN BISHOP	Golden Valley	(1945)	49 years
BERNARD PARKER	Mid-Devon	(1957)	37 years
W. J. WALKINSHAW	Mid-Antrim	(1959)	35 years
JOHN HENRY	Meath	(1959)	35 years
JIM LANG	Bur ton	(1961)	33 years
ROBERT PROUD	Bewcastle	(1961)	33 years
J. TINDALL	Glaisdale	(1962)	32 years
W. E. PORTER	Eskdale & Ennerdale	(1963)	31 years
MARTIN LETTS	College Valley	(1964)	30 years
DON CLAXTON	Percy	(1965)	29 years
ALEX SNEDDON	Holcombe Harriers	(1965)	29 years
BRUCE DURNO	Fernie	(1966)	28 years
SIDNEY BAILEY	V.W.H.	(1966)	28 years
MALCOLM WING	Co. Down	(1966)	28 years
EDMUND VESTEY	Thurlow	(1967)	27 years
GARETH MORGAN	Pentyrch	(1967)	27 years
STAN LUCKHURST	West Kent	(1967)	27 years
MICHAEL FARRIN	Quorn	(1968)	26 years
MICHAEL ROWSON	South Shropshire	(1968)	26 years
PETER JONES	Pytchley	(1971)	23 years
DENNIS BARROW	Ullswater	(1971)	23 years
IAN LANGRISH	Garth & S. Berks	(1971)	23 years
TIM UNWIN	Cotswold	(1971)	23 years
BARRY DONOGHUE	Ballymacad	(1971)	23 years

LONG SERVING MASTERS
(ACTIVE)

(Extracted from Jackson's Hunting Handbook 1993/94)

J. MURPHY	N. Kilkenny	(1941)
Mrs. E. GINGELL	Cambridgeshire Harriers	(1942)
VIVIAN BISHOP	Golden Valley	(1945)
Capt. C. G. E. BARCLAY	Puckeridge	(1947)
Sir ROBERT BUCHANAN-JARDINE	Dumfriesshire	(1950)
E. O'DRISCOLL	Carberry	(1952)
P. O'DRISCOLL	Carberry	(1952)
I. L. HEDLEY	Border	(1952)
A. W. LOCKWOOD	Burton	(1959)
Capt. J. E. FOSTER	Wheatland	(1961)
J. A. COLLINSON	Staintondale	(1962)
MARTIN LETTS	College Valley	(1964)
Rt. Hon. The Lord DAVIES	David Davies	(1964)
J. GRAY	Hampshire	(1965)
J. E. BROCKBANK	Cumberland	(1966)
EDMUND VESTEY	Thurlow	(1967)
R. M. OLDER	East Kent	(1967)
Hon. Mrs. P. HOTHAM	Flint & Denbigh	(1967)

THE ESTABLISHMENT OF HUNTING
(Extracted from Burrows and Baily's – whose dates sometimes vary)

1739	CRAVEN
1745	HAMPSHIRE
1750	PYTCHLEY
1750	BELVOIR
1753	QUORN
1758	MILTON
1760	OLD BERKSHIRE
1763	CHESHIRE
1764	MIDDLETON
1775	HATFIELD
1777	LUDLOW
1778	BICESTER
1780	NEW FOREST
1780	WARWICKS
1784	DUKE OF BEDFORD'S . . . (Later OAKLEY)
1785	ESSEX
1786	BEAUFORT
1786	PUCKERIDGE
1798	OAKLEY

Jan.ry 28th 1809

We found a fox in Norton Oxier bed and went away at the best pace to Welton where we came to hunting and hunted on by Ledger Ashby to Kilsby Lodge where we lost him. We then drew Ashby Fallows bed, and Daventry Wood without finding but found in Badby Wood but the scent was so bad we could not do anything. Dainty, Regent, Rummager, Frolick, Arrogant, Boxer, Stroker, Standard, Cowslip, Candour, Malchem, Whynot, Atropos, Advised, Cressida, Fanciful, Fugitive, Labourer, and Legacy distinguished themselves.

Hunt Report from ??????? - 1809

"Mr. Bragg's Equestrian Portrait" by John Leech
(Reproduced by kind permission of the R. S. Surtees Society)

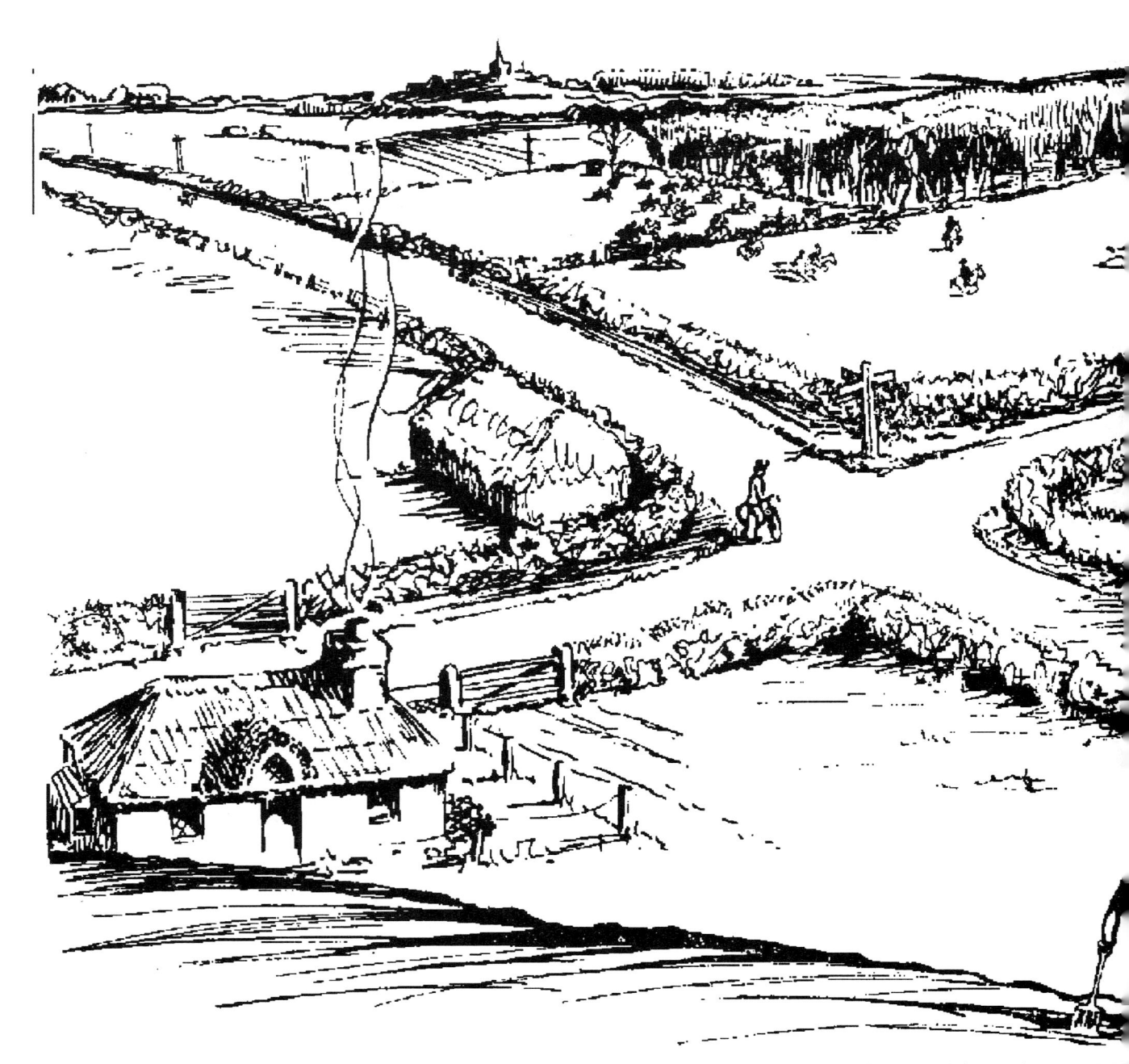

From an illustration by Helen MacGregor in 'The Foxhunter's We by David Brock, MFH, published by Seeley Service & Co, 1939

WHAT DO YOU KNOW?

Test your knowledge of Hunting and Win a signed author's limited edition copy of "Hunting Tales".

Simply answer all the questions - you'll find the answers all in the book
and send them to:
- Hunting Quiz
- Maverick Sporting Publishers
- 65 St Giles Street
- Northampton NN1 1JF

by the closing date of 20th December 1994. The first all-correct answer drawn will be notified by 31 December 1994. Good luck!

PART ONE
GENERAL KNOWLEDGE

A) Who did Prince Charles first hunt with?
B) The youngest ever MFH was only eight. Who was he?
C) Who were known as the Blue-Bloods?
D) Who hunted with his cat and pet monkey, both on horseback?
E) Who kept a pack of dwarf foxhounds?
F) The Earl of Darlington holds the record for miles travelled on horseback. What is it?
G) Who were the "Stars of the West"?
H) Whose is the monument on the A508 between Pitsford and Brixworth, in Northamptonshire?
J) Who was killed at Yelvertoft when hunting from the Coach & Horses, Brixworth?
K) What is a VULPICIDE?
L) Who was England's youngest ever whipper-in?
M) Who was Merry Tom?
N) How far did Squire George Osbaldeston ride in 8 hours, 40 mins?
P) How many children did John Peel have?
Q) What is the legend of Gelert?
R) What were Warde's Jackasses?
S) How do you get room service in an Irish hotel?
T) Who did Capt. Bay Middleton "pilot" with the Pytchley in 1877?
U) Who was "Skittles"?
V) Who was "Handsome Jack"?
W) Who invented the modern riding boot?
X) What did Beau Brummel call the farmers?
Y) The Middleburg Hunt in Virginia, USA, has one famous ex-First Lady as a member. Who is she?
Z) WHAT DO THE FOLLOWING WORDS MEAN?
SOIL
BILLET
BALL
DRAG
FROG
BYE-DAY
BARS

PART TWO
FAMOUS QUOTES

WHO SAID:

"Women have no business out hunting"
WAS IT...Max Hastings_____
................R. S. Surtees_____
................Michael Bletsoe-Brown_____
................Ronnie Wallace_____

"Like Foxhunters, you should buy Old Masters.
They fetch a better price than old mistresses"
WAS IT...Woody Allen_____
................Bob Andrews_____
................Lord Beaverbrook_____

"It was a horsewoman that drove me to drink, and you know, I didn't even thank her"
WAS IT...W. C. Fields_____
................Oliver Reed_____
................David Bletsoe-Brown_____
................Dudley Moore_____

"Certain Horse Women should be struck regularly, like gongs"
WAS IT...Noel Coward_____
................Sean Connery_____
................Harvey Smith_____
................Prince Charles_____

"A Horse Woman is only a woman, but a good cigar is a smoke"
WAS IT...Richard Burton_____
................Charlie Simmons_____
................Rudyard Kipling_____

"In spite of his taste for throwing Christians to the Lions, the Roman Emperor, Caligula, loved horses and was therefore all right"
WAS IT...Jenny Knight_____
................Michael Clayton_____
................Rintoul Booth_____
................Jane Spencer_____
................Captain Mark Phillips_____

"There are, they say, fools, bloody fools, and those who remount after falling over a five-bar gate on opening day"
WAS IT...William Shakespeare_____
................Peter Jones_____
................Willie Carson_____
................Joy Hawken_____

"This being Easter Sunday we will ask the Master's wife to come forward and lay an egg on the altar."
WAS IT...Church bulletin at Sywell_____
................The Vicar of Wakefield_____
................A complete invention, but it sounds funny_____

ACKNOWLEDGMENTS

The author and publishers gratefully acknowledge permission to use copyright material in this book. In some cases only a line or a phrase was used, in others a book was used for reference only. Whilst every effort has been made to secure permission, we may have failed in a few instances to trace the copyright holder. We apologise for any apparent negligence.

Riding in the Midlands: NHAGB 1940
The Woodland Pytchley Hunt: William Fawcett 1936
Memoirs of An Undistinguished Man: G.F.Lucas (Lynx) 1955
The Hunting Diaries of Stanley Barker: Stuart Newham, Standfast Press 1981
The Life of Frank Freeman, Huntsman: Guy Paget 1948
History of the Althorp and Pytchley Hunt, 1634-1920: Guy Paget 1957
High Days and Bye Days: Ralph Graves, Philip Mann 1933
Wit and Wisdom of the Shires: Walter Faber, Ed. Guy Paget 1932
Breakfast the Night Before: Marjorie Quarton, Andre Deutsch 1989
The Chase: Michael Clayton, Stanley Paul 1987
Mr Silas P. Mowbray Returns to Melton: Guy Paget, Edgar Backus 1940
Magic of the Quorn: Ulrica Murray Smith, J.A.Allen 1980
Diary of a Huntsman: Thomas Smith, Country Life Ltd, Tavistock Library Series 1933
Tom Firr of the Quorn: Roy Heron, Nimrod 1984
Fox and Hare in Leicestershire: Eric Morrison, Eyre & Spottiswoode 1954
British Hunts and Huntsmen: The Biographical Press in conjunction with
The Sporting Life in four volumes, 1908-1911, borrowed from the Peter Jones Collection
Famous Foxhunters: Lionel Edwards, Eyre & Spottiswoode 1932
Ask Mamma: R.S.Surtees, Bradbury & Evans 1858
Hillingdon Hall: R.S.Surtees, Methuen & Co 1904
Hunting with Mr Jorrocks: R.S.Surtees, Oxford University Press 1956
Market Harborough: G.J.Whyte Melville, Country Life Books 1861
Mr Facey Romford's Hounds: R.S.Surtees, Bradbury & Evans 1860
The Horseman's Weekend Book: Gordon Winter, Seeley Service & Co 1938
Foxhunting: Sara and Raymond Carr, Oxford University Press 1982
The Foxhunters Weekend Book: David Brock, Seeley Service & Co 1939
A Foxhunter's Anthology: Peter Lewis, The Boydell Press 1934
Regency London: Stella Margetson, Cassell 1971
Tales and Legends of Beds and Herts: Vic Lea, The Book Castle, Dunstable 1988
Foxhunting: The Duke of Beaufort, David & Charles 1987
In Praise of Hunting: David James and Wilson Stephens, Hollis & Carter 1960
The Horseman's Handbook to End All Horseman's Handbooks: Rintoul Booth, Wolfe 1975
Skittles, The Last Victorian Courtesan: Henry Blyth, Rupert Hart-Davis 1970